THE MYSTERIOUS BARRICADES:
LANGUAGE AND ITS LIMITS

ANN E. BERTHOFF

The Mysterious Barricades:
Language and Its Limits

UNIVERSITY OF TORONTO PRESS
Toronto Buffalo London

© University of Toronto Press Incorporated 1999
Toronto Buffalo London
Printed in Canada

ISBN 0-8020-4706-8

Printed on acid-free paper

Toronto Studies in Semiotics
Editors: Marcel Danesi, Umberto Eco, Paul Perron, and Thomas A. Sebeok

---

Canadian Cataloguing in Publication Data

Berthoff, Ann E.
  The mysterious barricades : language and its limits

  (Toronto studies in semiotics)
  Includes bibliographical references and index.
  ISBN 0-8020-4706-8

  1. Discourse analysis.   2. Semiotics.   I. Title.   II. Series.

  P302.B477 1999   404'.41   C99-931022-4

University of Toronto Press acknowledges the financial assistance to its publishing program of the Canada Council for the Arts and the Ontario Arts Council.

University of Toronto Press acknowledges the financial support for its publishing activities of the Government of Canada through the Book Publishing Industry Development Program (BPIDP).

Canadä

For Warner

Contents

Acknowledgments ix

Introduction: Triadicity and Its Consequences 3

I. Dyadic Misunderstandings 13

  1 Gangster Theories 15
  2 A Clean Machine and a Competent Operator 19
  3 Determinations and Indeterminacy 28
  4 Bottom's Semiology: The Duck-Rabbit and Magritte's Pipe 39
  5 Gaps, Abysses, and the Mysterious Barricades 48

II. Triadic Remedies 55

  6 Peirce and the Third 57
  7 I.A. Richards and the Audit of Meaning 72
  8 Schleiermacher and the Hermeneutic Enterprise 82
  9 Sapir, Cassirer, and the World of Meanings 102
 10 Susanne K. Langer and the Process of Feeling 112
 11 Walker Percy's Castaway 125

III. Kleist's Parables and the Fall into Language 137

 12 Marionettes and Automatons 139
 13 The Journey to the Back Door of Paradise 153
 14 Green Glasses, the Figured Bass, and the Brakeshoe 159

Notes 167
Index 189

Acknowledgments

While working on these essays, I have enjoyed many instructive arguments and discussions with Alide Cagidemetrio, Albert Divver, Mary Anne Ferguson, Joseph Frank, the late Arthur Gold, Beverly Haviland, Paul Kameen, U.C. Knoepflmacher, the late Gary Lindberg, Michael McCanles, Leo Marx, Cynthia L. Sears, Louise Z. Smith, Frederic C. Tubach, and Renée Watkins. There are few psychologists with whom I would trust matters of language and thought, but Phoebe Ellsworth is one. She has been unfailingly helpful in dealing with my questions about perception and concept formation, and I long ago learned to trust her sense of style. My brother, Dr. Frederic M. Evans, has instructed me on various questions of physiology and in far more recondite matters of hermeneutics. Neal Bruss has labored to help me see what linguistics, at its best, attempts to do. I have appreciated Thomas Sebeok's encouraging interest in my interpretation of Richards and Sapir in terms of Peirce's semiotics.

My attempts to understand Peirce's philosophy of representation were fostered by the late Carolyn Blackmer and the late Richard Martin, a Swedenborgian and a logician. When I tried to set forth to Professor Martin Carolyn Blackmer's understanding of the consonance of Swedenborg's idea of correspondence and Peirce's Thirdness, he urged me to pursue those ideas and invited a paper for the 1981 meeting of the Charles S. Peirce Society, a project which led to Chapter 6. I am grateful to these two philosophers for their encouragement and, of course, for their profound insights into Peirce's philosophy of representation.

In slightly different versions, "I.A. Richards and the Audit of Meaning," appeared first in *New Literary History*, XIV (1982); Chapter 4, in *Pre/Text*, 14. 1/2 (1993); Chapter 3, in *College English*, 58 (1996). The Sapir chapter incorporates passages from both "Sapir and the Two Tasks of Language," in *Semiotica*, 71-1/2 (1988) and "Semiotics and Sapir," in *The Semiotic Web 1990*, ed T.A. Sebeok and Jean Umiker-Sebeok (Mouton). "Walker Percy's Castaway" was first published in *The Sewanee Review*, 102 (Summer 1994). Permission to reprint is gratefully acknowledged.

I am grateful to the Department of English, University of Massachusetts at Boston for research assistance provided by Beth Bagley, Lisa Schwarz, and Lorraine Martin. And I appreciate the labors of Robin Humes and Joann Wynkoop, who, with their word-processing skills, made it possible for me to hold on to my outmoded habits of composition.

Couperin's *Les baricades mistérieuses* was compelling the very first time I heard it played (by Wanda Landowska on the old Couperin Society disks), but it was in listening to my friend Eugenia Earle that I first understood the paradox of those enabling limits by which form finds form. No other performance I have heard of this piece has so surely and sweetly represented its mysterious form and power.

I dedicate these essays to my husband, whose reservations (never merely skeptical) and affirmations (always inspiriting) have been an aid to reflection for more than forty years.

Ann E. Berthoff
Concord, Massachusetts

THE MYSTERIOUS BARRICADES:
LANGUAGE AND ITS LIMITS

Introduction: Triadicity and Its Consequences

A "barrier" that it is logically impossible to remove is not, in any interesting sense, a barrier at all.

– Max Black

L'espace pictural est un mur mais tous les oiseaux du monde y volent librement. A toutes Profondeurs.

– Nicolas de Staël

Before the *nouvelle vague* became a tidal wave, some critics, foreseeing disaster, began taping windows and nailing on the plywood. Others simply deserted the shore, moving inland out of harm's way. Donald H. Reiman was braver. On the model of "each one teach one," he made the following proposal:

It may be necessary for many of us to submit to the duties of our age to the extent of mastering (say) two or three fallacious arguments apiece and demolishing them publicly, until the pressure of informed opinion drives these mountebanks back into literary studies of some validity ... In doing so, we will dispell the illusion that an egregious display of erroneous novelty is the way to honour, power, riches, fame and the love of women/men.[1]

The idea that "many of us" should each demolish a couple of misconceptions never took hold, but I doubt that such truth squads would have been effective. More promising perhaps is the kind of analysis recently undertaken by Frederick Crews in *Skeptical Engagements*, John Ellis in *Against Deconstruction*, Raymond Tallis in *Not Saussure*, and Brian Vickers in *Appropriating Shakespeare*. In these lively books, we find a great deal of point-by-point refutation, but their real strength comes from the examination of radically flawed methods and self-serving styles of critical discourse in which presuppositions remain unacknowledged and assertion does the work of argument; in which contradictions parade as subtle apprehensions, and paradoxes, of the sort which should be resolved, only signal confusion. But have such witty and provocative commentaries reached those who could most benefit from them?

In the newest critical fashions, sociology – of an unhistorical positivist sort – has succeeded to linguistics as the chief source of models for literary study, which is approximating what it was in the days before the New Criticism – that is, a strange amalgam of reading for message (even for uplift) and an egregious literary history in which *race, moment, milieu* have been reinvented as ethnicity, gender, and whatever theme of oppression has gained attention for the time being. Contexts, the more obscurely coded the better, push texts to the margins, when they do not supplant them. But the new approaches only distract us from issues of the recent past. Geoffrey Galt Harpham puts it this way:

The general movement of the profession of literary study away from the entire project of a theory of literature based on a philosophically inflected theory of language and towards issues of identity, power and status has left the antagonisms and divisions of the recent past unresolved, like a live shell buried in the farmer's field.[2]

My chief purpose in these essays has been to claim that such resolution will be impossible unless and until we can account for meaning, representation, and interpretation in logical, not merely psychological, terms.

That is certainly a philosophical challenge and, insofar as it concerns the way we think about the sign, it is a semiotic challenge. Semiotics does not always enjoy a sound reputation. It includes in its purview everything from roadsigns to puppet shows and unconscious gestures though, as practiced, seldom what Owen Barfield called "poetic diction." But there are different brands of semiotics, different conceptions of the sign. The usefulness of semiotics in the study of meaning, representation, and interpretation will be determined by whether the meaning relationship is thought of as two-valued or three-valued. The recent study of language – once structural linguistics won out over Sapir's profoundly hermeneutical and anthropological philosophy of language in the 1930's – has been guided by a dyadic semiotic. There is a signifier and a signified, with the role of interpretation defined only in psychological terms. In contrast, the triadic semiotic of Charles Sanders Peirce accounts for interpretation in logical terms: interpretation is a constituent of the sign.

For Peirce, signification is a three-valued relationship: a *representamen* symbolizes an *object* by means of a meaning, which he called the *interpretant*, in contradistinction to the interpreter. To understand interpretation as the third element of the sign is to recognize mediation – and once mediation is understood not as constituting a barrier but as the logical condition of signification, there will be certain epistemological consequences, chief among them the recognition that all knowledge is interpretation and that all interpretation must itself be interpreted. In Peirce's terms, each sign requires another sign for its interpretation, the interpretant of one becoming the representamen of the next. Representation and interpretation thus constitute a process carried on among sign-users (who are themselves signs) and is thus necessarily social. This process (semiosis) is also necessarily open-ended and necessarily interruptible, since we live in a fallen world. The infinite regress is suspended when we follow the pragmatic maxim, asking "If we stop here, if we put it this way, what difference would it make to our practice?" Peirce's pragmaticism is thus entailed in his semiotics.[3]

To these consequences of triadicity – recognition of the logic of signification, of the social character of semiosis, of the role of pragmaticism – we must add the conception of the heuristic power of limits. The idea of "the limits of language" has been compromised, especially by those who have followed Wittgenstein's aphorism: "The limits of my language are the limits of my world." It has usually been interpreted in the light of the idea that language determines thought, the limits of what we can think corresponding to the limits of the language of whatever speech community we are born into. The result has been an uncritical acceptance of the idea of the identity of thought and language. This conception of the limits of language is consonant with the doctrine of linguistic determinism associated with Benjamin Lee Whorf and (wrongly) with Edward Sapir – "the Sapir-Whorf Hypothesis." Those who subscribe to this idea move easily from "If you don't have the words, you can't say it" to "If you don't have the words you can't think it." The identification of language and thought is one pole of current criticism; its polar opposite is that language corresponds to reality, representing it as a code. Both identification and correspondence are ideas underwritten by an understanding of meaning as a two-valued system, by the dyadic semiotic which has informed most linguistics since Saussure. By remembering the Third, we can reclaim the idea that the limits of language are enabling. "Semiotics," as it appears in this book, fosters a view of language as a system whose formal completeness is the source of its heuristic power, as a symbolic form whose limits make possible the apprehension of the world and the making of meaning.

Everyone who declares independence from Aristotle speaks of a "new rhetoric." In *The Philosophy of Rhetoric* (1936), I.A. Richards argued that a new rhetoric should "take charge of the criticism of its assumptions" – which is what he meant by "philosophy." Richards' continuing concern was with the problem of initial terms: where do we begin in interpretation? how do we understand what it is that is given for interpretation? how do we conceive of the interpreter? He decided that rhetoric – the study of "how words work" – should begin with "misunderstanding and its remedies."

I have chosen this as my point of departure, and in "Dyadic Misunderstandings" I examine the corrupting effects a positivist linguistics and the models derived from it have had on certain aspects of critical theory and practice in the past thirty years or so. I use the term "positivism" loosely, with no attempt to limit it to a particular philosophical method or school. But I have in mind certain specifications, including the following attitudes: a conviction that concrete particulars "come first," before concepts, and that they are more important than anything "abstract"; an ardent willingness to worship what Susanne K. Langer calls the "Idols of the Laboratory"; a fear or a contempt (or at least a distaste) for dialectical thinking; a distrust of the idea of "interpretation," which is set over against "explanation." The mirror image of this positivism is a corrupt mysticism, the radical skepticism of deconstruction: a rejection of the very idea of representation or of mediation and an ignorant disregard for the heuristic character of limits. My contention is that both hard-nosed positivism and its mystic variants are fostered by a view of the meaning relationship as two-valued.

I have focused on claims and disclaimers, explanations and disagreements, pronouncements and misconceptions which are expectable when meaning, representation, and interpretation are entertained in the perspective afforded by a dyadic semiotic. None of these misunderstandings is current: Kenneth Burke and René Wellek on what is determined in a text; E.D. Hirsch and Stanley Fish deploying information theory as interpreted in psycholinguistics; Jonathan Culler on the arbitrary sign;

Paul de Man decoding Proust; Wittgenstein on the supposed distinction between *seeing* and *seeing as*; etc. In returning to discussions which are no longer at the forefront of critical controversy or are indeed long-forgotten, I have tried to establish a critical distance from matters which are still very much at issue, though both the terms of argument and the terminology have changed – both contexts and the lexicon. "Structuralist poetics" or "affective stylistics," for instance, are no longer with us as programs or approaches (they were never pedagogies), but the problems they allegedly solved remain as challenging as ever. "Dyadic Misunderstandings" attempts to disarm some of these land mines.

I have not discussed the misunderstandings of gender studies or culture studies or the new historicism, but in defining "gangster theories" (I.A. Richards), I expect the reader to recognize whatever might be pertinent to a critical discussion of those fields of study and inquiry, to a critique of current attitudes towards history, the self, and the role of interpretation.

In Part II, I turn first to Peirce's triadicity and the consequences it has for a general theory of hermeneutics. Peirce is by now a show place on the guided tours conducted by contemporary critics. He is rather widely cited, though the same passages appear again and again, culled from anthologies and secondary sources; nor is it unusual for an American academic to rely for his understanding of Peirce's semiotic on a British explicator of passages previously selected and expounded upon by one or another European philosopher. In this way, certain misapprehensions of what Peirce meant when he spoke of community, the limitations of knowledge, undecideability, the classification of signs, indeterminacy, etc. are being institutionalized. There are, of course, contemporary interpreters of Peirce who have done wonders in making his thought accessible; I am thinking especially of Joseph Esposito and Umberto Eco, Max Fisch and Thomas Sebeok and Jean Umiker-Sebeok. In an attempt to describe Triadic Remedies for Dyadic Misunderstandings, I have turned to six philosophers writing earlier in this century (and one in the early nineteenth century), whose thought is consonant with Peirce's conceptions of the sign. (Only two – Richards and Walker Percy – were directly influenced by their study of Peirce.)

Richards' understanding of "the seemingly revolutionary doctrine of the Interpretant"[4] illuminates the difference between what the poststructuralists mean by "indeterminacy" and Peirce's semiosis, "the endless process of learning from signs." Richards' critique of the use positivist linguistics has made of information theory aids the effort to reclaim the distinction between variant readings and misreading, reminding us of the role of contexts, if interpretation is to be something other than solipsistic decoding. His "theory of comprehending" is a hermeneutic with the semiotic dimension made explicit. As a good pragmatist (in Peirce's sense, i.e. a *pragmaticist*), Richards believed that this confluence of hermeneutics and semiotics was the proper site for a practical criticism, though he was alert to the hazards of what has become known as "foundationalism" and preferred the metaphor of dependence.

If we return to Schleiermacher, freed from the dyadic presupposition that the hermeneutic circle is vicious or generative of one aporia after another, we will discover what he meant by method. The two "moments" of his hermeneutics are not linear steps or isolated scenes of interpretation but the motives of construing and constructing what is written and what is meant. They are separable for the purposes of analysis but their relationship Schleiermacher called an *Ineinandersein*. Schleiermacher's dialectic is thoroughly triadic and it offers further remedies for the misconceptions arising from a dyadic semiotics.

Neither Sapir nor Cassirer read Peirce (whose papers were not edited until the thirties), but there is a consonance among Sapir's philosophical anthropology, Cassirer's philosophy of symbolic forms, and Peirce's semiotics. Arguably the greatest linguist of the century, Sapir called for a general theory of signs and provided very powerful ideas by whose means it could be developed. He established linguistics as central to anthropological study and developed a method of inquiry which fosters questions of a sort disallowed by positivist linguistics. Everything to be said about the significance of cultural elements depends on cultural contexts which must be recognized and defined and taken into account methodically. That he could treat languages as cultural elements meant not that Sapir reduced linguistic forms to empty structures but that he saw all human acts and artifacts as symbolic forms which are at once instruments and products. This dialectical understanding is at the heart of Sapir's conception of linguistics as "a tool in the sciences of man." He shares it with Cassirer and all those whose basic premise is that we see man's life in "the mirror of culture."

Cassirer's conception of the two tasks of language – the universal logical task and the social task – makes it possible to differentiate language and discourse, the formal structures and what we do with them. (The conflation of language and discourse is perhaps the most destructive consequence of dyadic semiotics.) It also clarifies the fact that when

Sapir speaks of "the tyranny of language" he means the grammatical categories and syntactical orders which are, at once, unconscious, historical beyond individual control, and the source of heuristic power: fulfilling the universal logical task is the necessary condition for carrying out the social task, which is to create the means of building "the world of meanings."

Susanne K. Langer's *Mind: An Essay on Human Feeling* provides the biological foundations for the claim in *Philosophy in a New Key* that man is defined by a "need for symbolic transformation." The powerful working concepts by means of which she proceeds in this essay derive from her study of Cassirer's philosophy of language and myth; of Whitehead's understanding of the modes of thought; and from her own philosophy of art. Like Peirce, Susanne Langer was concerned with the architectonics of theory and, like Peirce, she knew that theoretical structures must be built with the most careful attention to fact, to method, and to seeing what difference to our understanding one or another claim might make. By way of an exploration of symbolization and imagination, of the powers of language and art, and of the process of feeling, her life work constitutes a genuine philosophical anthropology, the human science which fulfills the promise unrealized by psychology or linguistics.

Walker Percy read Peirce with affectionate admiration, seeing very clearly the consequences of the revolutionary doctrine of the Interpretant, which he called "the coupler." He understood the importance of triadicity for an appreciation of metaphor and its heuristic power – and, indeed, for any consideration of the human condition. His point of departure was to remark "how queer language is, how queer man is, and what they have to do with one another." Percy's castaway, doomed to patrol the shores, watching for "the message in the bottle," is a compelling image not only of our not being at home in the world but also of our capacity to recognize "the good news from across the seas." Dr. Percy's triadic remedies are old-fashioned but nonetheless therapeutic.

I have looked back in order to look forward – back to certain philosophers who, because they have understood the centrality of interpretation, can guide attempts to account *for* meaning, representation, and interpretation and might give accounts *of* meanings, the primary task of a re-claimed practical criticism. Those I have chosen are, of course, not the only ones whose thinking encourages ideas of how theory and practice can be brought into a mutually defining relationship. Support for the argument about the heuristic power of limits could be found in

Vygotsky and Bakhtin, Bachelard and Barfield – and so on. I mean the ones I have written about to serve as Representative Men – and a woman – in the exploration of the world of mediations which triadicity discloses to us.

In Part III, I have explored further the philosophical consequences of triadicity, by way of a reading of two of Kleist's essays. His very modern insight into the relationship of language and thought is subverted by his naïve realism; he describes precisely the operation of the mysterious barricades of language but turns abruptly away from appreciating the consequences. Thus Cassirer saw Kleist as a representative of those who cannot apprehend mediation. Kleist's narrator in "On the Marionette Theatre" declares that his argument about the puppet's recovery of grace cannot be grasped unless his interlocutor has read the third chapter of Genesis. The Fall of Man as both a fall from innocence and grace and a fortunate fall into language supports the idea that language is our salvation, but Kleist found no comfort in the doctrine of *felix culpa*: "The gate of Paradise is locked and barred; we must undertake a journey around the world to see if it is somehow open at the back." The works of his imagination tell the story of Kleist's attempted journey to the back-door of Eden.

Coming to grips with the revolutionary doctrine of the Interpretant involves certain fundamental revisions in received ideas of language and therefore of how we come to know the world and ourselves and of how we make sense of what we see and what we read: that doctrine will change everything, if we give it its way. Thinking of the meaning relationship as three-valued both requires and generates the ideas needed for developing a theory of literacy so that we can be well-guided in a study of what happens when we read. How we think about the sign determines how we think about the relationship of what we mean and what we say; the relationship of form and purpose; the relationship of one Man-Sign to other Man-Signs whom he interprets and by whom his representations are interpreted. Perhaps the chief reason for studying triadicity is that with its guidance, those responsible for literacy at all levels might yet forestall the political dangers of a citizenry which cannot read either in the sense of not being able to construe the written word or in the wider sense of being unable to read critically. The bond between teaching and philosophy is immemorial and the study of the relationship of language and thought, as even positivists occasionally agree, is necessarily carried forward in terms provided by a recognition of our life as social creatures. Peirce's characterization of Thirdness – the symbolization made manifest in and by the sign – as "the sense of learning" I take as emblematic of the enterprise of bringing theory to bear on practice: the theory of signs in conjunction with the practice of critical reading.

To reclaim criticism as a philosophical activity concerned with how words work, how dialectical processes can be represented, how purposes are to be taken into account, how definitions operate heuristically – this reclamation is itself a challenge to philosophy. It can be met only if we have to hand adequate ideas to think *with* – I.A. Richards' "speculative instruments" and Peirce's "instruments of thought," those representations of meaning by whose means we explore and create further meanings. I have tried to bring certain of these instruments to the test, to see what difference they make in the way we think about language and its limits, about triadicity and its consequences.

I. DYADIC MISUNDERSTANDINGS

1

Gangster Theories

And, as credulity is the cause of error, so incredulity oftentimes of not enjoying truth: and not only an obstinate incredulity, whereby we will not acknowledge assent unto what is reasonably inferred, but any academical reservation in matters of easy truth, or rather sceptical infidelity against the evidence of reason and sense. For these are conceptions befalling wise men, as absurd as the apprehensions of fools, and the credulity of the people, which promiscuously swallow anything.

– Sir Thomas Browne, *Pseudodoxia Epidemica*

I.A. Richards, who constructed more theories than most critics would ever see the need for, was also the man who reclaimed Coleridge's *practical criticism*. Richards' theory of theories was thoroughly pragmatic: "How we use a theory best tells us what it is." One of the chief uses of a theory, he held, is to protect the estate of discourse from "gangster theories." What he had in mind on this occasion – a preface to his own poems in 1960 – was "academism, punditry, fashion, faction, movements, modernities, and so forth." Elsewhere, he was more forthright: the gangster theories were "verbal behavior," the doctrine of usage, digestive theories of education, the apotheosis of misreading, the conception of language as "a sort of verbal butterfly net to catch non-verbal butterflies," and, most sinister of all, the misappropriation of information theory by psycholinguistics.[1] Since that time a generation ago, these gangster theories and many others have won power and respectability and are consequently harder than ever to defend against.

The power of a gangster theory derives from the style of argumentation, especially the bold refusal to acknowledge ambiguities, contradictions, and paradoxes of the sort which are symptomatic of confusion and should be resolved. When the exceptions threaten to overturn the law, when the formulation is shown to be fundamentally invalid, the positivist impulse is not abrogation but casuistry and equivocation. What had been declared irrelevant or superficial or invalid is surreptitiously brought back. A common sequence is for a theory to move from statements of the self-evident, based on incontrovertible fact, to pronouncements of absolute truth and then, gradually, to qualified and restricted application, not logically different from the original.

A gangster theory can start out as a reasonable analogy, with ambiguities noticed and limitations recognized, but then it will be "strengthened" by being pushed to an extreme, the qualifications dropped, the principles formulated as law. What happens to "strong" readings is an example of this typical course of development. A "strong" reading, it should be noted, is the antithesis of "strong" inference. Strong readings pretend to account for everything in text or picture or symbol. The cost may be the neglect of contexts or documented intention or other extrinsic knowledge; dependence on them is considered unfair, like having a net under the high wire. Strong inference also accounts for what there is, but it does so by demonstrating that one theory accounts more economically than another and that it passes logical tests which others do not. An hypothesis is tested not simply by experimental findings but by reasoning.[2] Applications of gangster theories in their strong form can sound like daring inferences, ones that nobody has hitherto been brave enough to formulate.

Gangster theories deploy dichotomies in a hazardous fashion. Now, a dichotomy is simply a pair of mutually exclusive categories. Susanne K. Langer explains the function of dichotomy this way: "Whenever we form a class within any universe of discourse, then every individual in that universe must either belong to the class or not belong to it."[3] Classifying, that is to say, entails differentiating *A* and *Not-A*, but to do so is not to make a claim that reality divides neatly into *A* and *Not-A*. It is not because they are two-valued that dichotomies are dangerous; it is because the categories they establish can so easily be confused with reality. If you claim that the only role of language is to correspond to reality and if you know there are no dichotomies in reality, then you will find no justification, theoretically, for dichotomies in language. However, dichotomy is not a linguistic but a logical concept: many linguists and many semioticians confuse language and logic. When these categories lead to differentiation in terms not of the logic of propositions but of experience and the real world, they are pernicious.

Killer dichotomies are especially notable in the life of a gangster theory in the first stages of the weakening that inevitably follows the strong phase – when the unitary absolute splits in two. They are easy to formulate; they lend themselves to the old rhetorical tropes and schemes very well. Chiasmus is especially popular, as when Paul de Man speaks of "the rhetorization of grammar and the grammatization of rhetoric." The memorable character and persuasive power of such formulations helps to institutionalize dichotomies so that they work their harm unheeded.

A match for the killer dichotomy, which is modelled by the binary oppositions of code, is the pseudo-concept, modelled by the dragnet. *Discourse*, for instance, has become a pseudo-concept in Vygotsky's sense: it has gathered to itself many analogous or at least comparable ideas and terms, but there has emerged no criterion by which to differentiate the members of this new class. The field of application of this pseudo-concept is virtually limitless; *discourse* can mean *language, procedure, culturally determined attitudes, historically determined conventions, unconscious habits, deliberate habits, rational conventions unconsciously followed, arbitrary conventions deliberately deployed*. Discourse analysis has thus become a safe house for gangster theories.

Even when gangster theories are brought to justice, killer dichotomies subdued by squads of *tertium quid*s, the perverse attractions of what Roland Barthes called *semioclastie* bravely rejected, there is a danger that fundamental attitudes will remain unchanged.[4] Once the view of language as an impenetrable barrier between us and reality begins to lose its appeal, a countervailing conviction that language corresponds in a point-to-point way to reality – that it *segments* reality, as Whorf put it – will appear. Or, indeed, these contradictory views can be held simultaneously, on the rhetorical model of *There is no God and Mary is His Mother*: there is no reference and it is represented by a code. In any case, the underlying conception of the sign as a two-valued relationship is likely to subvert any attempt to follow out the consequences of triadicity. Owen Barfield called these deep unexamined convictions RUP – *residual unresolved positivism*.[5] Its symptoms are everywhere to be discerned in current critical theory.

An adequate defense against gangster theories will necessarily have the support of a theory of meaning, of what Richards called a philosophy of rhetoric. Only if we account *for meaning* can we give an account *of meanings*; the demise of practical criticism which has accompanied the rise of "theory," as it is currently understood, is not merely coincidental. Theory and practice nowadays seldom bear one another a functional relationship: witness the complete lack of interest among critics, of whatever variety, in teaching. Contemporary theory sets meaning aside because it is "mentalistic" or because it is a delusion of a corrupt and oppressive humanism. And as the possibility of reference is discounted, the idea of representation equated with copy and dismissed, the idea of meaning itself alternately mechanized and mysticized – as the radical skepticism which substitutes "story" for explanation moves to foreclose the possibilities of answering (however hypothetically) any question of import, it becomes less and less feasible to imagine reading for instruction or delight. But the way we account for meaning, if indeed we feel compelled to do so at all, can be useful for the study of literature only if we acknowledge the centrality of interpretation, defining its place in logical terms; otherwise, *pseudodoxia academica* will remain as virulent as ever.

2

A Clean Machine and a Competent Operator

No one who follows the Cartesian method will ever be satisfied until he has formally recovered all those beliefs which in form he has given up.

– C.S. Peirce

In the title of Walter Benjamin's essay "On Language as Such and the Language of Man," the *as such* signals a phenomenological concern for essences, for whatever is universal, holding in all instances.[6] "Language as such" is Benjamin's term for symbolization: it is *code*, in the sense of a system of codified meanings in terms of which the world can be apprehended and thus represented to the mind. It differs from the "language of man," by which Benjamin means one or another code, in the sense of a formal grammatical system. Positivist linguistics and its progeny have muddled these two senses of *code*, aiming to eliminate "mentalistic" concepts in the belief that what is real (or "interesting") can be set forth unencumbered by whatever is inaccessible to empirical study.

Consider the confusions in the case of "structuralist poetics." The chief aim of a structuralist poetics is, as Jonathan Culler puts it, "to specify the codes and conventions which make meanings possible, just as linguistics, the systematic study of language, makes explicit the rules and conventions of language."[7] Just as it is not the aim of linguistics to establish the meanings of individual sentences, so it is not the aim of a structuralist poetics to interpret metaphors, to explain individual passages, to relate one text to another, to compare readings, to develop contexts. It is to define "the codes and conventions which make meaning possible." A curious thing happens when this critical method is dollied into place: when the codes and conventions which make meaning possible are studied without reference to the meanings made, they become not meaning-making systems called poems and stories but empty machines stalled or idling in vacant lots, awaiting their operators.

These positivist models of language are familiar in contemporary criticism. Roland Barthes's "empty sign" is one such clean machine; here is Frank Kermode trying to get it to run: "[We should consider] the structure of a text as a system of signifiers as in some sense 'empty,' as what, by the intervention of the reader, takes on many possible significances."[8] If Kermode means by "a system of signifiers" *notation*, this is a truism. The music on the piano rack is not the music we hear; notes are squiggles until they are played or sung or are heard in the mind's ear. (Toscanini's favorite bedtime reading was orchestral scores.) If, on the other hand, Kermode means by "a system of signifiers" bearers of meaning, his statement that they are "in some sense empty," pending "the intervention of the reader," creates a logical muddle, since the implication is that in another sense they are *not* empty, that signs can be significant without intervention. This is a replay of the puzzle of the tree falling in the forest: would there be a sound if there were nobody to hear it?

This unstable sense of "a system of signifiers" is the kind of ambiguity we should expect when dyadicists come to deal with the language of actual discourse, for how could an analytic method which has been developed to define phonological components and grammatical structures without attention to the making of meaning be adapted to the study of meaning-enabling codes and conventions? What we have in the theory of structuralist poetics – the practice is something else – is a version of the strategy of the behavioral psychologists who study *verbal behavior* because supposedly it can be delimited in a way that *language* cannot.

The empty sign is activated by an intervening interpreter. Now, since it is the maundering interpretations of actual readers which a structuralist poetics is meant to circumvent in its attempt to define "the codes and conventions which make meaning possible," actual readers must be supplanted by the fiction of The Competent Reader. But competence, insofar as it has to do with accurate expectations based on literary experience, is the antithesis of what is meant by linguists who use the term: linguistic competence is a predilection, a predisposition, a capacity to learn the language of whatever speech community one belongs to. The Competent Reader has nothing in common with The Competent Speaker, who is born knowing how, who is always (already) fitted with a Language Acquisition Device, who needs *society*, but not the society of the literate. Linguistic competence must be defined in terms of its effect: the concept of competence thus entails the concept of performance. The relationship between the two will remain obscure unless it is defined in terms of knowing, as for instance in the matter of knowing the rules of a grammar. But it is precisely this particular question about knowledge – the conscious and unconscious aspects of knowing – which Culler has set aside as a "supremely uninteresting question." Literary competence presumably is also to be defined in terms of its effect; it is, again, a matter of performance. But the performance of literary competence is interpretation, which structuralist poetics has set aside as trivial and subjective.

The pseudo-concept of "literary competence" allows the semiotician or literary critic to bypass the problematics of interpretation, just as the notion of the empty sign allows dispensing with the concept of representation. The competent operator paired with the clean machine is a problem-solver's delight, but it should be recognized for what it is: one more version of the ghost in the machine. Positivist epistemology constructs models which are entirely empirical, but then, when there is a failure to account for the phenomenon in question, various concepts are sneaked back into the model which has been developed precisely in order to get rid of them. The Competent Reader, like The Self, is one of those ghosts summoned when the positivist machine stalls.

Competence is, of course, the logically necessary condition of communication: there must be a competent signalman on board if messages are to be sent and received. The signalman has an intention, or he encodes the message of someone who does, but that message is not of a kind with the material means by which it is communicated. Differentiating signal and message, I.A. Richards called the *pons asinorum* of linguistics.[9] Reducing message to signal or conflating the two is encouraged by the fact that the terms and working concepts of modern linguistics are borrowed from communication (or information) theory in which no distinction is made between message and signal because none is needed. When critics use the term *information* instead of *meaning*, or *information processing* instead of *expressing* and *interpreting*, they do so because the jargon of computer science suggests well-grounded facts rather than mentalistic concepts. But *information* in information theory has nothing whatever to do with information in the other sense of what is meant or known or what is to be communicated; it has nothing whatever to do with structure or import or reference or designation: *information* means *absence of noise in the channel*.[10]

22 Dyadic Misunderstandings

The favorite term borrowed from cybernetics is *code*, and its several meanings are muddled in the same fashion as are *signal* and *message* and the two kinds of *information*. When Todorov or Genette or Barthes (or their American and British popularizers) speak of *codes*, they mean what is encoded – attitudes and presuppositions, ideologies and privileged perspectives. But the other meaning of *code* as the material means of representation hovers near, lending a spurious empiricality. The binary oppositions of information theory correspond to the negative-positive polarity of electricity which makes it possible to represent the alphabet (which is one kind of code) by means of the dots and dashes of Morse Code or by the binary digits (0/1) employed in all computers. Coding – or "Morsing," as Richards called it – depends on dots being differentiated from dashes. Identity and difference are the conditions of any system; it was Saussure's insight that because one sound – acoustic image – could be differentiated from another, there could be a linguistic system. But a system of meanings is not reducible to the means by which it has been realized: the Morse Code and a code of etiquette (Richards again) are not the same kind of code.

It is instructive to try to trace the sequence of mediations – the representational *screens*, as both Burke and Richards call them in recognition of the double sense of the word as *filter* and *background* for a display. When one composes a message which represents an intention formulated by means of the meanings represented by certain words, one has already been involved in a linguistic process which cannot be described or explained in the binary terms of a signal system. Once the message is composed and formulated, that formulation – the linguistic representation in oral or graphic form – can itself be represented in other terms: that process is properly termed *encoding*. A telegraph clerk knowing no English but familiar with the alphabet could transmit a message in English because what he must encode is not meanings but letters.

All codes are built on the logical fact that to say *A* is simultaneously to imply *not Not-A*. This is true whether *A* is a letter of the alphabet or a symbol standing for a definite object or measurement. All discourse depends on the possibility of establishing a system of such oppositions by means of a binary code, but the crucial point is that the system is not identical with the elements which enable us to construct the system – indeed, it is not a *system* at all until it is in operation. It is the linguistic process which defines the linguistic system; without a full account of the process of determination, linguistics is only a taxonomy. Borrowing the special terminology of linguistics forestalls attempts to account for process.

Consider the once ubiquitous dichotomy of surface features/deep structures. As a dichotomy, surface/depth begs the central question which any philosophy of language should pose, *viz.*, the question of the relationship of *what is said* and *what is meant*. Surface/depth is, of course a mythic polarity:

In the beginning God created the heaven and the earth. And the earth was without form, and void; and darkness was upon the face of the deep. And the Spirit of God moved upon the face of the waters.

The face of the deep: surface/depth provides the means of apprehending creation, but notice that the myth – the saying – provides a mediating term: "And the Spirit of God *moved* upon the face of the waters." The poet-philosopher who best understands the dialectic of surface/depth is, as it happens, a profound student of psychoanalysis – of *depth* psychology: Gaston Bachelard. In his essays on Monet's water lilies, the ambiguities of surface/depth provide superb hinges for thought as we come to realize that surfaces have structure and the deeps have features.[11]

The archetypal polarity of depths and surface provides a mythic means by which we can apprehend language and its reflective and reflexive powers. The best structuralists use it as an image of perplexing dialectic. Geological layers serve as an analogue for superficial meanings whose contours can be better understood in cross-sections revealing historical accumulations, deformations, and metamorphoses. The trouble begins when the metaphor of surface/depth is surreptitiously literalized: those who take this image as a model can thus bypass questions of meaning, thought, intention, representation and, of course, mind. Casuists who use metaphors as ways of avoiding the task of forming concepts are following the chief law of positivist model building: "Leave out the metaphysics." What that really means is "Leave out the concepts."

It is, of course, the purpose of any model to represent complex operations, structures, processes so that the essential form is clarified and defined, but the idea that particulars should not be multiplied, that economy of formulation is preferable – this sound principle of scientific method (and of critical philosophy and hermeneutics generally) is debased when it is taken as a license to set aside the complex. The scientism which has plagued psychology and sociology does not so much misappropriate scientific method as misunderstand it. For the challenge is not simply to reduce in order to build an elegant model, but to be clear about what the model is to represent and, more importantly, to know how to let the model serve heuristically. As Francis Crick observed of the most famous model of modern times, "You knew when it was working when you got more out of it than you'd put in."

But no model of language can be heuristic if it does not represent the linguistic process – the making of meaning. If process is not represented in some form from the start, we will never get to it authentically; it will simply be added in as another factor. In the study of language, it is what we start with that counts. What Richards saw as the problem of initial terms[12] is solved for the positivist by a manipulation of terminology. The psycholinguists study "language acquisition" and "readability" by measuring "short-term memory." In their clinical experiments, "language" is usually represented by words in isolation or by nonsense syllables. The literary critic who takes these findings as support for a theory of reading which makes the syllable the unit of perception and the word the unit of meaning will naturally be encouraged in a view of reading as an enterprise in which we are, in our simplemindedness, continually surprised by syntax – or sin. As Helen Gardner impatiently asks, after a critique of misreadings by Stanley Fish, "Who *is* this reader who can bring nothing forward?"[13] The answer is, the reader as conceived by psycholinguistics.

Psycholinguistics provides a great deal of information which certain rhetoricians and critics call upon, apparently without compunction. Here, for instance, is E.D. Hirsch, Jr.:

There is good evidence from recent experiments that we do take up meaning more securely from concrete than from abstract terms. It is usually better to say "The pen is mightier than the sword" than to say "Writing is more effective than warfare."[14]

The evidence Hirsch cites is in fact from psycholinguistic experiments in which language is treated as a signal code, even though it might be called a "symbol system." "Take up meaning" appears to be an adaptation (it certainly is not idiomatic English) of a phrase used in studies of perception, "information pick-up," which refers to electrochemical activity in the brain. But to model interpretation on the unconscious scanning and correction of vision is to muddle two kinds of code. "Take up meaning" is perhaps appropriate to an analysis of tachistoscopic findings; it is a very curious periphrasis for reading or interpretation. ("What meaning did you take up from that poem?")

"Usually," in the second sentence is a weasel word: whether one word or phrase is "better" than another depends entirely on context. The Bill of Rights does not list the sects which are or are not religious; that is what we have courts of law for, to adjudicate in particular cases. Whether or not we "take up meaning securely" is a function not of the relative degree of concreteness but of a capacity to understand the *relationship* of concrete and abstract: presumably, in this instance we would not take up meaning more securely from the statement "The Bic is more effective than the Cruise Missile." Indeed, even a moderate degree of concreteness seems to have misled Hirsch since *pen* in the aphorism is surely not a metonymy only for *writing* but for all rhetorical response – propaganda, oratory, and, of course, negotiation – or *parleying* in military terminology, a word which derives from the French *parler*: even psycholinguists know that speaking is not the same as writing. I leave further deconstruction to the reader. Take any aphorism or proverb, of the sort Hirsch confidently advances, and note the mysterious dialectic of concrete and abstract. Take, say, President Roosevelt's "We have nothing to fear but fear itself." Millions of Americans "took up meaning" very "securely" from those "abstract terms."

The positivist presupposition is that the concrete should be the point of departure for investigation because it is where experience begins. But human beings, in the exercise of intelligence, do not begin with the concrete. We would not be able to see, perceive, apprehend any concrete appearance or thing whatsoever unless we brought to that experience an idea, a schema, an abstracting capacity. As Rudolf Arnheim remarks, we couldn't see triangles if we didn't have the concept of triangularity to guide our recognition of particular triangles.[15] Triangularity is not tissue; it is not innate: it is an idea and it is *formed*. We are symbolically transforming our experience from the moment we are born – maybe before. These facts of concept formation have been formulated by Gestalt psychology and the theoretical implications have been explored by philosophers since the turn of the century, but the facts and their significance are ignored by psycholinguists and those who turn to them for guidance. Thus psycholinguistics misrepresents the reading process because it does not account for natural and necessary projection and anticipation which, when it is deliberately deployed as what Coleridge called "the forethoughtful query," is at the heart of practical criticism. We are able to read, we take meanings *from* texts because we bring meanings *to* them.

In her inquiry into why so little has been forthcoming from psychology in the study of mind, Susanne K. Langer lays the blame on a scientism which has set up the Idols of the Laboratory: Physicalism, Objectivity, Mathematization, Jargon, and Methodology.[16] She notes further the incapacity to develop working concepts which could supersede "What IS mind?" The focus on such questions was precisely what brought metaphysics into disrepute, but the methods and procedures of psycholinguistics are no advance. The assumption is that analysis should begin with the measureable, traceable, identifiable element. The search for a universal grammar has aimed for the same kind of essentiality as the eight basic sounds identified and analyzed by Jakobson; theories of poetic form – "verbal art" in Jakobson's phrase – have imitated phonological description. The attempt to find the smallest element, to identify the simplest and most accessible bit as the primary building block, has led to the absurd notion that the linguistic process begins with the means of recording. The graphic, neural, or electronic medium is taken for the basic, primary aspect so that it is now a commonplace to declare that writing is basically, or essentially, or really, graphite traces on processed pulp.

The mode of inquiry favored by positivists is problem-solving. The problem of problem-solving is that it so easily distracts critics and pedagogues, designers and investigators, politicians and strategists, from problem-posing; framing the question is much more difficult than proceeding as if it were self-evident. Following problem-solving procedures, whether algorithmic or "creative," is easier, more comforting, much more exhilarating than getting one's bearings, reflecting on presuppositions, drawing out implications, confronting the problem of initial terms. For this reason, even the idea of process is subject to positivist reduction. The positivist impulse is to move quickly to procedures and to spend time and energy on describing them; Methodology is one of the most demanding of the Idols of the Laboratory. And when procedures are thus refined and codified, it seems a shame not to use them; invention thus becomes the mother of necessity. Political examples are perhaps more easily recognized than rhetorical and critical ones, but in all fields, the temptation of problem-solving is to do what we already know how to do and to do it uncritically; to assume that because we are proceeding "methodically," the aim is beyond question.

Husserl's principle of bracketing (*epoche*) has been taken as a model for the style of modeling favored by psycholinguists. The term bracketing is sometimes used in contemporary criticism simply as a synonym for "setting aside" whatever might be considered inessential, for whatever reason. What gets bracketed – read out of court – is trivial, self-evident, not to the point, or merely distracting. At other times, bracketing is an overt ideological act, as when a certain idea is held to be contaminated and is thus treated as hazardous waste. Husserl's bracketing is more complex than this usage would suggest. The challenge for Husserl was to relate a particular experience or perception to universals, a problem familiar in theories of exegesis. But instead of developing a hermeneutic which could define the role of interpretation, he sought to obviate the need for admitting that role; he thus sought to isolate and empty out and reduce.[17] Bracketing, by enabling us to disregard what is inaccessible directly, would allow us, he presumed, to formulate statements about essences as strictly syllogistic as those of mathematics. But this solution does not recognize that *how* we account for how we know will determine the accounts we give of *what* we know.

A phenomenology of perception can not possibly provide ways of accounting for the ways we make sense of the world unless it offers a conception of the *process of determination*. Demonstrations of how concepts are formed in a continuing dialectic of particularization and generalization offer a corrective to any theory of reduction. Showing how the linguistic process and the process of perception are interdependent, how they unfold in social contexts, can guide us towards an authentic phenomenology of knowledge.

3

Determinations and Indeterminacy

It is very easy to fall into a metaphysical trap, to suppose that reality "has" only the forms we have provocation to see, or even into a slip-shod relativism assuming that the "real" form of Nature depends on someone's point of view.
– Susanne K. Langer

Like many a philosopher before and since, Husserl supposed that the phenomenon of the recognition and naming of colors could be analyzed and explained in simple terms and that the findings from experimentation could then serve as a "probe" (as psycholinguists like to say), as a way of exploring other processes inaccessible to empirical observation. A probe in the experimentation of natural scientists is an observable biological or chemical agent, the characteristic activity of which can be measured according to one or another scale. The careful differentiation of the probe and what it allows the investigator to trace and monitor is, of course, a central problem for phenomenological method.

When the subject of inquiry is literary meaning, developing the probe is a centrally important matter. "The task of criticism," René Wellek once declared, "will be a phenomenology of literature."[18] What is our point of departure for that enterprise? What do we bracket? The first question to be raised, one might think, would be how we are to determine what we are looking at. For Wellek, the work of art must be isolated and studied in its literariness, but there are, nevertheless, "limits set to the problem of interpretation: Hamlet is not a woman in disguise, nor is he, as Miss Winstanley proposed, 'mainly James I.'" This delightful *reductio ad absurdum* leaves unanswered, of course, the question of how we do decide. What for one critic is a highly probable allusion or subtext or reference strikes another as preposterous. Do we throw out of court the claim that Hamlet is suffering from an Oedipal conflict? Is that interpretation to be judged by the same criteria as the ones by which Miss Winstanley's is dismissed? For Wellek, what we are looking at is decided by what he called, in a later essay, "the structure of determination." Apparently, he saw no basic difference between the obsessive Miss Winstanley and those like Kenneth Burke who follow out the course of their quirky questioning. He excoriated them as follows:

These critics have lost all feeling for what I would call the structure of determination implicit in a text and have read into it almost anything which comes into their minds.[19]

I offer a close reading of this passionate sentence.

"The structure of determination implicit in a text" reads like an academic version of a familiar phrase, "straightforward meaning." Questions of method are disregarded and terminological ambiguities unacknowledged. Wellek's phrase could be taken to refer simply to formal limits of one kind or another, the kind of structure which in music determines tempo, for instance. The Boston Symphony Orchestra once planned a program in which dancers would perform as the orchestra played a Bach suite, thus dramatizing the fact that a suite is indeed a set of dances. In rehearsal, the dancers complained that the sarabande was entirely too slow. "After all," they complained, "you can stand on one foot only so long!" From such physical constraints derive enviably identifiable limits which in turn help to validate the interpretation represented in a performance. But are there comparable limits in linguistic structures, in a text? Rhyme and meter have famously served as guides in the recovery of the correct reading of Chaucer's verse, for instance, but they are explicit, measurable aspects, not something "implicit in the text." Words in an utterance of any kind are not lexical items whose semantic and syntactical roles can be studied in isolation from one another.

What is an "implicit structure" anyway? The model here would seem to be a skeleton, but a skeleton, though it specifically determines certain relationships, can be fleshed out in a number of ways which are subject to determinations other than those provided by bone structure. Nevertheless, a skeleton whose articulations did not determine in some fundamental respects, would not – could not – function: to call a skeleton a *structure of determination* is pleonastic. The point in question is how we are to conceive of the relationship of "structure" to the text in which it is supposed to be "implicit." It is tempting to conclude that Wellek's phrase is a version of a doctrine allegedly fundamental to the New Criticism: we read a poem as words on the page. The spatial metaphors of the transformational grammarians, who have located the darker meanings of *meaning* in depths below the surface, seem to legitimate moving the structure from "on the page" to "in the text," and declaring it then to be "implicit," something for which readers should have a "feeling."

That something so seemingly rigorous as a "structure of determination" is found in undialectical conjunction with something indefinably personal like *feeling* is the expectable consequence of seeing the meaning relationship in dyadic terms. When there is a failure to account for the process of determination, a "structure of determination" remains a clean machine.

Now, Professor Wellek believed that the study of literature would lose its center when it expanded to include the history of culture. He considered that a concern for the relationship to the life and times of an author is dangerous unless it is "internalized": historical study should be "an internal history of the art and tradition of literature."[20] What happens to limits, in what Wellek called the "intrinsic approach," is that they become an aspect of the object itself. The historicity of a work of art is internalized as genre; causes are kneaded in, showing up as determining structure. The work of art becomes, as it were, self-sufficient because the competent reader (a comparatist?) has converted cause to form, process to structure, context to text. Internalization assures a correct *reading out* and a rejection of all other (extrinsic) interpretive attitudes or approaches as *reading in*. When René Wellek claimed that readers like Kenneth Burke (but he was a class of one!), having lost their feel for implicit structure, are unconstrained so that they read into the text whatever they wish, the unspoken assumption is that they should read out instead of reading in, or at least that they should postpone reading in until they have read out – at which point, reading in becomes interpretation. It is ironic that Kenneth Burke stood accused of reckless reading in, when it is he who developed the concept of recalcitrance.

Critical reading does not occur as a result of some unspecified "competence," or a "feel" for structure. In the act of critical reading, we continue what we do in all our apprehensions: we make explicit our implicit recognitions. To act critically is to represent our intuitions – intuition itself being not a method but an event.[21] The common reader – any critical reader – discovers structure in one or another instance by seeing it in terms of other structures. That is one of the chief meanings of reading in context; to have had the experience of reading one sonnet sequence is preparation for reading another. The structures we thus recognize are conventional, generic, grammatical, syntactical, and so on; they are both linguistic and conceptual. Guided by our familiarity with other examples of a kind – tokens of a type, in Peircean terms – we can make those recognitions explicit and in so doing can provide ourselves with the means of drawing further meanings from what we read. Competence is thus a measure both of how adequately implicit recognitions serve the process of interpretation and of how our representations articulate those recognitions. When wide experience of literature and letters is reflected on imaginatively, it makes for valuable criticism – the kind we go to Kenneth Burke for.

The distinction to be made in the study of literary meaning is not between reading in and reading out, which are in any case inseparable, but between what Richards called "variant readings and misreading." Of course we need to have ways of demonstrating that a reading is wrong and we must be able to do so without appealing to unquestioned authority or a so-called "structure of determination": meanings are not discovered like Easter eggs; texts are not baskets. Reader response theory, conceived in dyadic terms, is no help either: the recognition that there is no direct knowledge of anything – bettles, bottles, or books – has led to the aberrant idea that all knowledge is mistaken and the related notion that all reading is misreading.

The contradictions of current theories of literary criticism are to be understood, I believe, in the context of what has happened once the ill-conceived idea of "the structure of determination implicit in a text" was supplanted by pseudo-concepts such as intertextuality, code, and indeterminacy. The post-structuralists claim to deal only with the codes and conventions, but by a process which Paul de Man, in "Semiology and Rhetoric," calls the rhetorization of grammar and the grammatization of rhetoric, they will also manage to analyze meaning.[22] This is accomplished by a sleight of hand whereby *grammatical* becomes the equivalent of *literal*, and *rhetorical*, of *figurative*. I will be concerned here with de Man's analysis of a passage from Proust, but only that part of it in which he demonstrates his technique of deconstruction and briefly alludes to his theory of texts.

Proust describes a cool dark room with only a ray of sunlight where the totality of summer can be recreated by his imagination, whereas outside, walking in the streets, there would only be fragmentary impres-

32 Dyadic Misunderstandings

sions. Just so, the repose, the tranquillity, allow him to read shocking adventures, recreating them in his imagination. That is not, strictly speaking, a paraphrase, but it is an interpretive overview of the sort which de Man categorically rejects; "freed from the burden of paraphrase," he will proceed to work only with the code. As he works out the ratios, he sets inside/dark/cool/totality/imagination over against outside/heat/fragmentary/senses, developing a dichotomy in terms of metaphor and metonymy. The concluding paragraph of Proust's description (in de Man's translation) is the target on which de Man focusses his deconstructive energies:

The dark coolness of my room related to the full sunlight of the street as the shadow relates to the ray of light, that is to say it was just as luminous and it gave my imagination the total spectacle of the summer, whereas my senses, if I had been on a walk, could only have enjoyed it by fragments; it matched my repose which (thanks to the adventures told by my book and stirring my tranquillity) supported, like the quiet of a motionless hand in the middle of a running brook, the shock and the motion of a torrent of activity.[23]

When de Man comes to the "motionless hand in the middle of a running brook," he notes that this water is cool and therefore misplaced: it is allied with the inside set but is clearly of the outside. And instead of considering that this asymmetry could signal a misreading or a mistranslation, that it might involve a shift in the logic of a metaphor which might not belong to his dichotomy, he steams ahead:

The natural, representational connotation of the passage is with coolness ... but coolness ... is one of the characteristic properties of the "inside" world. It cannot therefore by itself transfer us into the opposite world of activity. (135)

De Man sees the solution to his problem in the phrase "torrent of activity" which, he says, sneaks warmth into coolness, thus

closing the ring of antithetical properties and allowing for their exchange and substitution: from the moment tranquillity can be active and warm without losing its coolness and its distinctive quality of repose, the fragmented experience of reality can become whole without losing its quality of being real. (135)

It might first be noted that "therefore" here ("it cannot therefore by itself transfer") has no logical force whatsoever, since it is a common-

Determinations and Indeterminacy

place that one metaphor can interrupt another and turn an argument or a description topsy-turvy. (This is probably the chief rhetorical strategy in Shakespearean dialogue.) De Man's problem is spurious and his solution takes the form of a misreading, a faulty construction. For it is not the tranquillity of the writer, who is here a reader, which is "active and warm without losing its coolness ... and repose." There is an obvious grammatical difficulty is speaking of the *repose* of *tranquillity*, but there is a logical difficulty of more importance than this pleonasm. De Man fails to see the logical point of the "motionless hand"; his translation of *supportait* as "supported" (rather than "bore," in the sense of "endured") is one sign of his misconception. The clear sequence of equivalences is as follows: Marcel's repose is in harmony with the cool dark room where his imagination can make a totality of summer; his repose bears the shocks of the adventures he is reading, as a hand in a stream of water which, going with the flow, is buffeted but does not resist – is passive, "motionless" in that sense. In short, the "torrent of activity" is not part of the chain of binary oppositions of inside/outside but is a description of what his imagination brings to life as he reads. The fundamental consonance of the imagination of summer and the imagined adventures de Man misses entirely: *analogy* is a triadic conception which cannot be caught in a dyadic grid.

De Man, who began by declaring freedom from the bondage of paraphrase, now concludes with this remarkable claim:

The reading is not "our" reading, since it uses only the linguistic elements provided by the text itself; the distinction between author and reader is one of the false distinctions that the deconstruction makes evident. The deconstruction is not something we have added to the text; it constituted the text in the first place. (138)

This is the kind of language we find in the claims of religious fundamentalists for whom the inerrancy of the text is a cardinal principle. Paul de Man's deconstruction is the apotheosis of the Clean Machine: the competent operator merely switches it on and it runs by itself. De Man believes that it is possible simultaneously to bracket meaning and to recover it by decoding, and he apparently believes that he has shown how to do that.

In the absence of a philosophy of representation, gangster theories struggle for dominance and in the competition, the typical development of weak versions of strong ideas is dramatically highlighted. Absolute assertions are followed, first, by modifications which distract attention from contradictions and absurdities; then, by a proliferation of metaphors, neologisms, and opaque slogans which rehabilitate the original version in a weak form.

Like most philosophic aphorisms, "There is nothing outside the text" terrorizes by sounding self-evident. Eventually, certain counter-claims and questions become possible: if there can be *nothing* outside, that is tantamount to saying that there is *no* outside. And without an outside, it is impossible to entertain the idea of an inside. The *text*, defined in terms of an outside/inside relationship, disappears. Adjustment is called for; the text is re-instated – with a *context*. But this begins to sound like an "outside," so the context is renamed a *text*; context is thus supplanted by many texts, none of which has referential power. The re-formulation is now prepared: "Nothing, indeed, can be said to be not a text." Indeed. But if no negative is allowed, there is no way to define. More aphorisms, more slogans, more paradoxes will be required. Thus *pseudodoxia academica* keep themselves alive by an endless adjustment of terms, by an energetic and aggressive casuistry.

And in the absence of context – destroyed in defending the gangster theory of all-is-text – there is an expectable confusion of lexical definition with what would otherwise be identifiable as contextual definition. Indeterminists discover that words in the dictionary have quite a range of possible meanings. They marvel at the indeterminacy of words out of context, which are the only kind we have now.[24]

The chief source of these ideas about the non-existence of reference is Roman Jakobson's conception of the "poetic function" as self-referential. Other kinds of communication can be defined as focussing on *message* or on the *decoder*, but the poetic function is not primarily a matter of getting an idea across: it is the formulation of expression – of *what*, it is not necessary to speculate about. Jakobson's wiring diagram of the communication situation is the master model for all clean machines. Just as it allows – and indeed encourages as a matter of principle – the conflation of message and signal, so it legitimizes a separation of *expression* from *reference*. In other words, the signified could in some cases be said to point beyond itself to real world purposes or, in others, to call attention to itself, when there is nothing in the real world being indicated. These ideas go back to Russian Formalism, but the ease with which they are adapted to quite different purposes is intelligible because of the shared conception of the sign as a dyadic relationship.

Determinations and Indeterminacy   35

What happens, as we have seen, is that the poetic function is soon imputed to all discourse: a strong theory is born. First we have an analysis which foregrounds the poetic means of making meaning, defined in technical terms – metaphor and metonymy, motifs, prosody, imagery, etc. Soon we arrive at non-interpretations of poems in which words are treated as lexical items, as acoustic images, or as elements of binary code. Then we find that the calculated disregard of "message" has become a principle of all discourse, that there is no "representational" function because reference is only to other "texts."

Attempts to legitimate the conflation of language and discourse have also drawn on Saussure's understanding of the signifier as an acoustic image: *word* and *acoustic image* become interchangeable.[25] The idea that the sound of a word is absolutely arbitrary is identified with the notion that the meaning of a word is equally arbitrary, i.e., is absolutely dependent on how the reader takes it. In reaction against the theory that the origin of language was in imitation of natural sounds and the elaboration of expressive cries, Saussure had stressed another theory, as ancient as the one he hoped to bypass, *viz.*, that the relationship of the acoustic image and what it stands for is arbitrary. What started out as a way of denying the onomatopoetic theory of the origin of language became for the structuralists a key concept in the analysis of kinship systems and sonnets alike. The principle of the arbitrary sign was taken over from phonology and deployed as a model of all symbol systems and thus of interpretation.

Protecting this spurious conception of the arbitrary sign is a powerful gangster theory, the so-called Sapir-Whorf Hypothesis. That is in fact a misnomer since it is at odds with what Sapir held; properly, it should be identified as Whorf's "linguistic relativity." The doctrine of linguistic relativity holds that we are prisoners of the language of whatever speech community we are born into and that each world-view is determined by the particular language of the group holding it. Since a correlation of linguistic morphology and understanding is demonstrably untrue, the expectable consequence is that "weak" versions are developed in which it is alleged that *somehow* and in some cases the syntactical structures of one or another language correspond *somehow* and in some cases to the way we see reality.

These two gangster theories – the arbitrary sign and linguistic relativity – invading the field of discourse analysis together can be formidable. Here is Jonathan Culler Whorfizing the Saussurian arbitrary sign:

36 Dyadic Misunderstandings

A language does not simply assign names to a set of independently existing concepts. It sets up an arbitrary relation between signifiers of its own choosing on the one hand, and signifieds of its own choosing on the other. Not only does each language produce a different set of signifiers, articulating and dividing the continuum of sound in a distinctive way, but each language produces a different set of signifieds; it has a distinctive and thus "arbitrary" way of organizing the world into concepts or categories.[26]

Culler has dispensed with readers and speakers, putting language in their place. This personification makes possible the casuistry by which he muddles *arbitrary*, meaning random or irrational, and *arbitrary*, meaning decisive and deliberate. The quotation marks around the second *arbitrary* signal that this is a quite deliberate attempt to make the two terms synonymous. Lawyers are adept at this maneuver.

Culler then explains that just as "the sound sequences of *fleuve* and *rivière* are signifiers of French but not of English, whereas *river* and *stream* are English but not French," so "the organization of the conceptual plane is also different in English and French." The term *plane* activates the Whorfian conception of a *correlation* of language and thought-perception. He continues then towards the expectable conflation:

"Fleuve" and "rivière" are not signifieds or concepts of English. They represent a different articulation of the conceptual plane ... Not only can a language arbitrarily choose its signifiers; it can divide up a spectrum of conceptual possibilities in any way it likes. (15–16)

The conceptual *spectrum* parallels the sound *continuum* in a thoroughly Whorfian way and creates a thoroughly Whorfian muddle. Culler has simply identified "the organization of the conceptual plane" with the lexicon; he has taken as his point of departure the concept of an identity of thought and language, despite the fact that the idea of a "conceptual plane" which can be articulated (or "segmented," as Whorf would say) in different ways presupposes the prior existence of concepts.

It is no great step from this idea of an autonomous language arbitrarily dividing up "a spectrum of conceptual possibilities" to the idea that if your language does not provide the right band of the spectrum, you will not be able to entertain the ideas which constitute it. The dyadic insistence that the map is not the territory becomes the claim that without the map there is no territory. Thus Jacques Derrida has come close to asserting that without the word *apartheid* there could be no such political system.[27] This claim is logically the same as that made by Stuart Chase, who declared in the 1930's that there was no such thing as Fascism – only fascists. But it is not the availability of particular words which determines the ideas to which we have access: the relationship of language and thought is mediated by meaning and, as I have been arguing, meaning is not a concept to be defined in narrowly linguistic terms. Whorf's linguistic relativity has a great appeal because it at first appears commonsensical, but to continue to be guided by it in the face of clear demonstrations of its inadequacies is a "skeptical infidelity against the evidence of reason and sense."

Indeterminacy joins the (misapplied) doctrine of the arbitrary sign and linguistic relativity as a formidable gangster theory. Indeterminacy, taken to mean uncontrollable shifts in the meaning relationship, is the mirror image of the idea of a "structure of determination," whether conceived as a mystical skeleton or identified positively with one or another set of particular elements.

The Indeterminists have thought that a warrant for their claims could be provided by modern science, especially physics. When the scientist speaks of determinations, he refers to conclusions to be drawn from calculations and, both in theory and practice, the limitations of the means of calculation are taken into account. But Heisenberg did not intend his Uncertainty Principle to bring physics to a halt, as Indeterminacy has very nearly done to critical inquiry.[28]

A more explicit warrant is allegedly to be found in C.S. Peirce by certain critics who seem not to have read Peirce but Jacques Derrida attempting to read Peirce. For Peirce, indeterminacy was, in its metaphysical aspect, a characteristic of what he called Firstness, that essential ground of Thirdness. He differentiated indeterminacy (his word for vagueness) and ambiguity: "A sign is ambiguous if it is doubtful what it is applicable to and what it is inapplicable to, but the indeterminacy here spoken of merely consists in its being applicable to more than one possible object."[29] *Indeterminacy*, as it is now used, is a pseudo-concept – a catchall term, not a theoretically sound principle. And it has no methodological or pedagogical implications whatsoever: *placing under erasure* is no more a method than it is an English idiom. It is a pretentious mystification of certain acts of mind entailed in interpretation. For Richards and his famous student William Empson, ambiguity provided an invaluable speculative instrument for the study of the structure of complex words and texts. What has been learned about ambiguity in fifty years of practical criticism does need to be freshly formulated, but that task cannot be carried out in the terms provided by a dyadic conception of the sign.[30]

It is not indeterminacy which should supplant the doctrine of a structure of determination but the idea of a process of determination. So too, the conception of representation as copy or replication or substitution must give way to representation seen as Peirce understood it, as the symbolic means of bringing before the mind ideas we wish to identify and express (7.535). And these changes of perspective are possible only as we entertain a triadic conception of the sign. In the absence of triadicity, *representation* will remain problematical, serving equivocation and unrecognized ambiguity.

It is very difficult for those suffering from RUP to resist reducing equivalence to identity. The tendency is to conclude that because consciousness entails representation, they are the same; that because thought requires language for its realization, they are the same; that because a sign requires another for its interpretation, what it represents is only another sign. But pragmatistically – triadically – speaking, we can see that it is not representation which engages us but the representation of representation. That is how a triadic semiotics can guide a reconception of the hermeneutic enterprise. Rather than the spurious claim that interpretation can be set aside because proper decoding techniques allow us to work with the coded text alone, hermeneutics will be seen as a matter of representing our representations. As Michael Baxandall has it: "We represent not the picture but our thinking about the description of the picture."[31] We must learn how not to forget the Third.

4

Bottom's Semiology: The Duck-Rabbit and Magritte's Pipe

The apprehension of the particular *qua* "existence" involves apprehension of the possibilities of transformation which it contains ... Perception is not a process of reflection or reproduction at all. It is a process of objectification, the characteristic nature and tendency of which finds expression in the formation of variants.
– Ernst Cassirer

To define critical inquiry by analogy with vision is a commonplace. (The word *idea* derives from a pre-Homeric Greek root meaning both *I have seen* and *I know*.)[32] But the scientistic impulse is to wake up the dead metaphor in order to model "cognitive processes" by drawing on supposed facts of the physiology of vision. Attention is, however, more complex than such modelling implies. Jacques Derrida's notion that we should attend to the fringes, to the margins, by somehow bringing them into focus simultaneously with the center does not take into account the fact that focus is determined by what we center on: if we shift focus to the edges of our visual field, they are no longer the edges. Central vision and peripheral vision are in dialectic and one cannot be held in abeyance while a shift takes place. "Look to the left," says the ophthalmologist so that he can look at the right section of the eye; but *we* can't ourselves look at ourselves looking. Derrida apparently means nothing more than that we should attend to problematic and borderline cases and contexts, but when he attempts to model that attention by the unmetaphoric facts of vision, he gets them wrong and the resultant formulation is a contradiction in terms.[33]

Muddling what the brain does for us and the interpretations those perceptual forms make possible is one of the chief sources of misconceptions

40 Dyadic Misunderstandings

of representation. Attempts to deploy brain activity as a model of interpretation founder because those who believe that they have thereby grounded mental operations have not differentiated, to use E.H. Gombrich's terms, the sense of order we are born with and the sense of order we must learn.[34] The conflation of innate powers of perception with the culture-bound apprehension of forms helps to muddle the idea of representation as copy and the idea of representation as symbolization. Appealing to the psychology of perception does not automatically assure trustworthy guidance, for there is no fact or surmise in that field (or any other) which cannot be misconstrued, if taken in a dyadic perspective.

One of the most commonly cited – and most commonly misunderstood – exhibits in the gallery of perception studies is the duck-rabbit, a configuration which, if certain lines are taken to represent a bill, is a duck, but it becomes a rabbit, if they are construed as ears. The duck-rabbit is sometimes understood as providing evidence for theories of a radical indeterminacy, either in "the way things are" or in the way we see them. One popularizer of European critical theory has declared that this teasing configuration gives him a warrant for claiming that all interpretations are equally valid because nothing is *really* there! You can see it as a duck or as a rabbit and therefore it is not either one. The duck-rabbit thus allegedly shows that everything depends on our desires or presuppositions or whatever disposition, conscious or not, determines our apprehensions. Although the aim of such argument is to establish the concept of indeterminacy by demolishing the concept of an objective reality, the validity of the subjective-objective dichotomy is, nevertheless, presupposed. The duck-rabbit as an emblem of indeterminacy begs the questions we need most urgently to formulate.

In the following passage, Gombrich explains the significance of the duck-rabbit:

The impression has grown up that illusion, being artistically irrelevant, must also be psychologically very simple. We do not have to turn to art to show that the view is erroneous. ... Take the simple trick drawing which has reached the philosophical seminar from the pages of the humorous weekly *Die Fliegenden Blätter*. When we look for what is "really there," to see the shape apart from its interpretation, we soon discover [that it] is not really possible ... We cannot experience alternative readings at the same time. Illusion, we will find, is hard to describe or analyze, for though we may be intellectually aware of the fact that any given experience must be an illusion, we cannot, strictly speaking, watch ourselves having an illusion.[35]

For Gombrich, the duck-rabbit is an emblem of the principle that interpretation is a name for all acts of knowing. His use of the duck-rabbit to demonstrate the interdependence of shape and interpretation, of the particular configuration and what we see, is close to that of Joseph Jastrow, in whose *Fact and Fiction in Psychology* (1901) the duck-rabbit made its first serious appearance. Jastrow demonstrates how the viewer cannot *will* to hold just one determination, that he is surprised by the shifts as they come. For Jastrow, as for Gombrich, the duck-rabbit illustrates certain physiological and psychological constraints of perception: what we see is not simply a matter of conscious choice and we cannot watch ourselves watching. The fact that it is psychologically impossible "to separate the shape from our interpretation" will be fundamentally misconceived if it is isolated from these other considerations. The visual gestalt shift cannot serve as a model for the interpretation of texts any more than the Morse Code can model cultural codes. Because the gestalt shift is unwilled and uncontrolled, it is logically inappropriate as an analogue of concept formation or the development of ideas.

Nevertheless, the duck-rabbit shows up in discussions of paradigm shifts.[36] Thomas Kuhn has had doubts about this kind of analogy, but his warning is equivocal:

Scientists do not see something *as* something else; instead, they simply see it. ... In addition the scientist does not preserve the gestalt subject's freedom to switch back and forth between ways of seeing. Nevertheless, the switch of gestalt, particularly because it is today so familiar, is a useful elementary prototype for what occurs in full-scale paradigm shift.[37]

To say that "scientists do not see something *as* something else," that they "simply see it," is a way of putting the matter which is likely to cause trouble, since in one important sense nobody ever "simply" sees anything: all perception is of something *with respect to, in comparison with, in opposition to*. That is why it makes sense to claim that recognition precedes cognition; that anticipation is essential to all construing and constructing; that any act of identification entails an act of differentiation and thus of classification. Let us assume that Kuhn means that scientists "simply see" in terms of the governing paradigm, the terms provided by nameable expectations and identifiable presuppositions, and that seeing thus *in terms of* is different from seeing "the marks on the paper as a duck and then a rabbit." But this presents another difficulty, since we do not first see the marks on the paper and then a rabbit: we *see as* in order to *see* at all. When Kuhn goes on to allow "the switch of a gestalt" as an "elementary prototype" for a paradigm shift, he not only dismisses his own reservations; he also reduces the paradigm shift to a matter of code-switching. It is no longer a transformation of the meanings which have provided the means of making further meaning. He thus muddles two semiotic perspectives: a binary opposition cannot be the prototype of a triadic representation. Kuhn takes *seeing as* to mean taking one thing, and then construing and interpreting it in terms of another thing, but that is a dyadic view: it posits an X and proceeds to interpret it as a Y would be interpreted. In a triadic perspective, *seeing as* is not a matter of comparing an apprehended figure or object or form of any sort with another; it is a matter of apprehending in the first place. An aphorism of Paul Klee's gives cogent form to this idea: "Art does not render the visible; it renders visible."[38]

Seeing as, taken as a mode of deliberate interpretation, is one way to characterize invention; analogy, as Oppenheimer claimed, is the means of discovering new ideas in science.[39] But in a deeper sense, *seeing as* is the necessary condition of seeing at all. The duck-rabbit problem is often said to exemplify the beholder's share,[40] the constraints of context, cultural perspective and so on. But this is incorrect. The uncontrollable gestalt shift exemplifies the way that physiological coding works; it is representative of the operations of the sense of order which we do not have to learn, the innate sense of order which Gombrich differentiates from the sense of order which develops in the course of our lives. The sense of order which we learn is culture-bound and depends on our practice and experience. To model the sense of order we learn on the sense of order we are born with is as hazardous as seeing the codes which are culture-bound systems of meaning in the same terms as those codes by means of which they can be represented. These two different senses of order function interdependently, of course; or, we might say, the innate sense is the necessary condition for all symbolic activity, for which culture provides the sufficient condition. The dialectic of the two orders which constitutes the process of perception is precisely analogous to that of the formal system of any language and the mediations of the culture in which it functions.

When in his philosophical investigations Wittgenstein came to focus on the psychology and logic of perception, the duck-rabbit had a particular importance. He thought that it demonstrated the difficulties of defining the relationship of shape and interpretation. He did not consider them interdependent; that is to say, he did not see them in triadic terms: "If I saw the duck-rabbit as a rabbit, then I saw: these shapes and colors ... and I saw *besides* [my italics] something like this: and here I point to a number of different pictures of rabbits."[41] Wittgenstein is not concerned with the gestalt shift or with the question of control or will. He apparently considers seeing the duck-rabbit as analogous to sudden recognition of a pattern in what appears initially to be a random collection of lines – the Aha! reaction. What he thinks it shows is the difference between the act of perception and the report we make of it: "'Seeing as' ... is not part of perception. And for that reason it is like seeing and not like seeing."

Wittgenstein sets a behavioral *seeing* over against an interpretive *seeing as*; mere recognition over against acts of imagination and will, which are interpretive. Neither he nor those who deploy his investigations differentiate *seeing as* from *seeing X as Y*. He disregards the fact that *seeing* – perception, the sense of order we're born with – is necessarily *seeing as* and that it is only in this sense that it could possibly model the activity of the imagination. Being able to picture to ourselves what is not present is an essential condition of speech; this imagining is a capacity which entails remembrance which, in turn, is necessarily dependent on language. Wittgenstein tries to conceive of the act of seeing in terms of what we do: our behavior in pointing would be analogous, he thought, to recognition. But if Husserl did not see that the individuality of facts is based on complexity, Wittgenstein, we might say, did not realize the complexity of the simplest act of seeing nor did he take into account the role of other acts of seeing which have preceded and those that are to come. His dyadic understanding of the meaning relationship was essentially a behavioral one.

There is an interesting contrast in Wittgenstein's comments to the Viennese positivists, when they were finally able to persuade him to meet with them. It is reported that the conversation "strayed into the field of perception."[42] The question put to Wittgenstein was like the conundrums of the Enlightenment, those early versions of worst case scenarios.

You say that the colors form a system. By that, do you mean something logical or something empirical? Suppose, for instance, someone spent his whole life shut up in a red room, and could see only red ... Could he then say, "I see only red, but there must be other colors also"?[43]

Here is Wittgenstein's response to the question:

I do not see red, rather I see *that the azalea is red*. In this sense, I also see that it is not blue ... Either there is a state of affairs, which can be described, in which case the color red presupposes a system of colors, or alternatively, "red" means something quite else [sic], in which case there is no sense in calling it a color.

In his account of *seeing* a rabbit and *seeing* the lines *as* a rabbit, Wittgenstein deliberately separates interpretation from recognition, but here, in insisting on *seeing that*, he effectively argues that they are integral, that it is as absurd to speak of a particular color without regard to the system of which it is a part as it would be to try to identify a pitch (or any other kind of degree) without a scale.

Seeing as can describe both the sense of order we are born with and the sense of order we must learn. The *seeing as* of perception, insofar as it is the brain's work, is a matter of scanning schema which are coded in the cortex and of the corrections which the brain makes. This sense of order we are born with is manifested in electrochemical transfers which can be described as a "code" because electrical polarity is involved, but the "information" is only absence of noise in the channel. The sense of order which is learned is perception in the sense of mind work. The *seeing as* which is conscious recognition is a learned response in which culturally determined experience is in dialectic with linguistic forms. We are born knowing how to see by *seeing as*, knowing how to recognize. New representations – tokens of types, in Peirce's terms – can be recognized without deliberate direction or control, because types discover tokens. We learn to recognize the class concept implicit in its members and thus to discover other classes which are comparable in one or another aspect: we learn to recognize and to represent by analogy.

Analogy empowers mediation, the symbolic representation by means of which we recognize our recognitions and interpret our interpretations. For Peirce, interpretation *is* learning – and he characterized Thirdness (mediation) as "the sense of learning."[44] The usefulness of the duck-rabbit is that it can remind us of how the sense of learning differs from the unconscious ordering of the brain. Jastrow's presentation of the duck-rabbit is consonant with this distinction, probably for the very good reason that at Johns Hopkins he studied with C.S. Peirce.[45]

There are as many contradictions and muddles in Michel Foucault's disquisition on Magritte's pipe as we find in discussions of the duck-rabbit and they arise from the same sort of misconceptions. Magritte's pipe is depicted on a neutral ground and labelled "Ceci n'est pas une pipe."[46] It appears to be a poster from the elementary school classroom. The legend appears in a very legible script – not "childish," as Foucault and others say, but schoolish. It is the script which youngsters learning to read learn to read. *This is a dog ... That is a man ... Here is a house.* Magritte's delightful joke is to slip in the negative. Since learning to read the world – not just script – entails recognition of the opposite case and of the fact that recognition must be represented, an Empsonian reading might lead to speculations on mediation as what makes the *culpa felix*, on recognition of the negative as the sign of the happy Fall. What we have, rather, in Foucault's labored interpretation is a variation on the positivist theme of the curse of mediacy.

Foucault claims that the label is "so easily recognized that it excludes any explanatory or descriptive text."[47] To explain this perverse explanation, Foucault draws upon the idea of the calligram, a coupling of text and image which challenges "the oldest oppositions of our alphabetical civilization: to show and to name; to shape and say; to reproduce and articulate; to imitate and signify; to look and read." His claim is that there is an ambiguity between the habit of taking captions (text) as descriptive of pictures (images) and the impossibility here "of defining a perspective that would let us say that the assertion is true, false, or contradictory." Never mind that Magritte's picture is not a calligram: the strong theory Foucault wants to press is surreptitiously weakened to a claim that there are *some* aspects of a calligram in this instance!

Of course, to explain a joke is to kill it, but Foucault manages to kill the joke twice over: he explains it, but then he gets the explanation wrong; he doesn't get the joke. Words, not habits, are ambiguous. *Ceci* in its ambiguity creates a paradox of the sort which can be resolved: if the *this* is taken as a reference to the image, the statement is a version of the positivist slogan "The map is not the territory." In dyadic terms, the label is a tiresome reminder of the self-evident. But of course we are meant to be pushed to "Yes, but": "Yes, but in another sense, of course it is a 'pipe.'" If the *this* is taken as referring to the image, the statement is contradicted. Magritte is parodying, we might say, those statements which logicians torture in the course of differentiating *Sinn* and *Bedeutung*: "The King of France is bald." "All Cretans are liars." "The cockroach is not falling off the table."

Magritte's joke provides what all jokes provide, a chance to feel ourselves getting it: all jokes are built on the principle of the double-take. Sometimes the wordplay involves an ambiguity of sound, in which case we call it a pun; in other cases, it is a play on referents. But it is a principle of all jokes to allow us to discover the "perspective" in which to judge. Only a positivist habit of assuming that there is properly a one-to-one relationship between signifier and signified forecloses this possibility. Call it Bottom's Semiology:

> SNOUT. Will not the ladies be afeard of the lion?
> STARVELING. I fear it, I promise you.
> BOTTOM. Masters, you ought to consider with your [selves], to bring in (God shield us!) a lion among ladies, is a most dreadful thing; for there is not a more fearful wild-fowl than your lion living; and we ought to look to't.
> SNOUT. Therefore another prologue must tell he is not a lion.
> BOTTOM. Nay; you must name his name, and half his face must be seen through the lion's neck and he himself must speak through, saying thus, or to the same defect, "Ladies" or 'Fair ladies, I would wish or I would request you or I would entreat you not to fear, not to tremble: my life for yours. If you think I come hither as a lion, it were a pity of my life. No! I am no such thing; I am a man as other men are; and there indeed let him name his name, and tell them plainly he is Snug the joiner.' (*MSND*.III.i)

It is the chief consequence of triadicity that our knowledge is mediated by what we already know. The process of signification – of recognition, of interpreting, of making new meaning – is empowered by "the sense of learning." We learn by interpreting our interpretations, by seeing what we mean. If we are told, as we often are, that vision is a treacherous metaphor for knowledge, we should note that in such caveats, vision is conceived as a linear decoding, itself a hazardous metaphor, resting as it does on certain presuppositions about how language allegedly corresponds to reality. Thus it is that what is rejected is explained in a frame of reference which is scorned but not dismantled. To say that vision is outmoded as a way of modelling the process of understanding is to fail to understand the logic of the analogy in the first place. It is like saying that the body is outmoded as a model for representing experience to ourselves. The point is, rather, that physiognomic perception must be corrected and supplemented. Of course we project; of course we must re-consider.[48]

Seeing as is the way we see: recognition is entailed in cognition. If, following Gombrich, we take the duck-rabbit as an emblem of the impossibility of separating seeing shape from interpreting, we will have a talisman which can at least alert us to the spurious claims of gangster theories which purport to be grounded in the facts of perception. In the dyadic perspective, recognition becomes a kind of linear decoding rather than being seen as the dialectical interplay of the sense of order we are born with and the sense of order we must learn. Images – remembered and envisioned – are representations by means of which we recognize other images: "Those images that yet/ Fresh images beget." The facts of perception properly remind us that forms find new forms, that meanings are our means of making meaning. And the consequence is not a dizzying indeterminacy which drives us to throw ourselves into the abyss; it is that we must cultivate, as Peirce said, "a contrite fallibilism."

But talismans and careful allegories of the making of meaning are not enough to protect us from killer dichotomies like *semiology/rhetoric* and *discourse/practice*. The only real protection against gangster theories; the only real solution to the problem of initial terms, of deciding what is given to interpretation; the only generative idea with the power to withstand the radical skepticism and moral terrorism of contemporary critical theory, is a philosophy of representation. We urgently need to come to terms with the issues raised in any consideration of the relationship of the linguistic process and intention; it is that end which the concept of recognition can serve. Recognition is a "speculative instrument"[49] of prime importance for apprehending how, in the linguistic process, images are stabilized so that they can support those central acts of mind by which we exercise "the sense of learning."

5

Gaps, Abysses, and the Mysterious Barricades

In the dim recesses behind consciousness there is the sense of realities behind the abstractions. The sense of process is always present. There is the process of abstraction arising from the concrete totality of value-experience, and this process points back to its origin. But consciousness, which is the supreme vividness of experience, does not rest content with the dumb sense of importance behind the veil.

– Alfred North Whitehead

The idea that language is a veil between us and reality; that words erect barriers which prevent direct access; that any and all expression contains error – these notions are universal and perennial. We find them set forth by Karl Marx and Eastern mystics, by skeptics and sophists, as well as by the deconstructionists of the present day. Language is infected and unreliable or it is somehow to blame for the human condition. In myths of origin, language is somehow implicated in loss; somebody gets the message wrong or forgets it entirely. In later versions of a Fall, language is an analogue of sin and death; and reason, because of its dependence on language, is profoundly and irremediably inadequate. Only faith, grace, intuition, or Right Reason can assure redemption.

These representations of separation – the (paradigmatic) *fall* from grace, perfection, innocence, and the (syntagmatic) *gap* or *abyss* which divides the knower from the known – are subject, of course, to different interpretations, depending on the perspective in which they are seen. Gaps can result, simply, from a dyadic conception of signifier and a signified, with mediation disregarded or denied. Dyadic gaps can be spanned or closed only by means of casuistry and equivocation. Saussure's dichotomy of *langue* and *parole* creates the problem of relating these two aspects of language. Fredric Jameson approves Saussure's solution, which was to give *parole* to the speaker and *langue* to the audience, but that is like giving the positive pole to the light bulb and the negative pole to the socket.[50] And how are we to understand the relationship of the signifier and the signified? The difficulty is exacerbated by the contradictory force of the theory of correspondence and the doctrine of the arbitrary sign. Saussure's characterization of the signifier as an acoustic image has led positivist linguists into this trap: any idea of the correspondence of language and reality is undercut by the idea of an arbitrary relationship between the signifier and the signified.

In the perspective of a triadic semiotic, gaps function as part of the semiotic structure itself. Thus, for Ogden and Richards, a triangle with a dotted base line symbolizes a triadic meaning relationship in which a *symbol* refers to an object (*referent*) only by means of a meaning (*reference*, at the apex) entertained by the sign-maker, and it can be construed only by an interpreter who shares that meaning. The triangle with the dotted base line is an emblem of a triadic semiotics.[51] By differentiating referent and reference and showing their interdependence, the curious triangle reminds us that the heuristic power of the symbol depends dialectically on separation and conjunction.

The triadic sign seems to offer easy solutions to problems created by the dyadic sign. If the relationship of the signifier and the signified is somehow determined by the interpreter, constrained by his "discourse community," the dilemma created by the inconsonance of the doctrine of the arbitrary sign and theories of the correspondence of language and reality could be bypassed: meaning could be brought into the picture as a psychological concept; hermeneutics could supplant semiotics; critics could learn to love their chains, to rejoice in barriers and gaps. But triadicity has no explanatory power unless interpretation is seen as a logical, not a psychological matter. (Peirce foresaw the difficulty and spoke only with reluctance of interpreters rather than what he called the *interpretant*, the mediating idea held by the interpreter.) Triadicity – the recognition of mediation – is not a matter of defining two powers of language, one which separates and one which unites, as in Mauthner's image of the ocean as bridge and as barrier.[52] The point is, rather, that it is by being a barrier that it is a bridge: language *as such* – the formal system, the arbitrary structure, unconscious and historically determined – language is itself the great heuristic.

A philosophy of language as a process whereby both the self and the world are objectified and represented has been established most convincingly by the work of Vygotsky, Whitehead, Cassirer and Susanne K. Langer. But the ancient notion of language as a barrier between us and reality has rather surprisingly surfaced in contemporary critical theory where it enjoys favor along with the equally ancient idea of the identity of language and thought. Both views, though they are camouflaged in the distracting language of structuralism and post-structuralism, are fundamentally expressions of a naïve realism. The maxims and gnomic sayings which currently guide theory construction and deconstruction – there is nothing outside the text; there is nothing that is not a text; all reading is misreading; all knowledge is error – are variant expressions of a positivist understanding of language. Max Black, in rejecting the idea of language as a barrier, comments that "a barrier that it is logically impossible to remove is not, in any interesting sense, a barrier at all."[53] But it could be said that the idea of a barrier which is at once irremovable and *necessary* is indeed logically interesting: it exemplifies the kind of paradox which is insoluble but not irrational. *All discourse is partial*, as Peirce noted; but it is by being partial that it carries out its tasks.

I contend that the barriers language constructs are mysterious barricades which function according to this logic of necessity. They are like the plane of the canvas described by Nicolas de Staël as a wall through which all the birds of the world fly freely. Language provides forms which continually reform as we construe and construct them; they are like the figures of Couperin's *Les baricades mistérieuses*, those resonant suspensions which seem to block the basic harmony, even as they shape the melodic contour.

The disjunctions in which critical theory nowadays rejoices are the artifacts of a false consciousness of the limits of language. That is to say, without the concept of mediation, the heuristic power of formal constraints cannot be appreciated; without an understanding of separation as the condition of the making of meaning, there is no reason to account for mediation. Indeed, the dyadic sign encourages the mystical notion that beyond the formal structure there is *real* reality. For the naïve realist, "all symbolization harbors the curse of mediacy," as Cassirer wrote in *Language and Myth*. (It is his characterization of attitudes he rejects root and branch, but it has been misconstrued over and over again, for interesting reasons.[54]) There are positivist and mystical versions of the naïve realism which considers language a veil between us and reality: truth is seen as being on one or the other side of a barrier – *with* us and our empirical measurements, or *beyond* us and out of reach. It is notable that this dichotomy of language and reality is consonant with the idea that language and thought are identical. If a signifier stands in relation to a signified like a map to its territory – as it does in the dyadic perspective – then everything that is not territory is map, including both language and thought. (Typically, positivists denounce all "Aristotelian" dichotomies but their own.) If reality constitutes one half of a two-valued relationship, then it follows that all else must be conflated to constitute the other half.

The question of the identity of language and thought has been a philosophical conundrum for centuries, and like everything else in the philosophy of representation, the way we answer it will depend on how we conceive of the sign. Only the triadic sign can accommodate mediation, but triadicity degenerates very quickly to dyadicity, with a third awkwardly tacked on, unless signification is seen as a dynamic, ongoing, dialectical process of determination. It all depends on how the identification of language and thought is conceived: either it is presupposed, or it is seen as emergent in the linguistic process. This distinction, I take it, is the burden of Walter Benjamin's early and extremely opaque essay, "On Language as Such and the Language of Man." The presumption of identity he calls an abyss over which a theory of language must remain suspended:

> The view that the mental essence of a thing consists precisely in its language – this view, taken as a hypothesis, is the great abyss into which all linguistic theory threatens to fall, and to survive suspended over this abyss is its task. The distinction between a mental entity and the linguistic entity in which it communicates [itself] is the first stage of any study of linguistic theory, and this distinction seems so unquestionable that it is, rather, the frequently asserted identity between mental and linguistic being that constitutes a deep and incomprehensible paradox, the expression of which is found in the ambiguity of the word *logos*. Nevertheless, this paradox has a place, as a solution, at the center of linguistic theory, but remains a paradox, and insoluble, if placed at the beginning.[55]

To speak of an identity as an *abyss* is a dizzying paradox, but Benjamin's logic is as sound as his insight is shrewd. His argument is that only by differentiating thought and language at first will we be able to appreciate the dialectic whereby they work together in virtual unity to create meaning. Only the recognition of a primary difference can lead us to understanding the achievement of functional unity. It is to this

52 Dyadic Misunderstandings

secondary unity which Benjamin refers in speaking later on in the essay of the *immediacy* of mediation.[56]

For the naïve realist, entertaining such a paradox is out of the question. Mediation remains a barrier against which shins must be barked to prove that it is not accepted. Or, conversely, mediation is simply denied in favor of the pleasant horrors of the abyss. But once we accept the "immediacy" or necessity of mediation, the dichotomy of language and reality dissolves and we discover that this opposition is logically faulty. Mediation – that is to say, the acknowledgement of interpretation as a constituent part of the sign – converts dichotomies to dialectical relationships; it transforms dyadic structures to dynamic processes; it makes interpretation the motive power of symbolization. This is, indeed, what Richards meant in referring to Peirce's "revolutionary doctrine of the Interpretant."

Benjamin's *great abyss* – "the view that the mental essence of a thing consists precisely in its language" taken as hypothesis – highlights the ambiguities of one of Wittgenstein's aphorisms: "The limits of my language are the limits of my world." To identify the limits of "my language" with the limits of "my world" seems an early version of "linguistic relativity," but the possessive is unclear: does Wittgenstein mean the merely personal? the merely cultural? the merely historical? We may answer according to our reading of Wittgenstein's stance at the time, but when the aphorism is deployed by others, it is impossible to know what is meant unless we know what conception of the self is in play. A muddle of the psychological and the logical is the result when the identity of language and thought and the correspondence of language and reality are presupposed, as seems to be the case here. It is a major drawback of academic aphorisms that they do not serve those purposes of definition which they are seemingly called upon to perform. The obscurity of *language, limits,* and *world* makes this statement no more useful than another in the defense of any one view of how we make sense of experience, of how we interpret, of what is given to interpretation. If limits are understood as merely constraining, without a recognition of enabling function, then Wittgenstein's formulation is analogous to Nietzsche's image of the prison-house of language. And, of course, no formulation which omits process can account for the heuristic power of language.

Vygotsky is less equivocal than Benjamin or Wittgenstein when he insists that the study of thought and language must begin, not with the *elements* of thought and language, but with the *unit* of meaning.[57] But is this not to presuppose their identity, thus falling into the abyss rather than remaining suspended over it? The answer, I think, is clear when we remember that this unit is conceived by analogy with a living cell, no element of which can function in isolation from the others. For Vygotsky meaning is a *dynamic system*: it is like a cell because of the way it is organized and because it is in process. Vygotsky depends on organic metaphors to represent an understanding of semiosis – the making of meaning, the linguistic process – but he does not let metaphors do his thinking for him. Nor does he hold that one can move from structure to process simply by converting nouns to participles. His understanding is developed from theory and practice in lively conjunction and from a method which continually demonstrates the dynamic character of semiosis.

When he comes to discuss the character of play in the development of the child, Vygotsky speaks of it as a mediated activity which, incidentally, he represents by a triangle with a dotted line between *stimulus* and *response*, the apex being a "complex, mediated act."[58] The earliest instance of meaning making is seen not as a response to the environment or as an instinctual expression but as an *activity* of mediation.

From another quarter entirely, we find the same emphasis on activity when Whitehead defines the relationship of language and thought. Here is a passage from a lecture of 1937 which is representative of his thinking in this matter:

Let it be admitted that language is not the essence of thought. But this conclusion must be carefully limited. Apart from language, the retention of thought, the easy recall of thought, the interweaving of thought into higher complexity, the communication of thought, are all gravely limited. Human civilization is an outgrowth of language, and language is the product of an advancing civilization. Freedom of thought is made possible by language: we are thereby released from complete bondage to the immediacies of mood and circumstance ... The denial that language is of the essence of thought is not the assertion that thought is possible apart from other activities coordinated with it. Such activities may be termed the expression of thought. When these activities satisfy certain conditions they are termed a language ... Thought is the outcome of its own concurrent activities.[59]

These concurrent activities constitute symbolic action; the conditions they satisfy are that they are purposive and intentional. Insofar as they are our means of making meaning, they are forms. Sustained by a semiotics which recognizes the centrality of activity, we can remain safely suspended over Benjamin's abyss of identity.

But this is an inadequate response if we are concerned with the issues Vygotsky speaks of; if we are interested in the difference a philosophy of language can make to our understanding of human life, then mere avoidance of the trap of presupposing identity and thus short circuiting the study of the making of meaning will not serve our purposes. Benjamin's figure reminds me of a small animal frozen in fear or, more accurately, caught in the headlights and, without the capacity of rational choice, trapped there by the instinct to freeze. Suspension over an abyss does not suggest the reflexive and reflective means by which the study of language and thought proceeds. Benjamin's figure of suspension cannot represent the study of the linguistic process. The only way we can account for the emergent identification of language and thought is by taking semiosis into account. Thus, in a triadic perspective, all gaps and abysses, cuts and barriers, are mysterious barricades: by the logic of necessity, they define the heuristic power of limits, the very conditions of knowing.

II. TRIADIC REMEDIES

6

Peirce and the Third

> Charles Peirce was an unlucky man. His two most important ideas ran counter to the intellectual currents of his day, were embraced by his friends – and turned into something else. William James took one idea and turned it into pragmatism which, whatever its value, is not the same thing as Peirce's pragmaticism. Peirce's triadic theory has been duly saluted by latter-day semioticists – and turned into a trivial instance of learning theory. Freud was lucky. The times were ready for him and he had good enemies. It is our friends we should be aware of.
> – Walker Percy

From the first, the general opinion has been that Peirce is hard to read.[1] As an old man, he recalled a conversation with William Dean Howells whom he had met on the way to the post office. Howells, he wrote, "began criticizing one of my articles from the point of view of rhetorical elegance. I said to him, 'Mr. Howells, it is no part of the purpose of my writings to give readers pleasure.'"[2] This was not simply a youthful sobriety: throughout his essays and articles and papers, Peirce is faithful to the principle he goes on to recommend in the drafted letter quoted from above, *viz.*, that the idea to be communicated to readers is that "distinct positive discovery is what we are laboring upon." The corollary is that if readers find the account difficult – well, the matter is difficult. Sometimes Peirce is merely impatient or even amused by the supposed criticisms of his readers, but he can be sardonic, as when he writes that now, just as he is prepared to demonstrate in logical terms what his argument has been, most readers will abandon him; or when he dismissed humanists, psychologists, and *littérateurs* for their failure to exercise "the ratiocinative power."

But Peirce did recognize the difficulties of his style and he eventually came to see the illogical character of the attitudes which were responsible for them:

The greatest analyst of thought that ever lived might spend an indefinite amount of time in endeavoring to express his ideas with perfect accuracy ... But he would only make his thoughts so involved that they would not be apprehended ... Perfect accuracy of thought is unattainable – *theoretically unattainable*. And undue striving for it is worse than time wasted. It positively renders thought unclear ... After all we want to get our thought expressed in short metre somehow.[3]

He put it that way to Lady Welby, with whom he carried on a correspondence in the last decade of his life. (Lady Welby died in 1912; Peirce, in 1914.) Lady Welby knew Peirce from his encyclopedia articles on logic and arranged to have her publisher send him *What Is Meaning?*, which Peirce then reviewed along with a book of Bertrand Russell. When he sent her his approving review, along with several articles, she wrote asking for further elucidation of Peirce's views of "that practical extension of the office and field of Logic proper, which I have called Significs," commenting on "the triad of signification" (her phrase for the three modes of signification she had tentatively identified) and noting certain points about "triadic ideas."

His response was very quick and very genial: the correspondence was under way. As the years passed, her appreciation was often expressed; at one point Peirce drafted the following P.S. (which was not actually sent):

Well, dear Lady Welby, you deserve this infliction, for having spoken of my having 'always been kindly [!!!] interested in this work to which my life is devoted,' when I have myself been entirely absorbed in the very same subject since 1863, without meeting, before I made your acquaintance, a single mind to whom it did not seem very like bosh. (8.376)

Clearly, Lady Welby's letters were a godsend to Peirce. Like most others, including William James, she could not follow the logical demonstrations which he considered crucial (she found the Existential Graphs, which he could not resist deploying, positively bewildering), but her questions were sharp and, best of all, they were double-pronged: she wanted to know what and she wanted to know why. Her analysis remains, he notes without recrimination, focussed on the relationship of symbols (and for Lady Welby they were exclusively *words*) and the conceptions they represented. He will attempt to show her how her concerns are related to the larger issues and that will require that he set out some basic premises: "I think that I will today explain the outlines of my classification of signs" (*S. and S.*, p. 23). And on that day he found the short metre: Lady Welby's letters are thus a godsend to us too.

The short metre – relatively speaking. Peirce characteristically begins not with the classification of signs as promised – Icon, Index, and Symbol – but with his cenopythagorean categories which, in Quaker style, he had named Firstness, Secondness, Thirdness. They are modes of being, ways that both ideas and things exist in the world, and though the analysis of just how they are related involves Peirce in noting degrees and reciprocities which must be named and adjusted, he manages to proclaim more than once that for his ideoscopy, it is Thirdness which is all-important, chiefly because it allows him to define a sign: "A Third is something which brings a First into relation to a second ... A sign is a sort of Third ... A sign is something by knowing which, we know something more (*S. and S.*, p. 31)." The complexities soon produce perplexities as Peirce tries to work within self-imposed limitations, and in less than a year he drafts a letter in which various explanations subvert those so recently offered. Nevertheless, the outline of Peirce's *semeiotic* emerges in the correspondence with Lady Welby far more clearly than it ever did elsewhere.

Peirce offers Lady Welby an explanation all his readers may welcome, *viz.*, that the Interpretant is an idea we think *with*: it is the mediating idea which is hold by an interpreter. Peirce explains it best at the very moment he despairs of ever doing so, declaring that he will, as a "sop to Cerberus," allow himself to refer to the interpreter as a person rather than a Quasi-mind (*S. and S.*, p. 81). Just as he resisted the conflation of interpreter and interpretant, so Peirce devised ruse after ruse to avoid suggesting that his *semeiotic* was dependent upon the concept of *mind* (which he intermittently thought of as a woolly German mammoth); he considered psychological description a bar to careful logical representation, a way to sneak nominalist attitudes into what he wanted to be a thoroughly realist architecture of ideas.

Peirce generally characterizes his categories as a set: if Firstness is a quality or feeling, then Secondness is event or action and Thirdness is effect or conduct. If Secondness is compulsion or limitation, Firstness is freedom and Thirdness is law. If Secondness is the fate that snips, Thirdness is the thread of life and Firstness is indeterminacy. Thirdness is mediation, representation, transmission; it bridges. Most persistently, Peirce sees it as continuity. Mediation is necessarily a process, which explains the emphasis on semiosis, on making, finding, interpreting signs. We learn from experience – we take habits and break them, too – by seeing significances, thus learning and changing, growing: that "sense of learning" is Thirdness.

To appreciate Thirdness is to recognize that because all knowledge is mediated, all knowledge is interpretation. All interpretations must be interpreted: that each sign requires another for its interpretation is one of Peirce's best-known principles. As the interpretant of one sign becomes the representamen of the succeeding sign, semiosis entails not deferment but partiality: "our understanding is always a matter of degree" (1.541). This point has been thoroughly muddled by radical skeptics of the day who conflate the idea of partiality and the idea of error. All knowledge is partial, but that is not to say that all knowledge is error-ridden; nor does the process of interpreting our interpretations mean that we cannot know or that we cannot represent our partial knowledge. When Derrida quotes Peirce on how all symbols grow out of other symbols, he does so to knock out of commission the concept of representation. Here is what Derrida[4] quotes:

Symbols grow. They come into being by development out of other signs, particularly from icons, or from mixed signs partaking of the nature of icons and symbols. We think only in signs. These mental signs are of a mixed nature; the symbol parts of them are called concepts. If a man makes a new symbol, it is by thoughts involving concepts. So it is only out of symbols that a new symbol can grow. *Omne symbolum de symbolo.* (2.299)

Just before this passage, we find the statement that "the symbol is connected with its object by virtue of the idea of the symbol-using mind, without which no such connection would exist." Derrida leaves out the Interpretant. Peirce is claiming that meanings provide the means of making meaning. He identifies yet again the central character of Thirdness: it is both the condition and the consequence of knowledge. "Whatever is capable of being represented," he wrote elsewhere, "is itself of a representative nature" (8.268).

Derrida wants to marshall Peirce for his obsessive campaign against "presence," which entails a skepticism about the possibility of representation. But *representation* is the term Peirce used before he hit upon Third-

ness: the Representamen is dialectically related to the Interpretant, a conception which Derrida seems not to grasp: for all his censure of Saussure, his semiotics remains thoroughly dyadic. When Peirce writes that "the idea of manifestation is the idea of a sign," Derrida takes that to mean that "manifestation itself does not reveal a presence, it makes a sign." But that reading converts a dialectical interdependence to a positivist dichotomy. Derrida has no means of bridging the gaps he continually discovers because he rejects the logic of triadicity.

Taking Thirdness seriously requires apprehending "the revolutionary doctrine of the Interpretant" and that, in turn, requires an understanding of the relationship of the sign and indeterminacy. In contemporary criticism, it is often assumed that Peirce's semiotics offers a warrant for the claim that the sign is indeterminate and that indeterminacy should supplant ambiguity. For Peirce, however, indeterminacy is another name for vagueness, which is not the same as ambiguity. Because signification entails generality, which is dependent on future, unknown semiotic acts, indeterminacy is a necessary condition of semiosis. Ambiguity, on the other hand, has to do with appropriate reference: "A sign is ambiguous if it is doubtful what it is applicable to and what it is inapplicable to ..."[5] We confront ambiguity as we interpret our interpretations and we can eliminate it, if we can develop the appropriate contexts. But indeterminacy, like mediation, is entailed in signification. Like partiality, indeterminacy is a necessary cost, the price of meaning-making. In triadic terms, indeterminacy does not mean that we can't know what we're talking about or that we can't represent our interpretations or that there is nothing but a play of signifiers. Peirce was profoundly aware of the role of chance, but he saw it in dialectic with continuity and his aim was order.

The chief consequence of Thirdness is not the necessity of a doctrine of indeterminacy but the need to cultivate that attitude which Peirce called "fallibilism." Since "perfect accuracy of thought is unattainable," we must be on guard against claiming too much for our interpretations. We must cultivate fallibilism because it is practical, because it makes a difference in our logic. We need to keep things tentative by continually hypothesizing by the method Peirce called *abduction* (or *retroduction*), a means of representing our meanings so that we can draw out implications, amplifying inferences as a way of exploring the possible consequences of one or another formulation. Abduction is the logic of pragmaticism: *If we put it this way, what difference would it make to our understanding? to our practice?*

Such pragmatic maxims have reference not to an individual asking a metaphysical question but to the process of semiosis which takes place in a community of those concerned to know: Peirce is hard to read unless we know how he thought of community. Individual truth was no more attainable, Peirce thought, than perfect accuracy of thought:

Unless truth be recognized as public – as that of which any person would come to be convinced if he carried his inquiry, his sincere search for immovable belief, far enough – then there will be nothing to prevent each one of us from adopting an utterly futile belief of his own which all the rest will disbelieve. Each one will set himself up as a little prophet, that is, a little "crank," a half-witted victim of his own narrowness. (*S. and S.*, p. 73)

Peirce over and over again demonstrated that the relationship of the individual to others is a matter of logic. He saw the individual and the public each as encompassing the other: the particular and the universal are represented in one another because "absolute individuality in representation is merely ideal" (3.93). "The very origin of the conception of reality," he wrote, "shows that this conception essentially involves the notion of a COMMUNITY, without definite limits, and capable of a definite increase of knowledge" (5.311). Thus the relationship of the individual and society is not to be defined merely in psychological terms any more than are the elements of the sign: "It is not merely a fact of human Psychology, but a necessity of Logic, that every logical evolution of thought should be dialogic" (4.552). The dialectic of man and society is like that holding for the representamen, its object and interpretant; indeed, it is the same because Man is a Sign. Representation can not function without context, purpose, mediation which, for the Man-Sign, is other signs, other human beings.

This principle is illuminated by Peirce's lecture on consciousness and language (c1867; 7.579–7.596) which includes a disquisition on man as a sign. Peirce first declares that we must make logic our metaphysics and then make sure that the triadic character of metaphor is established: he emphasizes the difference between metaphor as "an expression of similitudes," and metaphor as "true analogy" – as "a broad comparison on the ground of characters of a formal highly abstract kind" (7.590). In his argument, the character of the analogy he is drawing between man and sign is developed so that we see that the comparison is in terms of the power of representation and of being represented. He shows how a word can be in several places at once and then continues:

I believe that a man is no whit inferior to the word in this respect. Each man has an identity which far transcends the mere animal; – an essence, a *meaning* subtle as it may be. He cannot know his own essential significance; of his eye it is eyebeam. But that he truly has this outreaching identity – such as a word has – is the true and exact expression of the fact of sympathy, fellow feeling – together with all unselfish interests – and all that makes us feel that he has an absolute worth ... Every symbol has an essential comprehension which determines its identity ... Man is conscious of his interpretant – his own thought in another mind ... is happy in it, feels himself in some degree to be there. (7.591)

Man is a sign because insofar as he is more than animal, he is spirit and spirit is analogous to meaning: it reaches out; it recognizes itself in its representations.

One of Peirce's editors, Arthur W. Burks, has written candidly of the difficulty he has in reading Peirce when he writes in this analogical vein. Burks undertakes a rhetorical anlaysis to get at what Peirce is really saying, but since for him rhetoric is decoration or glitter, the task of analysis is a matter of reduction: "When we strip the Emersonian-like rhetoric from Peirce's writing ... we will find an intelligible and interesting doctrine."[6] This procedure is consonant with the conception of language found frequently in classical rhetoric, namely, as the garment of thought, but it has nothing in common with the best literary critical practice, of whatever school, and it certainly is not consonant with what Peirce meant by *rhetoric* in philosophic usage.[7] After he strips away Peirce's allegedly transcendental rhetoric, Burks then proceeds to re-clothe the doctrine he has discovered, in fancy dress: Man is an information-processor; man is not a symbol but an algorithm.

This interpretive paraphrase misses the point of Peirce's analogy, insofar as semiosis entails consciousness. All information processing proceeds by means of binary opposition: there is neither room nor need for Thirdness in information processing. *Human information processing* is a contradiction in terms and as an oxymoron it creates the same sort of muddle we have when terms from linguistics are simply transferred to the study of discourse – "literary competence," "cultural literacy," "interpretive communities," "literacy acquisition." Peirce grumbled to Lady Welby that he saw "a great many thinkers who are trying to construct a system without putting any Thirdness into it" (*S. and S.*, p. 28). I doubt if he'd have been surprised at Professor Burks's attempt to take Thirdness out of his.

Certainly, insisting on a semiotic description of man and society led

Peirce to some curious declarations. But the eccentric notions Peirce developed about the relationship of one mind to another or, rather, one individual to others, have great heuristic power: if we are alert to their complex dialectic, Peirce's formulations can generate new ways of thinking about the relationship of personal knowledge to the social construction of knowledge. He held that "man's circle of society ... is a sort of loosely compacted person" (5.421). And for Peirce, defining community was impossible without working concepts of generality:

The consciousness of a general idea has a certain "unity of the ego" in it, which is identical when it passes from one mind to another. It is, therefore, quite analogous to a person; and, indeed, a person is only a particular kind of general idea. Long ago ... I pointed out that a person is nothing but a symbol involving a general idea; but my views were, then, too nominalistic to enable me to see that every general idea has the unified feeling of a person. (6.270)

And he goes on to cite Christian communities as exemplary of this idea that "every general idea has the unified living feeling of a person." Such statements provide important correctives to Habermas' misapprehensions of Peirce's realism.[8]

Truth for Peirce is the Daughter of Time; it is what will come out, what would be arrived at "in the long run." If you think of interpretation as coming to an end, that is to imagine an end of the linguistic process itself – and that, in turn, is *a moment out of time*, expressible only by such an oxymoron. We may see face to face, but not so long as we live in a dimensional world. But Peirce seems never to have let go the idea that there could be an end to the infinite regression of semiosis – and that we could be there to enjoy it. A command of the kind of paradox necessary to the very formulation of ideas of absolute knowledge is perhaps to be found only in great poetry – for instance, in the Mutability Cantos – but Peirce somehow accommodates "in the long run" to an evolutionary semiosis. In any case, in the context of pragmaticism, what we need to remember is that community is constituted by those willing and able to judge what difference it would make if we hold one or another idea to be true.

When they deign to consider Peirce at all, the new pragmatists ignore the architecture of his ideas. Peirce's pragmatism – his *pragmaticism* – is unintelligible without an understanding of his semiotics which, by making interpretation an integral part of the sign, entails the development of an extraordinarily rich and complex support system: fallibilism and abduction, among other ideas scarcely touched on here; mediation and the instrumentality of thought; a dialogic sense of the individual and the community; a profoundly dialectical sense of the intersubjectivity of knowledge. What is least understood is Peirce's idea of representation: given the radical skepticism of much contemporary criticism, perhaps representation should also be hailed as a revolutionary doctrine. But then so should semiosis: Peirce's emphasis on the process whereby one sign requires another for its interpretation leads to his very powerful idea of Synechism – the continuity of all things, including ideas including man. It is expectable, then, that he would transform the Riddle of the Sphinx – in a familiar variant, "What is Man?" – to the question of his becoming. The short response to Richard Rorty's insolent remark that Peirce never explained what he needed his *semeiotic* for[9] is that he meant it to guide the exploration of that question: "What is Man to become?"

When Morris Cohen prepared the first selection of Peirce's works (while the Harvard edition was in progress), he gave it the felicitous title *Chance, Love, and Logic*. This particular triplitude is not Peirce's own, though it usefully relates Peirce's *tychism* (chance) and *agapism* (love) to the essential principle of his logic, *synechism* (continuity). I will allude to Chance, Love and Logic in briefly discussing parables of Firstness and Secondness before turning to the recurrent image of Thirdness, Man's "glassy essence."

Peirce prefers mathematical demonstration and is sardonic about the failure of "the ratiocinative power" in those who are unable or unwilling to follow such proofs. But he does know how to work from equations as well as towards them, though unfortunately, once he departs from mathematics, he frequently depends on coin flipping and the probabilities in card playing. (It was a habit he learned at his father's knee: Benjamin Peirce would keep Charles up into the early morning hours playing rummy and quizzing him on the whys and wherefores of unsuccessful bids.) But occasionally he turns to parables and metaphors. For instance, when he wants to explain how natural causes are comparable to intentions, he puts it this way:

Nature herself often supplies the place of the intention of a rational agent in making a Thirdness genuine and not merely accidental; as when a spark, as third, falling into a barrel of gunpowder, as first, causes an explosion, as second. (1.366)

The gunpowder metaphor lets us understand how Thirdness is the condition of Secondness without actually coming before it. Peirce spends a great deal of time and energy explaining how this works and to do so he constantly must speak of process: *semiosis* is of the essence of semiotic.

Probably the most useful gloss Peirce provides for the categories is that Firstness is Quality, Secondness is Event, while Thirdness is Mediation. A chance event is somehow between Firstness and Secondness: lacking Thirdness, it lacks even genuine Secondness. Earlier in this same gunpowder passage, Peirce turns to a myth-y story by way of explaining that genuine Thirdness entails intention:

"How did I slay thy son?" asks the merchant, and the jinnee replied, "When thou threwest way the date-stone, it smote my son, who was passing at the time, on the breast, and he died forthright." Here there were two independent facts, first that the merchant threw away the date-stone, and second that the date-stone struck and killed the jinnee's son. Had it been aimed at him, the case would have been different; for then there would have been a relation of aiming which would have connected together the aimer, the thing aimed, and the object aimed at, in one fact. What monstrous injustice and inhumanity on the part of that jinnee to hold that poor merchant responsible for such an accident! I remember how I wept at it, as I lay in my father's arms and he first told me the story. (1.366)

The story of the merchant and the jinnee is one Peirce tells many times; it is as if he struggled perennially against the idea of the merely accidental, seeking to identify the happy promise of indeterminacy to offset the sinister effects which could be realized by chance.[10] When he speaks of Firstness, it is generally to recognize the quality of freshness:

Stop to think of it, and it has flown! What the world was to Adam on the day he opened his eyes to it, before he had drawn any distinctions, or had become conscious of his own existence – that is first, present, immediate, fresh new, initiative, original, spontaneous, free, vivid, conscious, and evanescent. Only, remember that every description of it must be false to it. (1.357)[11]

False, not because language or any other sign is inadequate to it, but because the act of description presupposes an object or an event or an idea – a representation of some sort; and Firstness has no such character. Peirce has the same meaning in mind when he remarks that "Indeterminacy affords us nothing to ask a question about" (1.405). Nothing to describe, nothing to question: Firstness remains mysterious. Secondness, on the other hand, is "brute action" which, though it is not explainable in itself, is certainly describable:

The idea of second must be reckoned as an easy one to comprehend. That of first is so tender that you cannot touch it without spoiling it; but that of second is eminently hard and tangible. It is very familiar, too; it is forced upon us daily; and is the main lesson of life. In youth the world is fresh and we seem free; but limitation, conflict, constraint and secondness generally, make up the teaching of experience. With what firstness
  'The scarfed bark puts from her native bay;'
and with what secondness
            'doth she return,
With overweathered ribs and ragged sails.' (1.358)

Chance, like Firstness in its indeterminacy, is at once the release from necessity and the condition under which the tendency to habits eventuates in the establishment of laws.[12] Both chance and habit-taking entail process, which Peirce often calls *continuity* or *synechism*; and process is always identified with the idea of generality. The tendency of ideas to spread, to detach themselves from the particular, to be cultivated by the community of those who take them up: this spreading, this nurture and cultivation, Peirce called *agapism* or evolutionary love, which advances "by virtue of a positive sympathy among the created [i.e., the creations reproduced in this evolutionary development] springing from continuity of mind" (6.304).

The third of Morris Cohen's terms, Logic, is most closely related to Thirdness: Peirce's logic is a logic of relatives, which is precisely what Thirdness is intended to represent. Including intention means that the sign is dynamic; semiotic thus entails semiosis. To represent the paradoxes of the process of signification, Peirce frequently turns to the phrase *man's glassy essence*.

In his proto-farewell to philosophy, Richard Rorty surveys uses of the metaphor of the mirror which he construes as representative of a naive copy theory of knowledge, the conception of mind he considers dominant in the Renaissance. He notes that "the phrase *man's glassy essence* was first invoked in philosophy by C.S. Peirce in an 1892 essay of that title on the 'molecular theory of protoplasm,' which Peirce strangely thought important in confirming the view that 'a person is nothing but a symbol involving a general idea' and in establishing the existence of 'group minds.'"[13] Rorty is truculent about a rather carefully developed argument. In the essay bearing the title "Man's Glassy Essence," Peirce seeks to define the relationship of the psychical and physical aspects of a substance. He begins with molecular theory and its application to protoplasm in order to examine the meanings of such terms as *force* and *constitution, energy* and *resistence,* and to establish the claim that "a physical property of protoplasm is that of taking habits." He discards mechanistic explanations and concludes that there is evidence of "a primordial habit-taking tendency." The subdued but glowing conclusion is as follows:

> It is clear that nothing but a principle of habit, itself due to the growth by habit of an infinitesimal chance tendency toward habit-taking, is the only bridge that can span the chasm between the chance-medley of chaos and the cosmos of order and law. (6.262)

"Man's glassy essence" does not appear in this essay, but the fact that Peirce chose the phrase as his title is significant: it provides a gloss on the central argument he is making about the relationship of habit and order and how this reflects both the character of that universe towards which our ideas evolve and our role in a process to which we remain insensible.

Just as the tale of the merchant and the jinnee appears frequently in Peirce's explanations of the character of Firstness, so reference to "man's glassy essence," a phrase occurring in *Measure for Measure,* serves him to express an important aspect of Thirdness. Before turning to the other instances of the appearance of "man's glassy essence" in Peirce's works, we should look at Shakespeare's lines. One reason that Rorty doesn't understand what Peirce meant is that he doesn't understand what Shakespeare meant.

Isabella, pleading for her brother's life, turns to the tyrant Angelo who has refused mercy, crying that heaven's thunder cleaves only the oak, sparing the myrtle,

> but man, proud man,
> Dress'd in a little brief authority,
> Most ignorant of what he's most assur'd –
> His glassy essence – like an angry ape
> Plays such fantastic tricks before high heaven
> As makes the angels weep; who, with our spleens,
> Would all themselves laugh mortal. (II, ii, 117–123)

Rorty writes that the commonplace notions associated with mirrors do not seem to play any role in Shakespeare's figure of "man's glassy essence": "Shakespeare here seems to be simply original, rather than using a stock trope." This insight does not preclude Rorty's use of the phrase as if it were "a stock trope," in his pleonastic characterization. And he interprets Isabella's meaning as a stock idea.

Construing these lines requires a speculative instrument which the editors of the Riverside Edition, for instance, did not find. Here is their gloss on "glassy essence": "i.e. man's essential being or rational soul, which, mirror-like (glassy) will show the man who contemplates it what he is. Glassy has probably the additional sense of 'fragile, highly susceptible of damage.'" This leaves us with the central question unformulated: we must be able to account for the opposition of assurance and ignorance. I.A. Richards, for whom this passage was especially resonant, perhaps because he understood its significance for Peirce, comments on it in explaining his choice of *Complementarities* as the title of his uncollected essays. He begins with a comment of Niels Bohr: "When new discoveries have led to the recognition of an essential limitation of concepts hitherto considered as indispensable, we are rewarded by a wider view and a greater power to correlate." Richards then continues:

Does there not seem a sort of poetic justice about this? That, when we have brought ourselves, somehow at last, to acknowledge an inadequacy in our conceivings we should be *rewarded*, not penalized; that the outcome should be a gain, not a loss of power. It has its resemblance to the Sermon on the Mount, or to Isabella on that Representative Man, Angelo:
>   man, proud man,
> Drest in a little brief authority,
> Most ignorant of what he's most assured –
> His glassy essence ...

It is like Shakespeare to make ignorance and assurance thus vary together. And to hint that the last thing we may know is that whereby we know.[14]

Aided by that reflection, we can now ask how glass could symbolize that which enables by being a barrier. No modern critic is more skillful than Richards in laying bare the logic of metaphor. Here is a second gloss:

Glassy essence. Modern editors want to make this a looking glass or mirror. But isn't it rather that central mystery of our being: that activity *through which* we see whatever we ever see, our very self – a medium so transparent, like the lens of

the eye, that ordinarily we know nothing about it?
> Most ignorant of what he's most assured
> > His own focusing mind.[15]

This construction advances our understanding by reminding us of the ambiguities of the word *glassy* and by transforming an inert image, a mere decorative or "rhetorical" flourish, to an emblem, to a representation of a deeply felt idea. The one point which is not quite clear is the term *ordinarily*: if this means "generally speaking," the logic is wrong. We will have to take it in the Peircean sense of *regularity* to make it consonant with the paradox of an ignorance of the assured: by the law of our means of knowing, "we know nothing about it"; *ordinarily*, necessarily, we *can know nothing* about it. That this is, indeed, what Richards means is suggested by a third aid to reflection, another passage from Shakespeare, which Richards, earlier in his discussion, had juxtaposed to Isabella's speech; it comes from *Troilus and Cressida*:

> nor doth the eye itself –
> That most pure spirit of sense – behold itself,
> Not going from itself; but eye to eye oppos'd
> Salutes each other with each other's form;
> For speculation turns not to itself
> Till it hath travell'd and is married there
> Where it may see itself. This is not strange at all!
> > *Troilus and Cressida* (III, iii, 105)

Richards insists on *married* and chides nineteenth-century editors who emended it to *mirror'd* for wanting to make Shakespeare "obvious," but I think that he is led to this rather perverse reading by reason of wanting to strengthen his claim that *glassy essence* is a lens rather than a mirror. But he forgets, momentarily, the dialectic of seeing and reflection. *Speculation*, as it catches both thought/vision and mirror (speculum), prepares us for *mirror'd*, but, more importantly, these words together precisely represent the dialectic of representation:

> For speculation turns not to itself
> Till it hath travell'd and is mirror'd there
> Where it may view itself.

Could there be a more succinct expression of the idea that recognition is the condition of thought? We are *ignorant* of our *glassy essence* because we cannot see ourselves looking: the activity of seeing can only be completed in representation. The reason we are *assured* of our *glassy essence* is that we are made in the image of our Creator. The seeming contradiction of assurance and ignorance is thus resolved: our mirroring serves as a lens.

From occasions when Peirce incorporates Isabella's lines or notes them in the margins, we can see that ignorance sometimes means simply a failure to remember that "man is essentially a soul" (7.580). That in his ignorance man's imitation takes the form of aping does not gainsay the fact that man does have the power to represent heaven on earth. (The irony of Isabella's passionate philosophy turns on the fact that the deputy Angelo is no angel; his actions betray the truth that man is capable of reflecting heavenly virtues like magnanimity and mercy.) But man can mediate chance and law by love; he can do so because he is Thirdness to the facts of the universe in their Firstness and Secondness: Man is a Sign. Salvation lies in agapism:

The individual man, since his separate existence is manifested only by ignorance and error, so far as he is anything apart from his fellows and from what he is to be is only a negation. This is man,
>   proud man,
> Most ignorant of what he's most assur'd
> His glassy essence.   (5.317)

Thus the riddle of *most ignorant of what is most assured* can be answered in the light of Peirce's ideas of the continuity of mind and of evolutionary love. The agapastic process moves beyond individual man and out of our circle of society, that "loosely compacted person," into futurity: we are most assured that our ideas develop intersubjectively, but we remain ignorant of beginnings and ends. To represent this paradox, Peirce calls upon Emerson's lines as often as he does Shakespeare's:

A symbol, once in being, spreads among the peoples. In use and in experience, its meaning grows ... The symbol may, with Emerson's sphynx, say to man,
>   Of thine eye I am eyebeam.   (2.302)

We cannot grasp Firstness nor can we apprehend futurity: we cannot know the end of semiosis any more than we can know immediately, without representation. Ortega has put it in the very idiom and voice of Peirce:

Man is not a first man, an eternal Adam: he is formally a second man, a third man.[16]

7

I.A. Richards and the Audit of Meaning

> Though all organisms are critics in the sense that they interpret the signs about them, the experimental speculative technique made available by speech would seem to single out the human species as the only one possessing an equipment for going beyond the criticism of experience to a criticism of criticism. We not only interpret the characters of events (manifesting in our responses all the gradations of fear, apprehension, expectation, assurance, for which there are rough behavioristic counterparts in animals) – we may also interpret our interpretations.
>
> – Kenneth Burke

The theory and practice of I.A. Richards demonstrate the consequences a triadic semiotics has for criticism. Richards defined rhetoric as both the study of "how words work" and "a study of misunderstanding and its remedies." The first definition echoes what he and Ogden had said in explaining their call for a science of signs, while the second is virtually a paraphrase of Schleiermacher's conception of hermeneutics. If its dependence on a triadic semiotics is appreciated, then I.A. Richards' philosophy of rhetoric could be a powerful antidote to the radical skepticism which infects contemporary theory.

One of the interests Richards' career has for us is the exemplary character of his life-long search for ways to make interpretation central in criticism and pedagogy alike. His explorations led him, first, to a rejection of his own mystical scientism and subsequently to the development of his philosophy of rhetoric, to an important critique of positivist linguistics and a general theory of interpretation, which he called a "theory of comprehending." All along the way, his pragmatism yielded

I.A. Richards and the Audit of Meaning 73

an array of inventive triadic remedies for dyadic misunderstandings.

Since it has so often been claimed (by those who have read him shallowly or not at all) that Richards was an elitist or a degenerate Romantic, interested only in the private, psychological response to literary texts, or a formalist with a narrow interest in "the words on the page," it is worth noting that at the outset – in *Practical Criticism* – he considered language a "social product"[17] and that he devoted thirty years of his life to the problem of illiteracy around the globe. No linguist, no other critic has so tirelessly sought to follow the pragmatic maxim, insisting that any theory was worthwhile – or even intelligible – only if we could demonstrate the difference it could make to our practice. In *Mencius on the Mind*, he makes the case for interpretive paraphrase and multiple definition, which are central to his theory of translation:

New hypothesis is but old dogma writ large. Unless we do actually and constantly sketch out alternative definitions using different logical machinery we shall not gain the ability to *experiment* in interpretation which comparative studies require.[18]

Nothing Richards argued about language and literature, discourse and rhetoric, is cut off from what he had to say about learning, value, or the aims of "general education in a free society."

Richards saw very clearly from the first that Peirce's pragmaticism is entailed by his semiotics. The principal challenge to critical inquiry was for Richards a matter of bringing theories to the test, of showing what difference they could make to our practice. In *How to Read a Page*, he put it this way:

We are seeking *stabilities*, [but they] are not gained (as in the elementary parts of the sciences) by building them *up* from foundations of defined assumptions but through their *dependence* from a first principle or master rule of all being. As gravitation – that sketchy image of dialectic Reason – keeps the universe stable in its freedom; rather than the Elephant standing on the Great Turtle's back which supports the world in the old fable. But how to keep our philosophy from becoming a Great Turtle is always our problem.[19]

No fundamental principle of Richards' philosophy of rhetoric is at odds with Peirce's semiotics. The only way to get from symbol to what is symbolized is by means of a mediating idea which must, in turn, be interpreted. When Peirce declared that each sign requires another for its interpretation, he was showing that the interpretant of one sign becomes the representamen of the next. Richards' recognition of the importance of this interdependence of symbol and meaning (or meaning-making) is reflected in his circular formulations (*thinking* he defined as "arranging our techniques for arranging"), as well as in his emphasis on the fact that all critical inquiry into functions of, and factors in, language must be conducted by means of language. A central principle of Richards' philosophy of rhetoric is that we think not just *about* concepts but *with* them. This instrumentality was at first represented mechanistically; Richards adapted LeCorbusier's famous definition of a chair as a machine for sitting in as the opening sentence of his *Principles of Literary Criticism*: "A book is a machine to think with." Later, when he had read Coleridge, he came to call such ideas "speculative instruments," and he means precisely what Peirce meant by "instruments of thought."

Richards defined *dialectic* as an audit of meaning carried out by attending to *what is said* and *what is meant* as mutually constraining functions. Since all import is mediated, we must explore contexts and perspectives, situations and purposes, thus auditing accounts of what may be meant. When the emphasis is on the continuing audit of meaning, there is every chance to exercise and to learn control of the reflexive capacities of language; for Richards there never was any danger that this would become, as it has in certain circles today, a narrow, spirit-killing interest in language about language, with never a concern shown for *purposing*.

For the dialectician, beginning with meaning entails recognition of the fact that we cannot get under the net of language; the correlative is the discovery that language is not simply a medium but a means. Because we can have no direct, *im*mediate (unmediated) knowledge of the world, we cannot claim absolute truth for our statements; we must, therefore, cultivate what Peirce called "a contrite fallibilism." I do not think that Richards is ever contrite, but the idea of keeping things tentative is at the heart of his pedagogy. As nothing in the triadic relationship is stable, we must learn to take advantage of that fact. Only in the exploration of the open-endedness of the process of comprehending can the learner – the reader, the interpreter, the writer – discover the heuristic powers of language itself.

The triadic nature of Richards' theories is perhaps best exhibited in what he called his theory of comprehending. Its development suggests how his ideas of language and discourse, language and learning, language and thought evolved in ways which put him at odds with every-

I.A. Richards and the Audit of Meaning

thing the "Linguistic Scientists" were engaged in. It is commonly stated that Richards came under the influence of information (or communication) theory, but that way of putting it is misleading. The point is that information theory offered him a new way of setting forth his perennial concerns about the relationship of language and thought. Of all the schemata he employed, that of the communication situation as modeled by computer engineers is surely the most mechanistic, but it was for Richards a machine to think with, a speculative instrument.

Richards was first attracted to this model because he saw it as a way of defining the complexities of translation. As early as 1950, in the introduction of his version of the *Iliad* (*The Wrath of Achilles*), he printed the diagram which was to become so familiar in all discussions of semiotics.

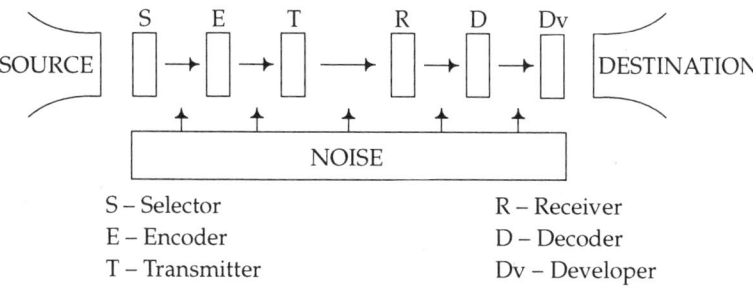

S – Selector
E – Encoder
T – Transmitter

R – Receiver
D – Decoder
Dv – Developer

Here is part of his comment:

Here Homer (whatever that might be) is the *information source*. I (certain subsystems, rather, in me) am the *transmitter*. I encode certain things my information source seems to give me in a *signal* which keeps up through the printed pages that follow. You (certain subsystems, rather, in you) are the *receiver*. You take in the marks on the paper which you recode again as sentences and hand on to the *destination*. This destination is the part of the diagram that has most of the appropriate poetic indefiniteness. It balances the mystery of the source which was "Homer."[20]

Richards uses the diagram, not to model the communication situation as the Linguistic Scientists were soon to do, but to problematize it.

The diagram in Richards' hands becomes a reminder that the language we use about language must itself be included in the audit of meaning. Thus, in his important critique of Roman Jakobson's version of the diagram, Richards comments: "Jakobson rightly remarks that the nomenclature of 'referent' is somewhat ambiguous. It is. But so too is that of 'context' and that of 'code' and those of 'message' and 'meaning' themselves."[21]

The chief role of information theory in Richards' thought is to identify ambiguities, "the very hinges of all thought."[22] The four concepts of context, code, message, and meaning were formed anew as he considered their ambiguity in working out his theory of comprehending. I will consider them briefly, in the order in which Richards lists them above.

Context. Richards begins with the idea of context as the surround of an utterance and then makes it complex again by showing us how this context of situation, of the originative circumstances as well as those of interpretation, is the "comparison field" in which the active mind operates, sorting and gathering as it apprehends *likes* and *differents*. The perception of similarity entails the power to differentiate; together they yield that "primordial abstractness" on which the mind's activity depends. Richards often described this activity as a matter of recognizing *tokens* of a *type*, Peirce's terms for particularities or exemplifications and the generality which they represent. Context is that which enables "a sign to stand for an instance of a sort."[23] In Richards' theory of comprehending, context becomes the scene of the process of construing and constructing, of interpretation and the making of meaning. He had moved from the substitution theory of language toward the idea that we know in terms of what we have construed. Recognition thus becomes a centrally important term in describing the activity of interpretation.

Code. To represent an abstract, conceptual entity by a term which usually names the means by which it is itself represented – that is the kind of game Peirce plays with *type*. The success of the game depends on being in control of the meanings. Richards continually sounded the warning that ambiguities cannot function heuristically if they aren't recognized as ambiguities. *Code* means one thing in the phrase "Morse Code" and quite another when we speak of a "code of behavior."

Many dilemmas familiar in contemporary critical theory are artifacts of descriptions in which the two senses of code are confused and opposed illogically. To say, for instance, that "a poem taken purely objectively is nothing but specks of carbon on dried wood pulp" leads to a quagmire; the common rhetorical trick of reduction (meiosis), used without decorum, only creates logical muddles.[24] A poem is not to be identified with the graphic means of representing the words which constitute the text and certainly not with the *graphite* which physically constitutes the graphic representation. It can be rhetorically effective, perhaps, to speak of music as the effect of a conjunction of horsehair and cat intestines, but the reduction does nothing to clarify the character of music or the problem of defining it because mere sound cannot be the initial term in describing musical form. Another muddle results when we are told that the aim of an authentic criticism should be to study not meanings but "the codes and conventions that make meaning possible." Insofar as *code* here has to do with something other than phonology or syntax, it must have to do with meanings. Further, there can be no way of determining *what is said* without considering simultaneously *what is meant*. That is because *what is said* is irreducible to phonological and syntactic elements. In a theory of comprehending the initial terms are meanings, the relationship of an utterance and what is uttered.

Message. The chief name for "what is meant" is *message*, but it is no help in forming the concept of message to identify it with what is transmitted: that is *signal*. Here is Richards' comment:

Messages are generated by Contexts; they are conveyed by signals. Messages are living. They are animated instances of meaning, determinations from the context field; the signals which convey them are dead ... It is essential to a Message that what forms in the Addressee (or other recipient) should be of the same order of being with what has formed in the Addresser. He may get it all wrong (and often does) but there is an IT. The two apparitions are both meanings. But a sound track and a system of meanings are not things of a sort, able to agree or disagree. The distinction between message and signal ... is indeed a *pons asinorum* in linguistics.[25]

The figure of messages as apparitions, as ghostly presences which must be realized, is a useful corrective, I believe, to the thingy notion of "getting at the message of a text." That common way of putting it suggests mining, and indeed the expression is usually supported by geological figures of depth and surface, layers and hidden structures. Richards speaks of composition as a process in which an "unembodied something ... finds itself in its words by finding the words for itself."[26] That circularity is entailed in realizing intentions, and it was a fundamental principle for Richards.

Meaning. Richards was intensely aware of the discontinuities in any representation of the communication situation. In order to understand how and why he revised the diagram which has been under discussion, we should turn to the concluding observation in the introduction to *The Wrath of Achilles*:

78   Triadic Remedies

Further reflection on this diagram makes us aware that its great central gap is repeated; that between the information source and the transmitter, between the receiver and the destination, as between the transmitter and the receiver, come the noises – with an iteration most incident to hollow men.

What some take for articulations, Richards recognized as gaps, but of a peculiar kind. They are necessary, constitutive: they are not abysses to be spanned; like wedges, they can unite because they separate. "The great central gap" between transmitter and receiver is seen as of a kind with that between the Representamen and its Object, in Peirce's terms. Richards read the diagram of the communication situation triadically: the gaps in the information theory schema are perceived as analogous to the dotted base line of the Peircean triangle. When he came to devise his own versions of the diagram, five years later in *Speculative Instruments*, they looked like this:

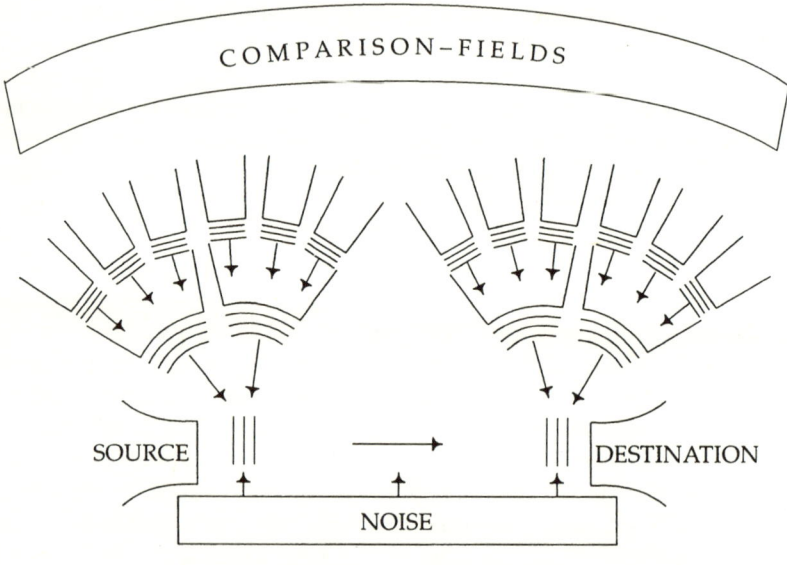

UTTERANCES-in-SITUATIONS

Richards's version can remind us that any linear diagram of "the communication situation" must be interpreted with a full awareness of the ease with which *message* can be confounded with *signal*, one kind of code taken unwittingly (or surreptitiously) for the other; of the hazard of neglecting to take utterances in context, which is to say in the "comparison field" made up of other utterances, actual and possible; or the danger of forgetting that our means of making meaning are themselves meanings. The wiring diagram of the information theorists inspired Richards to think not of one or another circumstance but of the universal situation, the "necessary conjunction and opposition of any utterance and what it would utter."[27]

Richards' interpretation of interpretation is based not on the notion of "psychological indeterminacy" but on the logic of triadicity. All hypotheses must be used tentatively, but that is not the same thing as saying (as Altieri does) that meanings are "in large part created by the individual reader" (72). (Insofar as they are "created" by the reader, they are *completely* created by the reader.) In "Variant Readings and Misreading," Richards outlines the reasons for claiming that, generally speaking, it is possible to differentiate "diverse understandings from the mistake, the inadmissible interpretation," remarking that we are "short of means" for doing so. This leads him to an analysis of what is wrong with reading instruction and to a recapitulation of his claims for the efficacy of multiple definition, interpretive paraphrase, and other procedures for comparing meanings and the ways they are controlled. He rejects firmly the notion of a critical consensus, just as he always does "the Usage Doctrine." "What we should seek [in interpretation]," he wrote, "is not the sense that is, or would be, most widely accepted, but that which most fully takes into account the situation the utterance is meeting and the integrity of the language."[28]

Just so, a triadic conception of representation kept him from entertaining as an interpretive touchstone the notion of authorial intention, which is only the obverse of psychological indeterminacy: both are consequences of a dyadic conception of meaning.[29] The assumption that there is a right meaning, that it is identified with the author's intention, and that we can "get at it" is founded on certain ideas which are fundamentally at odds with Richards' philosophy of rhetoric. His observation that no sentence ever says all it could applies as much to criticism as it does to works of art: all discourse is partial. This is a necessary, not a contingent, condition of the meaning relation. Triadicity thus protects us from one of the most dangerous of the gangster theories:

Modern historical scholarship ... terrorizes us with the suggestion that somewhere in the jungle of evidence there is something we happen not to know which would make the point clear, which would show us just what the author did in fact mean. That suspicion of a missing clue is paralyzing – unless we remember firmly that from the very nature of the case essential clues are always missing.[30]

To differentiate meaning and significance by identifying the first with "the text" or "the words on the page" or some other entity and the second with some indeterminate response finds no basis in Richards' theory of comprehending. He held that *what is said* can be construed only by means of hypothetical readings, tentatively posed versions of *what is meant*: the audit of meaning is always dialectical.

For Richards, considering the meaning of meaning always entailed the study of "how words work," but I think it is fair to say that in the later books the emphasis is less on the *how* or the *words* than on the *work*. Richards never lost his fascination with words as lexical items, never failed to enjoy "the endless paronomastic play of the Dictionary."[31] His sense of the ways in which the interinanimation of words and sounds and syntactic structures create meaning in poetry led him to make the case for "poetry as an instrument of research:" the *how* of poetry could illuminate all meaning-making. But he concentrated more and more on the *work* words do, the purposes language serves. He was brought to this new emphasis partly because of his disgust (always disguised as perplexity) with the attempts of Linguistic Scientists to consider utterances without reference to the kinds of context he had labored to define; to proceed as if the making of meaning were "a sort of catching a nonverbal butterfly in a verbal butterfly net;"[32] to set meaning aside as of no scientific interest or, only a slight improvement, to salute its importance without attempting to address the problems. The chief value of his theory of comprehending, which he developed out of thinking about the implications of information theory, was that it supported his continuing inquiry into the meaning of meaning as the TYPE of which all the problems of interpretation and representation he had ever investigated were tokens.

I.A. Richards is certainly in eclipse, as indeed he was throughout the last thirty or forty years of his life. He has long been blamed for some of the extreme stands allegedly taken by the New Critics – unjustly, as his views of paraphrase and "the words on the page" suggest. Attempts to rehabilitate him as an important forerunner of Deconstruction would be misguided, but so too is the contempt shown by those who proclaim as brand new certain ideas which Richards was hard at work on half a century ago.[33] His importance for criticism is that in his life work – in his philosophy of rhetoric and his theory of comprehending – he continually explored triadicity and its consequences. All that we know is mediated: all knowledge must be represented; all representation is interpretation; all interpretation must itself be interpreted; all knowledge is partial; all that we know should be brought to the pragmatic test – else, "new hypothesis is old dogma writ large." Richards' fallibilism, his pragmatism – maybe even his incurable optimism – all derive from his understanding of "the seemingly revolutionary doctrine of the Interpretant." He entitled one of his last essays, written in his eighties, "Powers and Limits of Signs." The revolution comes in the recognition that the limits provided by the sign are "virtuous and necessary." Richards typically draws practical, which is to say pedagogical, conclusions:

We must recognize that Peirce's doctrine, along with its encouraging positive aspects, has a negative interpretation which can be grimly forbidding. Many have taken it as denying that we can do more in exploring our meanings than switch from one phrasing to another and on again to yet others. Positivists, Behaviorists and their Nominalist allies, who make it a point of conscience to enact and obey self-denying ordinances in matters such as the occurrence and use of concepts and of images ... have seemed to wish to empty the mind of all but verbal equivalences and to substitute word-play for thinking. But SUBSTITUTABLE and EQUIVALENCE ... are terms whose meanings are as explorable as they are important. Human education might well be described as learning how to explore them.[34]

I have been claiming that Richards' practical criticism, his philosophy of rhetoric, and his theory of comprehending are all informed with a triadic semiotics. Richards learned from Peirce that pragmaticism and fallibilism are the necessary consequences of a recognition of mediation: his theory and his practice depend on (or from) an understanding of the logical role of interpretation. But I do not mean to suggest that Richards read widely in Peirce; indeed, I can find no evidence that he ever read anything beyond the selected passages from Peirce's correspondence with Lady Welby which constitute one of the astounding appendices in *The Meaning of Meaning*. It is the depth of his understanding which is the distinctive factor, not any wide familiarity. The reason for studying what Richards has to say about the meanings of meaning is that he saw that "the revolutionary doctrine of the Interpretant" changes the way we think about the way words work, guiding us to the discovery of remedies for misunderstanding.

8

Schleiermacher and the Hermeneutic Enterprise

> All knowledge is an interpretation, and we must choose such perspectives as will yield meanings of the universe which interest us ... Understanding is *systematic* interpretation, the discovery of syntactical meanings in the world. It is the recognition of truth-forms, of symbolic relationships, of which there may be many – even as it grows more and more general, and we come nearer and nearer to the ideal of philosophy, the appreciation of all-connecting orders in the world.
> – Susanne K. Langer

Hermeneutics is not a term used by C.S. Peirce, probably for the very good reason that it would have been, in his mind, firmly identified with theology. The idea of a hermeneutic method would have been for Peirce a contradiction in terms. He once observed that the reason philosophy had for so long remained without a proper method was that philosophers had more frequently come from the theological seminary than from the laboratory. Philosophers had seldom proceeded so that assumptions could be identified, analyzed, modified, or rejected: disputation, Peirce held, was no substitute for experimentation or, indeed, for a logic of inquiry. It is a fine irony that hermeneutics, which had its origin in theological exegesis, sometimes pretends to status as a form of inquiry not less rigorous than laboratory experimentation.

Considered historically as the theory and practice of interpretation, hermeneutics bears a curious relationship to semiotics, the science of signs. As *practice*, hermeneutics is older. One might expect that theories of intention, causality, purposiveness would be antecedent to formulated rules for construing and judging, but ways of interpreting and their regulation have preceded ways of accounting for motive and design. In contemporary theory, the term *hermeneutics* is sometimes synonymous with interpretation seen in psychological terms and opposed to a structural linguistics (or poetics) in which meaning is not a focus of interest. The dichotomy of hermeneutics, psychologically conceived, and the study of formal structure, is only a variant of the opposition of subjective and objective perspectives, a consequence of conceiving the sign dyadically.

From earliest times, hermeneutics has had an important role to play in certain disciplines where it has generally served two different but related purposes, protective and heuristic: to guard the code and to provide discovery procedures, a method of inquiry. In any of its forms, ancient or modern, hermeneutics suggests that to those in the know, all can and will be revealed; whereas, those with uncircumcised ears will forever be outsiders. Hermeneutics can be virtually sacred knowledge, and this aura of exclusiveness remains, even when hermeneutics has been reduced to a matter of problem-solving; of unlocking a door, never mind to what. But whether it has become a matter of decoding or a way of maintaining a body of special knowledge given to a special few, hermeneutics is always centered on interpretation. It is this character that explains why traditionally the hermeneutic sciences or arts – one of the perennial debates begins right there – have been medicine, law, and theology.

Medical diagnosis is an interpretation of symptoms. If swelling (*tumor*), heat (*calor*), redness (*color*), and pain (*dolor*) are present, there is evidence for the judgment that infection is present. The causes of infection – of any infection or this particular one – may not be known, but infection is recognized and identified as such. Legal interpretation of one case or another involves casuistry, the art of recognizing ambiguities of formulation and intent, and of manipulating them to your own or your client's advantage. (*Case* and *casuistry* are cognate.) Jesus's rabbinical answer to the Pharisees in the matter of the tribute money – "Render unto Caesar the things which be Caesar's, and unto God the things which be God's" – is casuistry with the power to become new law. In scriptural interpretation, the text is construed by both diagnosis and casuistry: a reader with a Biblical text is partly a physician identifying symptoms and partly a lawyer arguing a case. In modern times, hermeneutics has developed as a generalized method of interpretation with a much wider application, but, interestingly enough, it is in the traditional hermeneutic fields of medicine, law, and theology that this method is most significantly employed, with theory and practice maintained in a lively and fruitful dialectic.

In medicine, the art of diagnosis has been turned over to the computer. Whereas the measure of skill once was provided by the chief physician in Grand Rounds, it is now the program which scans, eliminates, focuses, calculates, inducing and deducing its way to a reading of the symptoms in order to identify the disease. When reliance on the printout apparently obviates the need for interpretation, it will seem also to make observation almost unnecessary. This is one source of hazard (and surely one cause of the dramatic increase in malpractice suits); furthermore, technological advances in medicine can do nothing to direct the choices to be made. The dilemmas which are the artifacts of technology can not be confronted in technological terms: brain death can be defined and identified, but not what to do about it. In making decisions, the physician, the family of the patient, sometimes the patient himself, the civil agencies and institutions involved will need a warrant – an explicit set of assumptions and definitions which can validate judgments. At this point, the questions are necessarily hermeneutical: physicians grow cosmographers; their patients, maps.

It is not surprising that the technologizing of medicine has been accompanied by a return to sometimes forgotten precepts – of treating the patient, not just the disease; of spending time and energy and money on preventive medicine, on the development of clinics and hospices and home care, for the newborn and the dying. Perhaps it is inaccurate to call these new or recovered attitudes hermeneutical, but they are certainly outgrowths of new ways of looking at the purposes of medicine, new ways of interpreting its ends and means.

Hard cases, it is said, make bad law: that aphorism represents the positivism which the movement known as Critical Legal Studies is committed to exposing. For the burden of the saying is that the intricate argument necessitated by highly complex and problematic cases creates interpretations and judgments which in turn necessitate further complex construction; with the result that the allegedly normal, actual, expectable or even self-evident congruence of fact and legal opinion, of informed judgment and reality, is not as clear as it should be. Equivocation and polysemy give certainty a bad name – and certainty, it is held, should be, and normally is, the defining characteristic of judgment. The comparable idea of a "strict constructionism," which treats the Constitution not as the representation of principles that must be continually interpreted but as words on the page with definite and limited meaning, makes a method of literal-mindedness.

Positivism is certainly not residual in modern religious expression, but in theology itself attitudes and enterprises are on the whole remarkably free of RUP. Modern developments in hermeneutics have concerned texts – translation and explication, as well as linguistic analysis, in the interest of reclamation, which is sometimes considered recovery but which is more likely to take the form of de-mystification and de-mythologizing. And in what is perhaps one of the most significant alignments in our time, texts and literacy have been seen in a very dynamic dialectic in the movement known as "liberation theology." These texts are not exclusively scriptural nor are they always verbal. In Paulo Freire's "pedagogy of the oppressed," one of Liberation Theology's chief supports, reading the world is taken as the model for reading the word. Primers in the Freire culture circles (literacy classes) can include passages from Scripture, but they are aimed at establishing very explicitly the contexts for all texts, the first of which is created in a process of dialogic action from the "generative words" which are collected by the illiterate learners. The problematizing of emblematic pictures, the interpretation of scenes and artifacts of daily life, bring full circle the process by which Scripture came into being as the record of parables and of an interpretative memory of events.

In the larger hermeneutic field of reading theory, literacy studies, and literary criticism, there are few signs of anything comparable to holistic medicine, Critical Legal Studies, or Liberation Theology, though of course that sort of claim has been made for the whole range of spurious doctrines, gangster theories, and other institutionalized "skeptical infidelities to the evidence of reason and sense," from "affective stylistics" to "cultural literacy." The claim is fraudulent because instead of encouraging the development of an understanding of interpretation in teaching; instead of making texts accessible to new and different kinds of readers; instead of finding ways and means of helping our fellow citizens reclaim the powers of language – instead of going forward with the enterprise of an authentic practical criticism, contemporary theory has usually contented itself with a variety of semioclastic exercises, serving no purpose beyond those narrowly defined by academic politics, and carried out in "a collective stupor of self-esteem."[35]

The question which generates the wildly conflicting taxonomies and programs of current critical theory is "What is given for interpretation?" Since it presupposes the reality of an object of interpretation, the question is intolerable to the radical skeptics who have extended the doctrine of the arbitrary sign. But their vociferous opponents, though eager to entertain the question, have no way to answer it except in the same dyadic terms in which the antagonistic gangster theories have been formulated. The question of what is given for interpretation can only be entertained by means of certain speculative instruments which have been deliberately abandoned – I mean *representation, context, intention, meaning,* for starters – but the point is that without a warrant, there can be no argument. What we have are proclamations and gnomic utterances.

A warrant is a Third, an Interpretant, a mediating idea: it is a deliberate appeal to the authority of habit, convention, the evidences of reason and sense; to historical context as well as present circumstances; to personal conviction, well-founded in the assumptions of what is now called a "discourse community." A warrant is a means of making meaning by enabling acts of interpretation. Without the Third, we lose the possibility of accounting *for* meaning, without which there is no way of giving an account *of* meanings. We are supposed to be content, instead, with an account of the codes and conventions which make meaning possible. But it is, of course, impossible to render that account in the absence of meanings themselves.

Method is the nexus of theory and practice and necessarily incorporates a reflective and reflexive motive. Without the warrant of a Third, hermeneutics is not authentically methodical because there is no way to account for interpretation, except in psychological terms. Without a Third, any opposition, instead of acting as a dialectical polarity, as a *coincidentia oppositorum*, becomes a killer dichotomy. Thus explanation is privileged over description, with no recognition of mutual entailment. Or it is held that understanding must precede interpretation. Or that the social must take precedence over the individual or that the personal outweighs any alleged innate and universal capacity. In such circumstances – and they typify modern critical theory – hermeneutics has become merely procedural, an algorithmic problem-solving or a riddling theorizing, without regard to practice or pragmatics, without cogency or purpose.

The rise of hermeneutics as a general theory of interpretation came in response to a crucial question of the Enlightenment: what is the appropriate method for the study of man and his works? Should it be – can it be? – the same as that for the study of nature? Cassirer notes an early formulation of the problem:

The Berlin Academy of Sciences had proposed, for the year 1763, a topic that immediately attracted the attention of the entire German Philosophical world, "Are the metaphysical sciences," it asked, "amenable to the same certainty as the mathematical?" ... Is the method of metaphysics – this is how the question must now be posed – interchangeable with that of mathematics and empirical science, or is there a fundamental opposition between them? And if the latter should be the case, have we in general any guarantee that thinking, purely logical deduction, is able to express fully the structure of "reality?"[36]

Kant's claim was that the human studies must be set on a sure path and that such a path would necessarily be scientific, *ein sicherer Gang des Wissenschaften*. In Hegel's view, the way for *Geisteswissenschaften* could not be scientifically sure: it must of necessity be a groping way. One response to this distinction has been to start out with allegedly scientific rigor and then soften according to the recalcitrance met. This is the attitude which produces "weak" versions of "strong" theories in linguistics and the social sciences. Occasionally, method is simply denied to the humanities altogether: *method*, it is held, yields empirically justified statements of science, not the unfortunately (or fortunately, depending on perspective) intuitive, personal, indeterminate perceptions of the human studies.

The very idea of a *groping way* proves intolerable to those who consider that only the natural sciences can provide appropriate models for any and all inquiry because they are objective and value-free. But it often turns out that those who model their research on what they take to be scientific method are only following a science which, as Robert Oppenheimer memorably put it, is no longer there.[37] Until this century when the concept of relativity came to influence metaphysical formulation, the method of the natural sciences was assumed to be epistemologically distinct from that of the human studies. Thus when Oppenheimer identified analogy as the chief heuristic of scientific investigation, he reversed the direction familiar from the Enlightenment, *viz.*, the attempt to adapt scientific procedures to the humanities.

When Peirce disdained theological disputation as a model of philosophical inquiry, he did not imply that scientific ideas were adaptable to all purposes: "Every attempt to import into psychics the conceptions proper to physics has only led those who made it astray" (1.255). The point is not that method belongs to science, with intuition or insight or inspiration left to the humanities; both are modes of inquiry and therefore both are methodical. What is essential to philosophy, as it is to science, is a practiced understanding of the necessary limitations of any representation of knowledge. The illusion of an objectivity which could bypass these necessary limits is the consequence of positivist conceptions of method, interpretation, and meaning – all underwritten by a dyadic conception of the sign. To see method as central to all inquiry is the essential principle of a general hermeneutics in which all knowledge is interpretation.

In this perspective, such a dichotomy as explanation/description appears absurd. It is often remarked that some statement or passage is "mere" description, but it is never said of explanation that it is "mere." It is generally presupposed that if you can explain, you must be able to describe and, further, that description would be supererogatory, given the explanation. Actually, it is as probable that any given explanation will be poorly supported as it is that a description will have inadequate explanatory power. If description and explanation are separated, converted to a killer dichotomy, the problem of explaining explanatory power becomes acute. The reason is that explanation is extended definition and definition requires both classification and differentiation, neither of which can be soundly or authentically developed without conceptualizing. And concept formation depends, as Vygotsky demonstrated, on a continual movement from particular to general to particular. The hermeneutic enterprise is dialectical and it founders whenever particularization *or* generalization – description *or* explanation – is either "privileged" or "bracketed."

The doctrine that holds explanation as altogether superior to description is at root an expression of a fear of abstraction. This paradox – for is not explanation, by definition as it were, more abstract than description? – is expressed in a privileging of particulars which somehow can be brought to constitute explanation. Explanation controls, it is held, the instability of abstractions by anchoring them in particularity – in facts and data and the evident findings of context-free investigation. Explanation is commonly associated with fact, whereas description is a matter of subjective judgment; indeed, it was this suggestion which led Wittgenstein to declare description superior to explanation: It was authentic – like art – because it kept us in touch with particular detail. Those who separate explanation from description and hold it as the higher good tend to consider it as the identification of cause: a valid explanation lays out a sequence, culminating in the explicandum. No such power is claimed for description. It is expectable that in the dyadic perspective, explanation will be considered public, logical, objective, whereas description seems personal, psychological, and subjective.

Such attitudes are familiar in contemporary Marxist analysis where the conception of interpretation is that because it is "subjective," it is arbitrary or, worse, a class-determined evaluation which depends on description, which is necessarily self-serving. Explanation, in contradistinction, is held to be in a dialectical relationship, not with interpretation but with reality. The rejection of interpretation as a contaminated judgment is consistent with the view that language itself – language *as such* – is a barrier between us and the reality which calls for explanation.

Marxist anxieties are fixed not so much on the privileging of the concrete in the interest of explanation as on the possibility that the abstraction might become synonymous with the concrete. It is permissible – indeed, it is considered a requirement – that the concrete be seen as an exemplification of the abstract; this is why the concept of code is so useful to dialectical materialists. But the obverse – reification – is disallowed. The result is that privileging particulars and declaring that they constitute an objective reality, independent not only of evaluation but of formulation itself, creates for modern day Marxists the problem of the subject. Thus they are busily smuggling the interpreter back into the Clean Machine of Explanation.

For both Marxists and their deconstructionist adversaries, the sign is a two-valued relationship. Reference for one camp is to reality, access to which is prevented only because interpreters, unwilling to acknowledge privileged terminology, refuse the task of explanation. For the other camp, reference to reality is impossible because language itself forbids it: the referent of language is language and representation is therefore out of the question. No matter how elaborate the idiosyncratic strategies or how specialized the abstruse terminologies, what is shared is a view of meaning as an object and of language as a barrier.

When explanation and description are seen as antithetical, it is a symptom of the absence of a philosophy of representation. Consider Wittgenstein's dilemma. The common interpretation of his turn to silence in the closing statement of the *Tractatus Logico-philosophicus* – "wovon man nicht sprechen kann darüber muss man schweigen" – has been that metaphysics is absurd. Any question about value is unanswerable; since there is no way we could know, we should not ask. But Toulmin and Janik argue that this is not what Wittgenstein meant.[38] His search was for a science of language, but he realized that such a stance was entirely inappropriate for works of art: since they were inaccessible to logic, one should remain silent before them. What Wittgenstein abhorred was the idea that saying – and for him *saying* means propositional logic – could represent value, ethical ideas, etc. Instead of addressing himself to the need for another means of conceptualizing the representation of value, he dismissed the very idea of an attempt, counselling silence.

Recent solutions to this problem, which remains framed in dyadic, positivist terms, have not so much reversed Wittgenstein's solution as they have developed variants of it: now what is silenced is the author and the idea of the representation of intention. The structuralist definition of the "poetic function" as a matter of the *how* rather than the *what* has gradually been adapted to all texts, poetic or otherwise. Guided by this strong theory, rhetoricians, semiologists, deconstructionists, and critics in many disciplines have arrived at the idea that all discourse is virtually poetic; indeed, Paul de Man has declared that the difference between literature and criticism is "delusive." The strong theory of discourse has culminated in the bizarre notion that story-telling should supersede explanation. The claim is that "philosophy" (but what is meant is Kant and Hegel, inter alios) exiled "rhetoric" (but what is meant is figurative language and narrative) in the vain attempt to offer general truths and abstract explanations. Thus Wittgenstein's call for description rather than explanation has taken a rather surprising turn. If philology and Biblical exegesis could model the art of hermeneutics, then narratology, it might be thought, could engender interesting ideas about the nature of discourse, but this is a futile expectation because narratology is itself a blueprint for constructing a Clean Machine and the conception of narrative it sponsors is as muddled as that of code.

Story is an ideologically freighted word which, in current critical discourse, signals a radical skepticism. It often represents the strong theory that since there can be no reference, it is futile to think of representing *findings*; that since knowledge is constructed, reality is therefore a fiction – whether it is the reality of a vision or of action, or the reality of a reading of laboratory results. In this perspective, magic and science, because they both express world views, are essentially the same. Everybody creates something that is not "there;" if it isn't "there," it isn't real. This logic eventuates in the contention that biochemists tell stories; to be sure, they do – if *story* has come to mean *what-we-do-with-language*. *Story* thus joins other pseudo-concepts in the family of *verbal behavior* and *language games*. What we have in *story* is not a new idea in terms of which we could discuss the aims of discourse. *Story* is simply a new bit of terminology; it does not provide conceptions in terms of which we could begin to develop ideas of representation.

The widespread use of *story* helps to institutionalize the muddle of *fact* and *fiction*, which are taken as equivalent terms because both facts and fictions are dependent on our doing. But that degree of generality makes for highly unstable terms and the rapid proliferation of pseudo-concepts. How can we articulate the relationship of agent and action, purpose and function, what and why? We will have to ask who formulates the facts, if we are to evaluate them. But there is a more fundamental logical problem: when fact and fiction are made equivalent, what is it that is formulated? What is transformed or seen as a fiction? Without that term, the ground of the analogy is obscured. Without a Third, the equivalence collapses into a dyadic identity rather than developing as a triadic analogy.

Story is, of course, a temporal term, but it can accommodate many different modes of telling, not just linear and not only fictional. A story is, after all, a kind of history, but the kind is what we need to conceptualize. We need *story* as a name for non-discursive modes of representation, a concept bound to cause trouble when the form is discourse. In this regard, it is useful again to recall Wittgenstein's dilemma. His conception of language as a picture of reality was an attempt to develop a philosophy of representation, but *picture* (*Bild*) is as liable to misconstruction as *story* or *code*, since it can mean image as well as model. We represent our ideas and feelings by abstracting, which is achieved by forming, but forming is accomplished in either of two modes: finding ways to differentiate them is a perennial challenge. The differentiation of *Vorstellung* and *Darstellung* – roughly equivalent to *image* and *model* – is centrally important to a philosophy of representation: using the word *story* to cover both is likely to foster the same confusions as were caused by *Bild* several generations ago.

If the question in 1763 concerned *which* method, the question in our time is often formulated so that the emphasis is on the definition of method *as such* – of any and all method. If method is understood as belonging to both the natural sciences and the human studies, it could be said that it is at once sure and groping – sure in that it is logical; groping in that it is necessarily partial. But of course those characterizing terms are infected with dyadic prejudice: both *sure* and *groping* presuppose a positivist epistemology in which meaning is thing-y and interpretation a psychological matter. The alternative conception of method is supported by a recognition of mediation as logically entailed in representation and of knowledge as necessarily partial. In a triadic perspective, method will be defined in terms of the meanings we use to discover, invent, and formulate new meanings.

For Peirce, method was not empirical measurement, nor was intuition a mystical power. He notes that "each step in science has been a lesson in logic," which he saw as "the philosophy of representation." The "instruments of thought" – the phrase occurs in his description of Lavoisier's method – include all means of representation. It is the representation of ideas with which interpretation deals and any representation is itself an interpretation (5.363). Peirce intended his *semeiotic* to guide ways of formulating representations – diagrams and graphs, extended metaphors and analogies, as well as all the conventional syllogistic forms – which could make apparent that process of determination in which we continuously and continually represent our representations and interpret our interpretations. This is the triadic response to the dichotomy of the sure way and the groping way.

In his own study of this problem of method (*Zur Logik der Kulturwissenschaften*, translated as *The Logic of the Humanities*), Cassirer argues that another kind of distinction than that represented by the sure way and the groping way was first developed by Vico in the *Principi di Scienza Nuova*. There the attempt was not to adapt the principles of natural science and mathematics to the analysis of human civilization but to distinguish two perspectives and to develop a logic which could account for man's creations in different terms from those appropriate for God's Creation. It was Vico's argument about the two worlds of nature and of man which first allowed, as Cassirer shows, the emergence of a logic of the humanities. God's design controls the natural world, but man's works are of a different order. It is principally his memory, his history, which make him man: these document the Fall. His records, whether in oral myths or in fictions written out at epic length, are the sign of his humanity.

Vico studied the law in order to answer the question of how it came to be that a universal principle, deeply instinctual in all peoples, could yet take so great a number of forms. His answer was that since law emanates from the human mind, changes in law must correspond to changes in attitudes over time. This theory he elaborated as a philosophy of history. Like all other human creations, history is dependent on language and the discourse it makes possible. Historical understanding, then, requires that we *read* the past. Vico can be seen as the forerunner of those for whom interpretation is modelled on the construing of texts, models themselves of all works of the human imagination.

Those who chart intellectual currents generally hold that the idea that hermeneutics or the theory and practice of exegesis could be generalized to a theory of understanding began with F.D.E. Schleiermacher, a contemporary of Hegel's and, like him, a theologian.[39] Friedrich Droysen first made Schleiermacher's ideas accessible to a wider public but it was Wilhelm Dilthey who developed the claim for Schleiermacher's importance to philosophy. Dilthey saw in Schleiermacher's hermeneutics a model for historiography which, in turn, could provide the guidelines for a method appropriate to the human studies. Far more attention has been paid to Dilthey's claims for the usefulness of Schleiermacher's hermeneutics as the model for a method of inquiry than has been given to his actual aims and procedures. It is notable that Schleiermacher did not himself publish a treatise on hermeneutics: the *Outline for a General Theory of Hermeneutics* is an editorial artifact constituted from his students' notes on a series of lectures delivered in 1819. The parallel with Saussure is interesting – the text of *Cours de linguistique générale* was constructed from notes of students who had attended his lectures – especially since neither scholar could be said to have concentrated his principal energies on the work for which he is chiefly known.

What makes Schleiermacher a different sort of theologian from those whose attitudes Peirce castigated, different certainly from Hegel, towards whom Peirce's remarks were directed, is his concern for the practical aspects of doctrine; more precisely, his sense of the interdependence of theory and practice. Schleiermacher wished both to develop a method of reading the Bible and to define its relationship to all understanding. He wanted to develop a theory of historical understanding which would take into account simultaneously human feeling and the facts of the natural world, in order that he might define a place for the church in the modern world. Hermeneutics is generally both conservative and exploratory, a way of guarding the given and of keeping it accessible to one or another constituency; it is notable that in his hermeneutics, Schleiermacher aimed to increase that constituency, that congregation. He wanted religion to be respected in a world in which scientific criteria were valued: he wanted faith to be accountable, though he would have agreed, perhaps, with Peirce that logic is but "faith come to years of discretion" (2.118).

The range of Schleiermacher's immense output – thirteen volumes of papers, sermons, essays, and letters – suggests the energy with which he pursued his goal of finding a firm ground for the church. He invented pedagogies and programs, designing curricula and organizing ceremonies. He set about creating an environment in which the church could foster a sense of continuity and community, one in which his parishioners could realize themselves in two dimensions – as an historical people with a past and future, and as individual creatures of the Lord. For Schleiermacher, the relationship in which the church stood to history and to the actual world was analogous to that of texts and their contexts, historical and actual. To aim at teaching a way of reading was therefore consonant with growing towards faith.

The interest in defining ways in which an individual could feel himself part of a community, both historical and actual, was the motive force of both philology and nationalism. Schleiermacher's program is in this sense comparable to Jakob Grimm's: the relationship of hermeneutics to dogmatics is analogous to that of philology and nationalism. The study of language offers an historical warrant for claims about national identity. It was in studying law that Grimm became interested in what was involved in studying anything whatever, in trying to find, as it were, the law of all laws. In his philological studies, his aim was to find the laws of language change, the laws of etymology. This led him to collecting samples of usage in the common speech of the peasantry, an enterprise which eventuated not only in his great dictionary but in the collection of folk tales which brought him greater fame than most philologists have enjoyed. By relating German to its past forms and by tracing its roots to more ancient languages, Grimm also sought to establish a German identity: his philology was politically motivated as well as being a matter of intellectual curiosity. This concatenation of philology and national pride suggests the dual function of hermeneutics, in which method is allied to high causes.

Hermeneutics is nothing if not methodical, though of course method can be narrowly conceived as a merely procedural matter. Schleiermacher's method – which is simultaneously metaphysical and practical, never merely procedural – is perhaps best described in the context of his thinking about how to think about the individual. Religious feeling – which is, famously, Schleiermacher's point of departure – is the sense one has of the universal, and the source of that feeling is a deep consciousness of self. Schleiermacher called it "immediate," meaning that it was not arrived at by a process of reasoning, though he could nevertheless explain such facts in terms of propositional logic: thus, since God does not admit of contrasts, He cannot be known by taking thought; He cannot be apprehended at will. However, the authentic proof of God's existence and of man's dependence on Him was not to be found in syllogisms but in ordinary, commonplace experience – in individual experience, shared by all. There was thus no sense of reaching to the universal from the vantage point of an antithetical individual experience; rather, the universal is entailed in the self's apprehension of dependence.

When Schleiermacher wrote that "we must seek to stir up in people the sense of the historical,"[40] the idea was to draw out what is there. The child is born with the capacity for religious feeling but realizes it in the process of taking his place in family, church, and state. Religious education was not to be a matter of indoctrination in the merely general. Schleiermacher's interest in Prussia rather than in some larger Germanic entity is best understood as exemplifying his distrust of anything abstractly conceived. More to the point is his rejection of catechisms. Luther had argued the need for catechisms on the ground that they were necessary because of ill-educated ministers, but, says Schleiermacher, there is no excuse for our depending on such ministers. If we do employ a catechism, "the more general it is, the more harmful; the more special it is, the more useful; the most useful is that which the minister makes for himself, while the most special of all is that which he makes every time for himself."[41]

For Schleiermacher, it was not catechism but hymnody which provided the way to grow towards faith, an idea which is central to the Moravian faith in which he was reared. Schleiermacher's well-known declaration of his sense of the individual is best read in the context of this Pietistic sense of the power of music and other principles, such as the importance of the fellowship of young and old. Here is the text from the Second Soliloquy:

Thus there dawned on me what is now my highest intuition. I saw clearly that each man is meant to represent humanity in his own way, combining its elements uniquely, so that it may reveal itself in every mode, and all that can issue from its womb be made actual in the fullness of unending space and time.[42]

The idea of representative man is, of course, centrally important in Romanticism, but in Schleiermacher's philosophy it has little to do with utopian thinking or, indeed, with transcendental notions: *representativeness* is here an intuition of the typological imagination. We find this "highest intuition" at the center of his thinking about the Christian faith and about language and literature. Schleiermacher liked to stress that *language* always presents itself to us as a particular language and the conviction that both the particular and the universal are represented in the individual is the model for his understanding of texts.

Schleiermacher's chief innovation was to bring to bear on theological exegesis the techniques of philology. In constructing and construing a text, Schleiermacher considered that there are two kinds of understanding in play: the "grammatical" and the "psychological," in his idiosyncratic terms. Grammatical understanding derives from a knowledge of words and phrases, of the outward appearance of the text and its contexts; psychological understanding is an apprehension of the inner form, the expression of the author's mind. The relationship of what-is-said (*Schrift*) and what-is-meant (*Rede*) is grasped in two different modes: by the comparative method – philological analysis which is at once formal and historical; and by the divinatory power – an intuitive apprehension of inner form, which it is given to us all to learn to exercise. Grammatical understanding depends chiefly on the comparative method, but it is also guided – necessarily – by the divinatory power, the enactment of those intuitions of inner form. And psychological understanding, though it is dependent chiefly on the divinatory power, springs from our experience as historical creatures and is, in a sense, another version of the comparative method.

In this double dialectic, the grammatical and the psychological approaches are not only interdependent but are, as well, dependent on that other interdependency of the comparative method and the divinatory power. Positivists who claim that first we must construe or first we must establish authorial intention or first we must identify the genre are incapable of taking advantage of Schleiermacher's dialectic, so powerful a propellant when it is allowed to function. The fruitless debates concerning validity in interpretation rarely engage the disputants in the authentic hermeneutic enterprise, which should mean a continuing audit of what it is we would know the meaning of.

Karl Barth's account of Schleiermacher's contributions to Protestant thought provides an emphasis interestingly different from that which Dilthey places on Schleiermacher's theory and method. Barth salutes Schleiermacher as one who did not forsake theology for the *history* of theology; he did not make theology a matter of source study. According to Barth, Schleiermacher "did not make things easy for himself," but sought continually to define the place of the church in the world and to make theology a science in the post-medieval sense, a responsible mode of thought, and to do so without making it merely philosophy. Barth, it is clear, is not satisfied with Schleiermacher's *Doctrine of Faith*, but he is full of praise for Schleiermacher's aim to keep theology theological, not letting it become mere epistemology or mere history. The other crucial point for Barth is that Schleiermacher preached every week; homiletics, we might say, was his pragmatics. It is the marriage of theory and practice that distinguishes Schleiermacher's hermeneutics, in either the narrow sense of exegetical procedures or as a general theory of interpretation.

Here is Barth's analysis of what is involved in the science of theology: "What decides whether theology is possible as a science is not whether theologians read sources, observe historical facts as such, and uncover the nature of historical relationships, but whether they can think dogmatically." (312) *Thinking dogmatically* gets at one of the chief roles of hermeneutics – the charge of keeping the code – and it suggests, further, the relationship of that function to the heuristic, pragmatic, and redemptive role of interpretation.

For Schleiermacher, God is both transcendent and immanent and it is this tenet which is at work in his discussions of language and discourse. Put "Meaning" in the place given to "God," and the dialectic of grammar and psychology comes right. What Barth means by thinking dogmatically is the antithesis of what Schleiermacher calls "careless interpretation." The pejorative meanings we now give the word *dogmatic* derive from the corrupt practice of treating doctrine superficially, without analysis, and of pretending that knowledge and understanding are independent of interpretation. Thinking dogmatically means knowing how to observe the constraints of *Schrift* and *Rede* alike, to interpret by attending to both the "grammatical" and "psychological." To think dogmatically is to identify implications and to explicate them; it is to draw inferences carefully and to represent them accurately. The third term is always there in Schleiermacher's exposition of how interpretation is enacted: it is a purpose entertained or suffered by the interpreter. Thinking dogmatically means honoring a commitment to the third way.

Schleiermacher's notion of projection (*Auslesung*) and a reconstruction (*Nachbildung*) is consonant with conceptions of mind which were not to be systematized for another hundred years. They can be found, for instance, in Cassirer's phenomenology of knowledge; in Sapir's conception of the linguistic process; in the tenets of Gestalt psychology and the later theories of perception which have been developed from the work of the Gestaltists. What Schleiermacher meant by the *psychological* was not a personal "reading in" which precedes "reading out;" it is not a matter of "guessing" which is then corrected, as Paul Ricoeur has it, but of envisagement. Divination is not a mystical counterpart of a scientific "grammatical" construing; we do not neutrally decode and then go into a trance. We anticipate, we expect, we project – and we meet the representations of those acts of mind.

It is important to stress the dynamic and dialectical character of interpretive acts in order to avoid falling into the trap of relying on certain unanalyzed metaphors, as Hans-Georg Gadamer has done with his notion of a "fusion of horizons" (*Horizontverschmelzung*). The idea of calling the limits or boundaries of a concept – the field of its application – a *horizon* is a commonplace, especially in German philosophical discourse. All metaphysical, epistemological concepts must be represented in spatial and/or temporal forms and remaining alert to the implications of those forms is crucial to the sound development of any theory. Horizons change, of course; horizons shift, expand or diminish, according to the observer's position. No one can see two horizons at once, in one scope; you can see different horizons only by changing the field of vision. You can watch the sun set from the shore and then race up the bank and watch it disappear a second time. The hiker can leave the path and climb a hill to see the lay of the land, but he cannot simultaneously regard the chipmunk along the trail. The military strategist surveys the topography from the heights because he can thus expand his horizon, seeing what is not to be seen at ground level. These self-evident points of logic are discounted in attempting to solve the problem of interpretation by means of metaphor – and metaphor which is illogically deployed. Only in a dyadic perspective could it occur to anyone to speak of a *fusion* of *horizons*. The concept of a horizon is inherently triadic; the surveyor's *triangulation* suggests as much. The horizon is defined by the point of view of the active spectator, the observer who actively interprets *with reference to* and *in terms of* position and angle of vision. The *fusion* metaphor simply begs the question of how we can entertain two points of view; it does not in any way explain how texts and contexts work together.

Schleiermacher's hermeneutics are thoroughly and consistently dialectical because, I would argue, both his theory and practice were underwritten by a triadic understanding of meaning which metaphors of fusion can not represent, as metaphors of incarnation and the sacramental can. The hermeneutic circle is as problematic a representation as the metaphor of fusion, but the figure of the circle can serve triadic conceptions, as I think *fusion* cannot. The hermeneutic circle in the dyadic perspective is seen as a diagram of *petitio principii*, the ancient logical device of question-begging; it represents a paradox which should be resolved. For those whose semiotic is dyadic, the hermeneutic circle is a vicious circle.[43]

Some critics impute to Schleiermacher himself feelings of dread and dismay at the discovery of the pervasiveness of the circle, its necessity. This is to ignore Schleiermacher's attitude towards all signs of our creaturely limitations – that they are potentially heuristic and redemptive. Many critics speak of the difficulty of breaking out of the circle. Heidegger's often-cited remark that the real problem is not the circle but where we enter it only subverts the idea represented by the circle, for to speak of entering a circle is like asking when Time begins: it destroys the logic of the figure. The aim of breaking into the circle is only the converse of the yearning to break out of it. In the triadic perspective, breaking in or out is not the point. The point is necessary engagement – a recognition of the constraints of interpretation as heuristic; of the interdependence of parts and whole as the necessary condition of knowing; of the dialectic of universal and particular in the individual moment or text or person. Seen in a triadic perspective, limitations are entailed in the very process of interpretation. Since that process can only be represented dynamically, the hermeneutic circle should perhaps be redesigned as a gyre or spiral, a self-generating helix.[44]

Schleiermacher on occasion deploys the figure of the circle in a way that bodies forth the dialectic – maybe even the dynamics – of representation. He speaks of the center and the circumference, and the necessary interdependence of that relationship suggests the methodical, not the vicious circle. It is not a dichotomy of inner/outer or part/whole which is defined but a dialectic in which one or the other may be emphasized:

Every creation of the human mind can be examined and comprehended from two points of view. You can look at it from its inner essence, and then see it as a product of human nature, grounded in one of man's necessary ways of behavior, or instincts. ... Or you can look at it from its circumference with reference to the determinate form it has assumed in various times and places; then you see it as a product of time and history.[45]

This passage illuminates the method Schleiermacher outlines in his lectures on hermeneutic. He observes there that "understanding *appears* (my italics) to go in endless circles, for a preliminary understanding comes from a general understanding of the language." He corrects this "appearance" by calling on the logic crucial for the hermeneutic enterprise, what Peirce called abduction: "The aim is to find the main idea in light of which the others must be measured." Representing "the main idea" hypothetically and tentatively is the means of making meaning; such representation is as necessary to interpretation as it is, in the first place, to the formulation by the author. In the task of understanding, the grammatical and the psychological bear one another the dialectical relationship Schleiermacher has defined as typical of "every human creation," but the crucial point is that they are simultaneous and correlative: "Understanding takes place only in the coinherence (*Ineinandersein*) of these two motives."[46] The point has been lost in the redactions we have had from positivist critics, especially insofar as they take "moment" as a temporal marker, without noting the complexity of the German *Moment*, which includes the idea of motive.

Schleiermacher is important for critical theory not because he stood in fear and trembling of the hermeneutic circle – which he did not – but because he insisted on the relevance of science to hermeneutics. And what Schleiermacher meant by science was method, that nexus of theory and practice which an authentic hermeneutics must take as its center. Observation, discovery procedures, formulation are essential in both scientific and philosophical investigation; the difference comes in the way findings and judgments are represented. This is not a simple question of modelling conventions; it is a question of defining the relationship of what is meant and what is said – and that is a matter of logic.

When Peirce defines logic as *the philosophy of representation* (1.539), he is acknowledging that ways of knowing can only be studied in terms of the way in which they are represented. *Representation* in this account entails recognition, the power of mind by which we see not separate aspects or parts but aspects *of* and parts *of*: Seeing is always *seeing as*. It is the power of recognition which defines the historical character of mankind: image-making is the primal symbolic act of mind; and the primal task of language is to stabilize our imagery so that we can remember. This conjunction of memory, language, analogy, and history is at the heart of Vico's new science, as it is of Schleiermacher's dogmatics; the rise of hermeneutics as a general theory of interpretation is from this complex.

The concept which binds them all is feeling. I think it is fair to say that not until Susanne K. Langer's masterful study, *Mind: An Essay on Human Feeling*, have we had the philosophical guidance needed to understand the biological and anthropological footing of this powerful idea. Schleiermacher claims feeling as the source of all our thinking; what Langer calls "the process of feeling" inspirits all thought. This premise assures that feeling will not be *added on*. Schleiermacher begins with feeling-forming and from it derives both the capacity to apprehend the formal and to understand significance. He thus avoids the mistake which Cassirer saw in Dilthey's conception of a form which is first apprehended and then humanized by empathy.[47] Schleiermacher avoids the dichotomy of abstraction and empathy by conceiving of form as the point of departure, just as he makes the immanence of God the condition of faith. Feeling is itself a forming power; for Schleiermacher, it was clearly the sign of our humanity, of what Coleridge called "the all-in-each of human nature."

9

Sapir, Cassirer, and the World of Meanings

The formal or logical analogy does not prove a material or ontological similarity in the subject matter of linguistics and biology. The linguist lives in a world of his own. His is a symbolic universe, a universe of meaning. We cannot analyze meaning in the same way and according to the same methods that we use in a chemical laboratory for analysing a chemical compound.

– Ernst Cassirer

Edward Sapir continually formulated definitions of language as a symbolic form and a symbolic activity:

Language is primarily a vocal actualization of the tendency to see realities symbolically.[48]
Language in its fundamental forms is the symbolic expression of human intentions.[49]
It goes without saying that in actual speech referential and expressive symbolisms are pooled in a single expressive stream. (1949:62)
Language is a purely human and non-instinctive method of communicating ideas, emotions, and desires by means of a system of voluntarily produced symbols.(1921:8)

His understanding of the dialectic of form and function enabled him to establish the importance of linguistics to anthropology:

The true locus [of the] processes which, when abstracted into a totality constitute culture is not in a theoretical community of human beings known as society, for the term 'society' is itself a cultural concept ...; it is in the interactions of specific individuals and, on the subjective side, in the world of meanings which each of these individuals may unconsciously abstract for himself from his participation in these interactions. (1949:515)

From the first, Sapir saw the methodological consequences of this view of language and culture: the centrality of interpretation must be recognized, the role of context appreciated. In "Why Cultural Anthropology Needs the Psychiatrist," he remarks on his own shock as a student when reading in Dorsey's "Omaha Sociology" such a statement as "Two Crows denies this," and continues with a revised judgment:

This looked a little as though the writer had not squarely met the challenge of assaying his source material and giving us the kind of data that we, as respectable anthropologists could live on. ... We see now that Dorsey was ahead of his age. Living as he did in close touch with the Omaha Indians, he knew that he was dealing, not with a society nor with a specimen of primitive man nor with a cross-section of the history of primitive culture, but with a finite, though indefinite, number of human beings, who gave themselves the privilege of differing from each other not only in matters generally considered as "one's own business" but even on questions which clearly transcended the private individual's concern and were, by the anthropologist's definition, implied in a conception of a definitely delimited society with a definitely discoverable culture. ... Unless one wishes to dismiss the implicit problem raised by contradictory statements by assuming that Dorsey misunderstood one, or both, of his informants, one would have to pause for awhile and ponder the meaning of the statement that "Two Crows denies this." (1949:569–70)

In the rest of this essay, Sapir considers what is involved in pondering the meaning of what anthropologists record.

Sapir saw the relationship of the historical and the psychological, of the systematic and the expressive, as dialectical, recognizing the essential role of perspective and context, and understanding that interpretation is entailed both in the linguistic process itself and in its study. Only this recognition enables the linguist to grasp the most important principle of all – that language is itself heuristic; that in the necessity of form lies freedom of symbolization. Sapir is never sardonic, never meanly polemical, but he is impatient with any view of language which precludes the apprehension of dialectical relationships. He thus habitually rejects dichotomies, always seeking an alternative which would be triadic – not simply a compromise but a way informed by semiotic principles: meaning is a relationship dependent on context and perspective; symbolization is an act of mind which is at once instrument and product; symbolic acts shape the individual and build the social world. In his theory as in his practice, Sapir recognizes the third term – the reference or interpretant, the purpose or activity which mediates the symbol and what it represents.

In 1923, Sapir reviewed what was to become one of the most influential books of the first part of the century, Ogden and Richards' *The Meaning of Meaning*. He proceeds with a typically astute redaction of the argument of this notoriously chaotic book, noting the crucial distinction Ogden and Richards make between the *referent* and the *reference*, which is the mediating idea that makes possible the representational function of the symbol. He then singles out what he calls "the originality of *The Meaning of Meaning*," *viz.*, the refusal "to see a ... special relation between symbol and 'referent' or thing (event) symbolized." (This is the doctrine of the arbitrary sign formulated here some years before Saussure's work was widely known.) Sapir mildly criticizes the authors for slighting the formal aspects of language, but then concludes with this strong statement that the book's real importance is that it is a harbinger:

New sciences are adumbrated in this book. They are a general theory of signs (a psychological approach to the problems of epistemology); a theory of symbolism; and, as the most important special development of a general theory of symbolism, a broader theory of language than the philologists have yet attempted.[50]

To chart the shifting meanings of the terms here would be to write the history of the philosophy of language in the past sixty years. "... the general theory of signs" is now given the name *semiotics*. By "psychological" Sapir meant all that is not covered in what he called the "historical;" it included both "form-libido" and the study of individual conscious and unconscious motives. The juxtaposition of *psychological* and *epistemological* is testimony to the fact that Sapir rejected the killer dichotomies of scientific critical inquiry. The theory of symbolism hinted at, which will go beyond the traditional concerns of philology by way of being "a broader theory of language," seems an accurate forecast of the advent of the New Criticism. That it is to be a "general" theory suggests an emphasis and an aim found from Herder and Schleiermacher to Einstein and Freud: I take its appearance here as a signal that Sapir wanted the study of signs and symbols to be perceived as including theory, practice, and methodology; he wanted linguistics to be seen as a philosophical enterprise with scientific implications.

The conclusion of Sapir's review is, as well, a fair summary of the program he had set for himself: to identify language as the primary study in the sciences of man; to define speech broadly and deeply in both psychological and historical terms; to demonstrate a method as fully dialectical as the conception of language it was meant to serve. Sapir's case for linguistics as a science is nothing less than a case for a general theory of signs; the status of linguistics as a science depends on its regard for the principles of semiotics – its faith in "the closest possible psychological scrutiny of experienced contexts" and a capacity to be guided by "the canniest 'canons of symbolization.'"

Sapir's allegiance to the principle of mediation is explicit everywhere in his linguistic and ethnological studies. He does not conceive of reference and representation as relationships holding directly between a signifier and a signified; the sign functions only because of the mediating idea which empowers and articulates the symbolic relationship of what represents and what is represented. Thus, in Sapir's anthropological linguistics, the meaning relationship is always given a social or historical context; when Sapir considers the making of meaning, whether in logical, methodological, or psychological terms, it is always by way of taking into account the Interpretant.

In the 1920s, Sapir's linguistics – his semiotics – was set aside as Leonard Bloomfield's structural linguistics won the field. This positivist linguistics derided any concern with intention or meaning or purpose as "mentalistic" and proceeded with scientistic conceptions of method – the kind which would have considered recording that "Two Crows denies this" as unprofessional. Though this bit of history makes it intelligible, it does not soften the irony of the fact that Sapir has survived chiefly because of his alleged association with Whorf in the formulation of a positivist view of language which has been institutionalized as the "Sapir-Whorf Hypothesis." Sapir's importance for critical theory lies in his conception of linguistics as a science of signs and in his conception of signs in triadic terms. Recognizing his achievement should begin with dissociating Sapir from Whorf.[51]

For Sapir, language is neither in its origin nor in its purposes essentially communicative or physical or classificatory: fundamentally, speech is a symbolic act and language is a symbolic form: "Language is primarily a vocal actualization of the tendency to see realities symbolically" (1949:15). *Tendency* I read as a term given special meaning by the

Gestalt psychologists, a way of suggesting the dynamics of the apprehension of form. It also suggests that a predisposition to symbolization is the species-specific character of *language*: to say "human languages" would have been redundant in Sapir's eyes, since the symbolic character of language radically differentiates it from animal communication. From his earliest discussions in his essay on Herder down to the last articles he wrote (many published posthumously), Sapir assures that the symbolic character of language is not limited to indicative reference and other narrowly limited expressive functions but is always represented, as well, in its heuristic role. The metaphors of interpenetration and molding, if read aright, define this active character of language: it works, produces, creates, shapes, and transforms.

Early and late, Sapir held that it is the formal, systematic character of language which allows our intuitions to be expressed, our experience to be represented, our thinking to be articulated. In his explanation of linguistic form, we find Sapir continually stressing the relationship of the "symbolic inventory" language provides and its heuristic power; form is more than "formal," so to speak. It is both instrument and product, and it has its origin in both the individual imagination and a social motive Sapir called "form-libido" (527). He notes that language in its origin *welled up*; that the needs it answers are not those initially of thinking but of feeling. An appropriate method of language study would recognize the dialectic of feeling and form. It would lead to an acknowledgement of the vital role of the speech community which tacitly accepts the categories provided by the language by which it is itself defined.

It has been observed that it was no accident that Sapir's interests developed as they did, that is in the direction represented by the sequence of terms in Mandelbaum's title: language, culture, personality.[52] Although it would take a Paul Klee to suggest the intricacies and surprises of all the connections among the foci of Sapir's interests, his cultural anthropology can be said to depend on a single, fundamental principle. Expectably enough, it takes a dialectical form: the linguistic process is necessarily social; the locus for the study of culture is the individual. In the dyadic perspective, such an apposition is simply contradictory, but in triadic terms, it is sound. The cogency of the argument that culture must be studied in the focus provided by the individual depends on the concept of the individual as representative of a group, of all mankind. Sapir's explanation (quoted in part above) follows:

The true locus of these processes which, when abstracted into a totality, constitute culture is not in a theoretical community of human beings known as a society, for the term "society" is itself a cultural construct ... The true locus of culture is in the interactions of specific individuals and, on the subjective side, in the world of meanings which each of these individuals may unconsciously abstract for himself from his participation in these interactions. Every individual is, then, in a very real sense, a representative of at least one sub-culture which may be abstracted from the generalized culture of the group of which he is a member. (1949:515)

In speaking of the individual as the locus for a study of culture, Sapir is careful to note that "the terms 'social' and 'individual' are contrastive only in a limited sense" (544). He notes, too, that although the idea of the individual as an abstraction is generally accepted, it is less commonly recognized that culture, too, is a "statistical fiction" (516). Each participates in the other, as it were; each can represent the other. Indeed, the interdependence of the individual and society is an idea which entails the concept of representativeness. In the dyadic perspective, this is only a mystical notion, but in a triadic perspective, representativeness is as clearly a logical condition of signification as is interpretation. Representativeness, which Peirce discusses as a matter of tokens of types, is for Sapir central to language, culture, and personality.

Both Peirce and Sapir rejected psychology practiced in accordance with positivist principles, because both rejected the dichotomous view of man and society which such psychology fosters. Sapir reclaimed psychology from positivist contexts in which it was combined with mechanistic views of the psychical. He spoke of the psycho-spiritual, in contradistinction to the psycho-physical. Sapir's interest in psychiatry and social psychology was strategic: he found there the speculative instruments needed for exploring the unconscious, psychic forces which determine in large part the forms of culture and language. He found the necessary protection against the "evolutionary prejudice" of the social sciences (1921:123) surviving into his time from nineteenth-century positivism. Sapir held that historians who neglected unconscious compulsions would provide inadequate accounts, just as psychologists would, who disregarded social and cultural contexts. When the abstractions necessary to critical analysis are mistaken for the real world, the result is "mythology," whether on the part of historians or of psychologists. But Sapir rejects the contention that an acknowledgement of unconscious forces is a resuscitation of the "mythology of the 'soul;'" he dismisses those who "tacitly assume that all experience is but the mechanical sum of physiological processes lodged in isolated individuals" (1949:512).

The complex dialectic of the relationships Sapir saw among language, culture, and personality culminates in the idea that language is "the most significant and colossal work that the human spirit has evolved ... the most massive and inclusive art we know, a mountainous and anonymous work of unconscious generations" (1921:220). The "latent content" of this "collective art" is the same in all languages: it is "'the intuitive science of experience'" (218). When Sapir speaks of language as the work of the human spirit, he is following out the implications of claiming symbolic transformation as a species-specific power and of his conviction that language is a "pre-rational function" (1921:14): "We must imagine that thought processes set in, as a kind of psychic overflow, almost at the beginning of linguistic expression" (17).

Sapir's reclaimed psychology depends on the same principles we find in his linguistics and his cultural anthropology: his interest in language, culture, and personality is semiotic. Sapir's subject is always "the world of meanings."

Sapir could not write about language without writing philosophically. His technical papers do not lose sight of larger issues, as he clarifies in case after case the formal completeness which gives language its heuristic power. The articles he wrote for the profession continually monitored the possibility that linguistics had reached scientific maturity. In *Language: An Introduction to the Study of Speech* and his more speculative essays and reviews, he never condescended or obfuscated in the attempt to explain why a literate public should be interested in the study of speech. His success in establishing certain truths about language and principles of linguistics has been long-lasting, as a review of course syllabi can attest. And then there is his eloquence:

> Both simple and complex types of language of an indefinite number of variations may be found spoken at any desired level of cultural advance. When it comes to linguistic form, Plato walks with the Macedonian swineherd, Confucius with the head-hunting savage of Assam. (1921:219)

That passage, among several others, found its way into Ernst Cassirer's *An Essay on Man*, written in English and published in 1944 in the United States, where the author had come as an exile from Nazi Germany. There is a consonance in the views of the philosopher and the linguist about language and the sciences of man, but Cassirer's name is generally linked with Sapir's on the grounds, simply, that they were both influenced by Herder and Humboldt, or, more frequently, because of a commitment they both allegedly had to something called "linguistic determinism." Since that phrase is often another name for the strong version of the so-called Sapir-Whorf hypothesis, the strange triumvirate of Whorf-Sapir-Cassirer has emerged: nothing justifies it.[53] There could be nothing in common between the engineer who gave the name "linguistic relativity" to a conception of language modelled on point mechanics, and the philosopher of science, whose studies of substance and function in modern physics provided the context for a logic of the humanities and a philosophy of language as symbolic form.

I offer a few passages which testify to Cassirer's and Sapir's understanding of what Cassirer called the two tasks of language. Here is a late formulation of an argument he had been making for forty years:

The idea of a general philosophical grammar is ... by no means invalidated by the progress of linguistic research, although we can no longer hope to realize such a grammar by the simple means that were employed in former attempts. Human speech has to fulfill not only a universal logical task but also a social task which depends on the specific social conditions of the speaking community. Hence we cannot expect a real identity, a one to one correspondence between grammatical and logical forms.[54]

It is not that grammar belongs to one and logic to the other task but that human speech is the logically necessary means of our construction of social reality and that a grammatical system is the logically necessary condition of the function of speech. The universal logical task of language is to provide for response to the necessary condition of our life in the fallen world, *sub specie temporis*. We do not see face to face but in a glass darkly; there is no unmediated vision and it is only a naïve realism that holds out the possibility of direct access to the objects of knowledge. The universal logical task of language is to free us from the momentary – the eternal present of the beasts. Language recreates us as historical beings and enables us to live in a human world, not only in nature. "Human speech," Cassirer declared, "always conforms to and is commensurate with certain forms of human life" (136). The conformity is between language and "human life" – our perceptions, memories, feelings, thoughts, visions – all of which take place in a social world. If the universal logical task of language is to provide the *necessary* condition of human life, then the *sufficient* condition, we might say, is exemplified in the social task.

The two tasks are analogous to Sapir's dialectical pairs, the formal completeness of language and the creation of the social world; the self-contained system and "the ultimate psychological determinants of cultural form" (527). Indeed, there is scarcely an essay or article in which Sapir does not in some way examine the process by which the two tasks are fulfilled by the formal, systematic character of language and its social purposes.

For both Cassirer and Sapir, defining the two tasks of language requires an understanding of the idea of language as energy, as power. (Ironically, *tasks* should be taken not, as it generally is, as "jobs of work" but as "purpose.") Here is one of several passages in which Cassirer draws on Sapir in arguing the heuristic power of language:

If we wish to understand language, declares Sapir, we must disabuse our minds of preferred values and accustom ourselves to look upon English and Hottentot with the same cool yet interested detachment. If it were the task of human speech to copy or imitate the given or ready-made order of things we could scarcely maintain any such detachment. We could not avoid the conclusion that, after all, one of two different copies must be better; that the one must be nearer to, the other farther from, the original. Yet if we ascribe to speech a productive and constructive rather than a merely reproductive function, we shall judge quite differently. In this case it is not the "work" of language but its "energy" which is of paramount importance. In order to measure this energy one must study the linguistic process itself instead of simply analyzing its outcome, its product, and final results.(131)

For Cassirer and Sapir, language, like perception, is constructive, not merely reproductive, and reality is not given but is apprehended, not a *Gegebenes* but an *Aufgegebenes*.

Apprehension in the linguistic process is a profoundly dialectical act constituted by action and reflection, by the projection of our expectations of the shapes and forms of utterance. Our apprehensions are continually shaped dialectically; our projections are checked and modified, as they are inspirited, by the constraints of grammatical categories. And because the linguistic process is through and through a social process, our apprehensions are continually affirmed or rejected by those present and those who historically have built the culture in which a particular language is spoken.

What Cassirer calls a "philosophical grammar" seeks to define linguistic universals, but they are not found by setting meaning aside as a way to purify by abstraction, but by studying "the linguistic process." For both Cassirer and Sapir, the conception of language as heuristic had an important methodological consequence: language, they held, should be studied as a *process of determination*. The linguistic process is one which does not simply label objective entities but actively brings them forth as objects of knowledge; it is defined by the active forming powers of language, *viz.*, the power of naming and the power of articulation. They are, of course, dialectically related. The hypostatic power, by stabilizing our imagery, gives us our memory and makes possible analogy and thus the power of envisagement. Naming – identifying – entails recognition of both class and the negative: it is in the process of determination that these implicit logical relationships are recognized and articulated.

Both Cassirer and Sapir considered that the unity of language lies in the heuristic powers of naming and articulation which constitute "the linguistic process." It is here that the search for linguistic universals begins and ends. Both claimed that the unity of language is functional and not to be identified by a correlation of logic and grammar. Language mediates experience, individual and social; the meanings it provides as means of making further meanings cannot be reduced to the patterns of sound and syntax which constitute the self-contained system, but that is not to deny that concepts are logically dependent on language. Sapir observes that logic must be "freed from the trammels of grammar" (165), but that does not mean that logic and grammar would otherwise be identical.

If Cassirer is read in the light of Sapir's conception of linguistics as a "tool in the sciences of man," it will be easier to differentiate the flattened, lifeless, literal-minded versions of what he said from his actual argument, which is that in the linguistic process we construct the human world. And if Sapir is read in the context of Cassirer's powerful conception of the two tasks of language, we will find illuminated both what he meant by the "tyranny" of the formal completeness of each language – the necessary condition of its heuristic power – and why it was that he took the construction of social reality to be the proper focus of study for the human science of linguistics.

10

Susanne K. Langer and the Process of Feeling

It should be the task of the philosophical schools of this century to bring together the two streams [introduced by Descartes and Leibnitz] into an expression of the world-picture derived from science, and thereby end the divorce of science from the affirmations of our aesthetic and ethical experience.

– Alfred North Whitehead

Mortal Socrates has other fish to fry.

– Josephine Miles

For Susanne K. Langer, paradox is a symptom of confusion and as such should be resolved. She began as a logician and throughout her career argued with cogency and passion for the importance of feeling in any account of mind: to understand why that is not a paradox would be to understand the argument. Her third book, *Philosophy in a New Key* (1942), was widely influential (for a time it held the record for paperback sales); whereas her magnum opus, completed forty years later, *Mind: An Essay on Human Feeling* (1982), remains unread, uncited, and even though recognized as a powerful and beautiful work by scholars in quite different fields – among them, Clifford Geertz, C.H. Waddington, and L.C. Knights – it has been virtually without influence. The usual attitude towards Susanne Langer (especially among aestheticians and most especially among British aestheticians, who have misunderstood the little they have read) is condescension. Feminists would have ready answers for the question of why she has suffered neglect, but the fact remains that feminist theory on the whole has not benefitted from so much as a glance at Susanne Langer's philosophy of mind, in which the idea of "women's ways of knowing" plays no role whatsoever. The reasons for the neglect are more complex, though doubtless being a woman, and especially a woman philosopher, was disadvantageous. I believe that Susanne Langer lost influence because her enterprise of developing an aesthetic consonant with Cassirer's philosophy of symbolic forms, a biology of feeling, and a philosophy of mind ran counter to the scientism which in the post-war years was everywhere on the rise – in structural linguistics, in ethology, in both behavioral and cognitive psychology, and in all other disciplines for which "the end of ideology" was a slogan. And in the current climate in which humanism is derided, philosophy declared bankrupt, and the enterprise of reasoning is itself suspect, her latter-day attempts to sketch a philosophical anthropology have expectably found no audience.

There is in Susanne Langer's[55] work an extraordinary convergence of aesthetics, biology, psychology, and anthropology, but for all the theoretical support for interdisciplinary research, outsiders, unless they exercise uncritical attention, are unwelcome. When this philosopher turned to psychology, for instance, observing that it was about time that psychologists developed working concepts (her term for speculative instruments) to guide their research, there was no interest in the charge. Every year there are reviews of books in a variety of fields – psychology, cognitive science, anthropology, and, indeed, in philosophy – in which the reviewer expresses gratitude that someone at last has attended to questions and problems which, as it happens, SKL was addressing thirty-five years ago and, in some cases, as long as fifty years ago.

It must be said that SKL is hard to read (or, rather, hard to remember) – not because, like Peirce, she over-categorizes and digresses, and not because of her prose style; indeed, she writes some of the best philosophical prose since William James. It is her style of argumentation that is forbidding. She is no phrase-maker; there are no Delphic pronouncements and very few memorable aphorisms or set examples which, like Heidegger's hammer, can be dropped into a discourse in lieu of working with the ideas they purport to represent. SKL is hard to remember having read because of her explanatory style: she defines very rigorously, exemplifying and documenting her claims; she develps analogies, drawing out the implications, all the while making the case so thoroughly that the reader can remain unengaged, there being so little work for him to do. Like Cassirer, she patiently unravels the arguments she wishes to discard, anticipating defenses in the course of developing a counter-argument. For attitudes she dismisses, she often makes the case more cogently than the proponents themselves. It must be said, however, that she has no interest in demolishing theories which she finds are set forth in equivocal terms; thus Piaget and Chomsky appear in footnotes only and Heidegger makes no appearance at all.

Each of her books stems from its predecessors: *Philosophy in a New Key* develops the distinction between ways of thinking made in *The Practice of Philosophy*. Taking the chapter "On Significance in Music" as the point of departure, she then proceeds in *Feeling and Form* to show how art takes its place alongside language, myth, history, and science as a symbolic form. Virtual form, which has been developed as an aesthetic concept, becomes the chief speculative instrument for a meditation on vital process which constitutes the first volume of *Mind: An Essay on Human Feeling*. In the second and third volumes of that work, she offers brilliant critiques of the claims and demonstrations of ethology and certain schools of anthropology, arguing that the role of symbols cannot be defined in terms developed in the course of studying seagulls and molluscs, or even the higher apes.

"Symbolic logic," SKL observed, "is an instrument of exact thought, both analytic and constructive; its mission, accordingly, is not only to validate scientific methods but also to clarify the semantic confusions that beset the popular mind as well as the professional philosopher at the present time."[56] It was her mission from the first to set us straight – all of us: from the first, her tone was magisterial. What sympathetic readers construed as lively instruction (or wittily expressed impatience), others took as plain arrogance. In her first published articles – on the logic of verbs and on "form and content" – she noted that Wittgenstein was misguided in what she called his turn to "Mysticism." "Mr. Wittgenstein," she wrote, need not "despair of any philosophical, that is to say, truly general propositions." And she proceeds with an explanation of logical form and logical language.[57] Fresh from Henry Sheffer's logic seminars, this protégée of Alfred North Whitehead's knew what she was talking about and by the time of her second book she had learned how to talk about it. She managed to write both for "the popular mind" and "the professional philosopher," if not simultaneously, then contrapuntally.

Throughout all her books, SKL put her logical skills to work, quickly learning to move beyond abstruse formulations. Her chief method was to desynonymize[58] the terms of the argument. She rehabilitated *intuition* – usually a synonym for *not-thinking* – to name the fundamental act of mind. Intuition, she notes, is not a method but an event – and she goes on to define a syllogism as a device for getting from one intuition to another.[59] What we intuit is form and this is achieved by "spontaneous and natural abstraction."[60] Desynonymizing sometimes leads to such concatenations as this:

The perception of forms, or abstraction, is intuitive, just as the recognition of relations, of instances, and of meaning is. It is one of the basic acts of logical intuition, and the primitive and typical occurrence is in the process of symbolization.[61]

Out of context, we might easily be persuaded that a pseudo-concept is in the making here, with anything having to do with abstraction inseparable from anything else. But in fact, having desynonymized *abstraction* and *generalization*, SKL has begun to make *abstraction* the mother term with two daughter terms: *abstraction by means of generalizing* and *abstraction without generalization*.[62]

Early on, SKL had suggested *insight* and *understanding* as terms for kinds of knowledge, but she soon abandoned them, shifting the focus instead to the representation of mental acts which she distinguished as *presentational* and *representational* or *non-discursive*. The analysis offered was influential, but the terminology proved unwieldy. Further, defining in negative terms suggested secondary status for "non-discursive" symbolism; like I.A. Richards' *pseudo-statement*, *non-discursive* undercut the argument being made. SKL finally declared that there was no really acceptable name for abstraction without generalization and settled for "presentational abstraction."[63] Definition, in any case, was not a final goal. SKL understood what Peirce meant by calling logic "the philosophy of representation" and she sought pragmatically to demonstrate what difference certain differences might make – differences of form and purpose articulated in conceptual definitions, established by terminology, and ready to be put to work.

Probably the most important influence on SKL's thinking about symbol came from Cassirer, whom she had read in German in the 1920s. In 1946, she translated *Sprache und Mythos* and in her Translator's Preface she offered a cogent and stirring account of the inportance of Cassirer's *Philosophie der Symbolischen Formen*, for which *Language and Myth* was a kind of proto-gloss. Cassirer had "struck a new note in so-called 'theory of knowledge;'" it became a "theory of mental activity." The focus was myth, usually accounted for as *mistake*. Cassirer undertook "a search for the reason and spiritual function of this peculiar sort of 'ignorance.'" He spoke of the commonality of language and myth as "metaphorical thought," arguing that both are abstractive processes which entail the apprehension of form and the articulation of elements. SKL could thus speak of the *logic* of mythic ideation. Summarizing the argument of the second volume of *PSF* (*Mythical Thought*), she writes: "The characteristic form ... of mythic thinking ... is a logic of multiple meanings instead of general concepts, representative figures instead of classes, reinforcement of ideas (by repetition, variation, and other means) instead of proof."[64]

The most compelling idea for SKL in Cassirer's theory of language and myth was that language has two offices, the first of which is hypostasis: "Language is essentially hypostatic, seeking to distinguish, emphasize, and hold the object of feeling rather than to communicate the feeling itself."[65] SKL saw that hypostasis builds on perception, "the natural abstraction" by which we intuit forms, and echoing Coleridge, she continues: "This hypostasis, entailed by the primitive office of language, really lies deeper even than nomenclature, which merely reflects it: for it is a fundamental trait of all imagination ... Imagination is the primary talent of the human mind, the activity in whose service language was evolved" (386). By stabilizing images of experience, language makes it possible to refer to them: "In its symbolic image the expression is conceived." (387) Articulation, the other office of language, is made possible by its syntactic structure: "It is the discursive character of language, its inner tendency to grammatical development, which gives rise to logic in the strict sense ... to reasoning" (399–400).

At one point, SKL suggests that abstraction acts like an armature for our creative and constructive thought; I think she saw hypostasis serving the same sort of role. Giving something a name she called "the vastest generative idea that was ever conceived."[66] Just as an image stabilized by naming enables us to recognize kindred images, so one name begets others. In the concept of hypostasis SKL found a generative power to match that of syntax, that discursive power which (moving along) brings thought with it. Both powers are active in metaphor, "the natural instrument of our greatest mental achievement – abstract thinking."[67]

Certainly in working out conceptual definitions of abstraction and symbolization SKL followed the leads of Whitehead and Cassirer, but in forming the concept of feeling and in considering the consequences of making feeling central to a philosophy of mind, she struck out on a path of her own. SKL was, of course, not the first philosopher to take feeling seriously. William James, for instance, had considered using *feeling* to serve the purposes for which he finally chose *thought*. To understand Peirce's Firstness requires a semiotic conception of feeling. Feeling is crucial to Whitehead's conception of the modes of thought. The achievement of SKL is to have seen the consonance of virtual form and vital process: her contribution to philosophy is to have demonstrated how certain principles of aesthetics and biology could transform our understanding of how the human mind creates the human world.

As I have noted, her disquisition on music led to *Feeling and Form* which bears the subtitle "A Theory of Art Developed from *Philosophy in a New Key*."[68] The claim is forthright: "To be able to define 'musical meaning' adequately, precisely, but for an artistic, not a positivistic context and purpose, is the touchstone of a really powerful philosophy of symbolism."[69] SKL analyzes and sets aside familiar, tedious arguments about whether or not music "expresses" feeling; whether it is the composer's feeling or the performer's; whether this feeling is real or formulaic, etc., etc. She discards two emotive theories of musical meaning, namely, self-expression and the logical expression of feeling, thus clearing the way for a new approach. Drawing on her extensive knowledge of music theory (especially the work of Heinrich Schenker), as well as her experience as a musician (she was an accomplished cellist), SKL formulates this odd definition: "Music at its highest, though clearly a symbolic form, is an unconsummated symbol. Articulation is its life, but not assertion; expressiveness, not expression" (240).

Joined to this desynonymizing is a terminological solution, the use of the term *import* for the "meaning" of an art symbol. A comment in "The Genesis of Artistic Import" tells us where it will take her:

I strongly suspect, though I am not ready to assert it dogmatically, that the import of artistic expression is broadly the same in all arts as it is in music – the verbally ineffable, yet not inexpressible law of vital experience, the pattern of affective and sentient being. (257)

"Verbally ineffable" is a pleonasm and, like *non-discursive* and *pseudo-statement*, it misses the mark, but a terminological difficulty should not be mistaken for a conceptual muddle. In order to deploy the speculative instrument of *import*, understood as following the pattern of sentience, she had to clarify the relationship of feeling and form. Desynonymizing is essential in the critique of pseudo-concepts; dismantling killer dichotomies requires an equally supple procedure. SKL first explains how the relationship of feeling and form has been misconstrued:

> Feeling and form are not logical complements ... Feeling is associated with spontaneity, spontaneity with informality or indifference to form, and thus (by slipshod thinking) with absence of form. On the other hand, form connotes formality, regulation hence repression of feeling, and (by the same slipshodness) absence of feeling. The conception of polarity ... is really an unfortunate metaphor whereby a logical muddle is raised to the dignity of a fundamental principle.[70]

With the publication of the first volume of *Mind* (1967) SKL was ready to develop the premise of "The Genesis of Artistic Import," and to use that concept of "the law of vital experience" for the larger purposes of her *Essay on Human Feeling*:

> My reason for entertaining the hypothesis of the derivation of all forms of human experience – self-awareness, *Weltanschauung*, mental suffering and joy, social consciousness or what[ever] you would name – from primeval feeling is the image of feeling created by art throughout its long, ramified history; that image seems to be capable of encompassing the whole mind of men, including its highest rational activities. (149–150)

How could a philosophy of mind grow from a theory of art? By way of a highly articulated analogy between virtual form and vital process, biology providing the Interpretant – *sentience* or *livingness*.

When SKL studies the forms of vital process, she finds the shapes and structures, the tensions and resolutions of art; motions grow like melodies. Her mission in the first volume of *Mind* was to demonstrate the mutual illumination of aesthetics and biology:

> We know that every form which seems to be charged with feeling also appears "organic," and makes the impression of "livingness." ... This semblance of organism is implicit in the artist's "Idea." ... It is this circumstance that really led me to think of feeling as a phase of vital process itself ... instead of as a new substantive element produced by such a process. (151)

Feeling does not "come first" in the sense that something entirely different comes next; it comes first the way song comes before prose, the way metaphor precedes discursive thought. By saying that thought is a phase of feeling, SKL sought to emphasize this kind of primacy. She had held that the study of mythic ideation would dispel the Darwinian notion that symbolization is an elaboration of animal behavior. Thus intuition is not a higher form of instinct, speech is not an adaptation of exclamatory cries, and ritual is a human, not an animal, acitivity. Her study of physiology likewise provided the ground for an argument that deciding on the primacy of a developed cortex or of speech is a dilemma to be avoided only by beginning at a point at which two elements are in dialectic.

The trick of abstract conception could never have been adopted for the sake of its practical advantages if it had not somehow occurred naturally in pre-human brains. It could only be put to practical use after it had evolved in the course of that cerebral specialization which made one primate genus become Man.[71]

The central argument of SKL's theory of mind is that emotion invests abstraction with the power of symbolic transformation. The physiological processes which account for recognition are necessary to abstraction but not sufficient: "They may indeed make conception possible, yet to make it actual requires something more. That further element, I maintain, is emotional" (73). "To make it actual": activity is felt process. Activity is central to Cassirer's philosophy of symbolic forms, as SKL noted in her Preface to *Language and Myth*; it is equally important to Whitehead's philosophy. What SKL contributed was a biological context in which acts could be identified at all levels of organization, from the firing of neurons to utterance. The act concept thus provides the framework in which to interpret the idea that thought is a phase of feeling. The first volume of *Mind* is devoted to the most careful investigation of the act concept and its derivatives. Only in Sapir, I believe, is there to be found so searching a study of the *Ineinandersein* of thought, feeling, and utterance.

The counterpoint of interpretation and speculation characteristic of SKL's *Essay on Human Feeling* can be exemplified by this passage:

The necessity of "living form" for any rendering of psychical events rests simply on the fact that such events are the very concentration of life, acts in which the deeper rhythms of the organism, mainly unfelt, are implicated so that the dynamic structure of the individual is reflected in the forms of feeling as it is in the form of every voluntary movement of the body. But in the development of cerebral activity to the human level, some characteristics inherent in all such activity become highly specialized and finally transformed ...: imagination, intuition and the whole gamut of new powers these engender, primarily of course speech and reasoning. These characteristics become paramount in forming the emotional patterns of man and even his perceptions, which are shot through and through with conceptual elements, so human experience is a dialectic of symbolic objectification and interpretive subjectification.[72]

The idea of dialectical process is dependent on the idea of heuristic limits: throughout *Mind: An Essay on Human Feeling*, SKL discloses to us that that interdependence is "the law of vital experience."

What happens in the individual brain is not "socially constructed," though the Lysenkos of the present day often seem to be claiming just that. But when the brain's process is felt, that is the mind's activity – and that activity cannot be simply personal. Individuation for SKL, as for Peirce and Sapir, is in dialectic with involvement. The third volume of *Mind* is given over to discussions of that dialectic; the second volume clears the way for a philosophical anthropology by offering, first of all, an examination of theories purporting to account for the social nature of our species in terms of herds and flocks or even of insect "societies." SKL never denies the continuities, but her conception of mind is at the service of explaining not only the commonality with the higher apes but the abyss between us and all other animals. Her contempt for the language and methods of scientific inquiry is unmitigated. I have mentioned her critique of the Idols of the Laboratory; here is a comment from the chapter "Interpretations":

In the early years of anthropological research it was often critically remarked that the scholars in that new field knew too little of animal ways to trace human characteristics to their prehuman origins. Today we have the counterpart of that failing in the presently new study of animal behavior; our ethologists know too little anthropology to realize the inadequacy of their definitions of those key words in application to human experience, and to foresee how, in our evolutionary picture of the hominid stock, the differentiae that distinguish the genus *Homo* from other high primate genera are perforce obscured and made ineffectual for the understanding of human life. Once "rites" and "ceremonies" are imputed to animals – not only to apes, but to gulls, ducks, lizards – all other distinctively human traits which actually underlie the occurence of ritual performance by men are gradually ascribed to non-human creatures: symbols, concepts, tradition, superstition, sham battles and tournaments, punishment to correct the young, and even principles of exogamy and special relations with aunts and uncles. All these findings rest on the interpretation of animal acts, which are behaviorally convergent with human acts, in terms of human motivation. (*Mind* II, 109–111)

In the final three chapters, SKL turns to the matter of human motivation, explaining how we might "recognize the critical point where an overcharged system of mental operations breaks over into imagery and symbolic conception, and the great shift from animal mentality to mind begins" (140). The idea of a great shift runs counter to current mythology in which the continuity of the species overrides (and outsells) the idea that Man is the animal symbolicum. The second volume of *Mind* helps offset the effects of certain popularizations, especially public television programs in which anthropomorphism is presupposed by the script and marvelously substantiated by photography in the wild, as well as by computer-generated representations. In these important chapters, themes which are recurrent in pop psychology and pop anthropology are touched on – brain hemispheres, dreams, the opposable thumb, the origin of speech, imagery, etc. The difference between most science writing for "the popular mind" and what we have in *Mind* II is that SKL understands the laws of evidence. She cites findings in a dozen fields, not as illustrative of unargued assertions, but as support for a philosophical argument. Her startlingly original conjectures are tonic because they are reasoned. The most important is the idea that the great shift was effected by the symbolic finish of impulses in the brain. She argues that symbolism first emerged as a saving action. But there is another danger, a match for the circumstances of the birth of symbolism: it is overspecialization, the danger of "excessive imagination," which is checked by what she will call in the concluding volume "the ethnic balance," the dialectic of individuation and involvement.

The third volume of *Mind* takes up an argument first made in "Man and Animal: The City and the Hive," a 1958 lecture published in *Philosophical Sketches*. The abstractive processes of perception and mythic ideation, in conjunction with hypostatic and discursive powers of language, make possible the fact that Man is the only creature who knows that he will die. By drawing out the implications of this startling fact, SKL shows that the foreknowledge of death is the paradigm of all mental acts in which we apprehend a case in point. And she finds here the human motivation which cannot be modelled by animal behavior. The

122 Triadic Remedies

recognition of individual mortality provides the impetus to form social institutions by means of which rights can be represented, authority delegated, and responsibilities shared. Her discussion of punishment suggests just how deeply rooted social forms are in feeling. "The ethnic balance" is explained as follows:

> The danger in every aberration from the instinctive round of hereditary behavior is that it is an act of self-assertion, and self-assertion is an overt sign of the agent's growing individuation. It is that basic, unconscious gesture of selfhood that has to be balanced by some display of the biological claims of the stock upon each living generation. (122–23)

Part V thus provides a speculative gloss on one of the central principles of *Philosophy in a New Key*, namely, "the need for symbolic transformation." Some readers confused SKL's scientific attitude with positivism, misreading "need" as a synonym for "drive." Throughout *Mind*, but especially in the third volume, we have the wherewithal for understanding this "need," both as it can be described in electro-chemical terms and as bearing a meaning close to what Sapir meant in speaking of "a tendency to see realities symbolically."

Part VI, unfinished because of increasing blindness, was to have been devoted to epistemology. The twenty-two page sketch which substitutes is entitled "The Open Ambient." We find there some of the most eloquent passages SKL ever wrote and, in every paragraph, illustrations of the power of her central argument that mind is a phase of feeling, that the body is not only the necessary condition for the emergence of mind but is itself our primary speculative instrument. The topic is the creative advance of natural science, which is founded on the concept of fact. After six pages in which she sets aside the claims of positivist linguistics "to narrow down the principles of ordinary discourse to scientific precision and fixity" (206), she turns to mathematics, "the instrument of scientific thought," and the origin of counting. One last time she comes to the Dance which plays so central a role in her thought:

> [The elements of counting] – similar conceptual units following each other in a series – are almost certainly first presented by the visual and kinesthetic perception of our own bipedal steps, under control of old cerebral mechanisms. ... The Dance ... animated the dancer's world at the command of his own voluntary movements, and must have been a magical activity from its beginning. All this seems, on the face of it, to have had nothing to do with mathematics, but it estab-

lished the reality of the whole realm of distinct, self-identical units on which that recently emergent technique is based. (210–211)

The leading motifs of *Mind* are resonant here: logical form, felt process, emergent new functions, the common source of non-discursive and discursive thought in mythic ideation. She observes that "fractions were danced for thousands of years without awareness of their relations to single (or, more often) dual steps," but notes that "as pure dance elements they might never have led even to the art of counting" (211). Only when people come to count on the fingers of both hands does there seem to be a development of "fertile ideas of relations among numbers." The concept of entrainment, the dynamic of evolutionary advance, is brought into play now; we should not be surprised to find where it takes her:

> If such basic patterns as the step – walking or dancing – were to be entrained by higher cerebral processes, something would have to effect a shift from footwork to a more versatile neuromuscular system which would entrain the precise, elaborate rhythms of the dance in a new activity. ...
> Now, there is just such a versatile system in our physiological makeup; it culminates in the expressive powers of the human hand, and the instrument which brought it into the center of communal life was the Drum. ... The drum abstracts the form of the dance and holds it when otherwise it might become frenzied; beats assert their character as a framework more forcefully than movements or voices. Above all, the early and apparently universal use of the drum drew the human hand into the techniques of its expression. (214–15)

In this concluding fireworks display, familiar ideas appear once more: the mediation of the body, the emergence of new activity, the control provided by the hypostatic function of symbols – all introduced with an unembarrassed reference to universals which are at once cultural and species-specific. It is saddening that SKL was unable to finish *Mind*; nevertheless, the concluding meditation on the Dance and the Drum sums the whole, inspiring a desire to start re-reading the entire essay.

SKL helped a generation of students in the 1940s and 1950s to understand the philosophical basis for claims being made for the autonomy of literature; to apprehend what it meant to claim that literature is a form of knowledge; to define the relationship of the forms of literary expression to other kinds of symbolism. She provided the speculative instruments for thinking about the arts, moving beyond the vulgarizations of the latter-day appreciators and the pedantry of those New Critics who still knew the notes but had lost the tune. She provided protection against the gangster theories of the day – "verbal behavior," C.P. Snow's conception of "two cultures," structural linguistics, scientistic psychology, etc., but that is not to say that her defense was widely adopted. By the time she began her work on *Mind*, she was beginning to lose her audience, though the lectures collected in *Philosophical Sketches* suggest that during the 1960s there were still people in the universities and in professional societies who valued the perspectives and insights she brought to philosophically defined issues.

Now, a decade or so after the third volume of *Mind* brought her work to a close, SKL can once again, I believe, help us reclaim ideas which recent criticism has misunderstood when it has not dishonored them. What is most urgently needed is a recovery of the authentic character of Romanticism, especially the concept of the organic and of the individual as representative, in the sense in which Schleiermacher and Peirce meant it. SKL can, better than any other philosopher of the second half of this century, show us how to find the footing for ideas of the organic, of the process of feeling, essential to the understanding of those powers of symbolization which define our humanity. From Alfred North Whitehead she learned how to think about process and act, about organic relations and the concept of value. She learned the importance of perspective, prehension, interest, and act as speculative instruments. I have stressed the ideas which SKL found in Cassirer's *Philosophie der symbolischen Formen*, but her debt to Whitehead is perhaps even greater. He wrote a Foreword to *The Practice of Philosophy* and SKL dedicated *Philosophy in a New Key* to "Alfred North Whitehead, my great Teacher and Friend." ("Friend" here has the full Coleridgean resonance.) It could be that with the recrudescence of interest in Whitehead among European philosophers, who have long since discarded the spurious claims, the sophomoric paradoxes, and the deadly jargon of Deconstruction and its successors – it could well be that Whitehead's great pupil will also come into her own.[73]

11

Walker Percy's Castaway

How dreadful it is when everything historical vanishes before a diseased probing of one's own miserable history! Who is to show us the middle course between being devoured by one's own reflections as though one were the only man who had ever existed or ever would exist, and seeking a worthless consolation in the *commune naufragium* of mankind? That is what the doctrine of an *ecclesia* should do.

– Søren Kierkegaard

The same freedom which Adam possessed when he created the first names for complex perceptions according to no other model than his own thoughts – this same freedom has existed ever since for all men.

– Ernst Cassirer

In his essays on the nature of language and the nature of man, Walker Percy amused himself with raising seemingly naïve questions, playing the fool in the face of other people's somber procedures, daring to speculate about ontology and servo-mechanisms simultaneously – all in the interest of exploring the human condition. His point of departure was to remark wonderingly "how queer man is, how queer language is, and what one has to do with the other," the subtitle of the first collection of essays, *The Message in the Bottle* (1975). Percy enjoyed looking at things as an outsider – pretend or real – and he continuously invented Archimedean points from which to gain a purchase on the questions he raised. He imagined what it would be like to be a castaway; how one would interview a Martian; how an amnesiac feels, or an astronaut lost in space or a shy person confronted with perplexing questions. Walker Percy could put himself in the place of people who habitually watch television talk shows and soap operas; in the place, too, of those he called "ex-suicides." Such exercise of his novelist's imagination allowed him to contemplate the mysteries of what it means to be "lost in the cosmos," the title of his second collection of essays (1983); of what is involved in construing "signposts in a strange land," the title given to the essays edited by Patrick Samway posthumously (1991).

No matter how whimsical or how sardonic the tone, his inquiry is always deeply metaphysical, in the old-fashioned sense of paying attention to matters of spiritual import. He may carry out the inquiry as a scientist or an artist (he was a novelist and a physician), a Southerner, a Roman Catholic, a Bourbon drinker, but the guiding motive is that he wants to know what the question means, what the premise entails, what an answer might conceal. He wants to read the symptoms, to work out a diagnosis and thereby to arrive at a therapeutic insight. (The medical imagery is his own.) He thumps and shakes us and our ideas (and his own) as a matter of course. The treatment is not always comfortable, but it is generally instructive and we might feel better when it is over.

In his essays on language and the human condition Walker Percy's style is personal and unacademic: sometimes he is talking to you on his verandah, but at other times he leads his readers on exhausting tramps through fields of physiology, theology, semiotics – not always avoiding swamps and quagmires, but we usually do come upon several bayous with delightful surprises. His range of allusion is very wide, from theologians to swamp hunters. His novelist's sense of event yields excellent representative anecdotes, in Kenneth Burke's sense: narrative accounts which symbolize logically defined relationships. In referring to Peirce, Buber, Whitehead, Sartre, Cassirer, or Marcel, he rarely gives chapter and verse because he does not need to: the references are there to lend support to an argument he is developing in his own terms.

In these essays, Walker Percy can remind us of another philosopher-physician, Sir Thomas Browne, author of *Religio Medici* and *Pseudodoxia Epidemica* – and of treatises upon gardens, numbers, burial customs, etc. The comparison certainly is not a matter of prose style: Sir Thomas Browne is generally recognized as one of the great prose stylists in English literature; Dr. Percy's style is usually graceless, if not awkward, contrived and oblique. The ground of comparison is metaphysical style – a matter of tone and an attitude towards inquiry and, most important of all, a delight in the play of the mind. It was a favorite idea of C.S. Peirce that the mind found its way; that in taking thought, we should follow where thinking takes us. *Musement* was his name for this course. In Sir Thomas Browne, it issues in fanciful allusions, sonorous cadences, and metaphysical conceits; in Walker Percy, musement takes the form of sardonic reflection, a kind of sweet hypothesizing, and a zany homiletic in which he seems frequently to be a talk show host who is simply talking to himself. Musement in Walker Percy's essays can be *a*musing as well as instructive.

Sir Thomas Browne was interested in antiquities and curious happenings of all sorts. He subjects claims to a searching analysis in terms provided by biology, logic, common sense, and by anyone who has noted careful observations. He condemns not only vulgar errors but an attitude endemic among the learned which he calls a "skeptical infidelity to the evidence of reason and sense." He steadfastly attempts to supplant unquestioned authority, and although his approach falls far short of scientific method, even in its crude Baconian mode, it is based on accurate, thoughtful observation. Walker Percy shared this respect for looking and looking again. He saw the challenge in Charles Morris' declaration that science can only deal with what is "observable behavior." Since he will have no truck with behaviorists, Percy sometimes is hard put to it to claim that his arguments about language and the nature of man are based on "observable behavior," but he manages by way of (usually) delightful casuistry. By observing what there is to observe, Dr. Percy carries out his diagnosis, reading the symptoms, drawing inferences. "There are," he writes in "A Triadic Theory of Meaning," "different kinds of variables in the communication process. Perhaps one may be taken as evidence of the other. Vapor locks, short circuits, transmission failures may be the best evidence that there are such things as carburetors, electrical systems, and gears – especially if the mechanic can't lift the hood."[74] Percy extends "observation" to cover what "interpretation" usually means; he is suspicious of that term, probably because it is so closely associated with "relativism." But of course evidence depends on interpretation, for physician and auto mechanic alike: diagnosis is paradigmatic of the hermeneutic enterprise.

Excellent diagnostician as he is, Dr. Percy nonetheless resists "interpretation" as a term even when it comes to Peirce's semiotics. Percy recognized as clearly as anyone who has written on Peirce the character of the triadic sign and the consequences for our ways of thinking about language. Percy calls the Interpretant "the coupler," insisting on the role of the Self in the activity of symbolizing. The crucial moment in the history of the cosmos is the entrance of "is." Naming is more than reacting or signalling, and it cannot be accounted for in dyadic terms. All symbolic acts – which of course means everything we do with language – are triadic events. This fact Walker Percy calls "the Delta factor," in honor of his fellow-Southerner Helen Keller and, of course, because the Mississippi Delta is a living emblem of triadicity. When it dawned on Helen Keller down at the pump house that what Annie Sullivan signed in one palm was the name of what gushed over the other, she responded to something other than a signal: recognizing a word as a name was a triadic event. Helen Keller coming out of her physical isolation into a world of meaning is the central image of Percy's philosophy of language. The Delta factor is what makes the study of language necessarily a study of Man. The lesson Percy teaches – the homily he preaches – is that the Delta factor is at once a divider and a gatherer: it separates us from all other creatures and it binds us to one another. Animals live in an environment, and so do we; but we live also in a world which comes into being in those acts of naming by which we language animals represent our knowing for one another:

The very act of symbolic formulation, whether it be a language, logic, art, or even thinking, is of its very nature a formulation for a someone else. Even Robinson Crusoe, writing in his journal after twenty years on the island, is nevertheless performing a through and through social and intersubjective act. (220)

Percy combines the social motive with what he persists in calling the "behavioral" in describing the activity of meaning-making which is at once communicative and expressive, always symbolic, always cognitive. He sees intersubjectivity as being entailed by consciousness:

The transcendental phenomenologist is seizing upon a social emergent, consciousness, abstracting it from its social matrix and erecting a philosophy upon this pseudo-private derivative. But the organism does not so begin. The *I think* is only made possible by a prior mutuality: *we name.* (275)

Percy depends on Buber for expression of the sanctity of the I–Thou, without recognizing that it finds logical support in Peirce's conception of the Interpretant. Percy's intersubjectivity echoes Peirce's synechism, the principle of continuity which is essential to his idea of community. Peirce declared that Man is himself a sign and since each sign requires another for its interpretation, each person requires others if he is to discover, define, or realize himself. We are ourselves triadic events.

Percy held that language enables us not just to understand how one or another thing hangs together but what it *is*. That identity is not a mystical, ineffable *Ding an sich* but an inscape which is to be sought in the process of naming, which for Walker Percy is a hermeneutic act. In articulating his idea that "is" is unique in the universe, he turns to metaphor, claiming that if we "observe" what happens there we will discover something about language and thought not otherwise accessible. This had been a commonplace ever since I.A. Richards had suggested (and demonstrated) in *The Philosophy of Rhetoric* (1936) that metaphor could provide a focus in which to study "how words work," but Percy argued that the examples usually chosen (including some of those by Richards) do not exemplify the creative, heuristic power of language. These examples are what rhetoricians call "dead" metaphors – the *leg* of the table, the *head* of the class – figures of speech which have become part of language and are used unconsciously. It was Percy's insight that the study of metaphor could best foster an understanding of how the nature of language and the nature of man are related if we begin, rather, with invented metaphors, especially those folk etymologies which he calls "mistakes." In this way, metaphor can serve us the way vapor locks and transmission failures do the auto mechanic.

A conventional view of mythic ideation is that it is a childish mistake, doomed to be corrected as the "primitive mind" is civilized. Percy took such mistakes not as aberrations to be grown out of but as representative of the heuristic power of language and the meaning-making character of the active mind – the capacity that defines us. In one of the examples which introduce "Metaphor as Mistake," Percy tells of hunting as a boy in south Alabama and of asking the Negro guide to identify a bird which flew straight and then suddenly dropped. He was told that it was a blue-dollar hawk; later his father tells him that it really is a blue darter hawk. Percy comments as follows:

The mysterious name, blue-dollar hawk, is both the "right" name – for it has been given in good faith by a Namer who should know and carries an *ipso facto* authority – and a "wrong" name – for it is not applicable as a logical modifier, as blue darter is immediately and univocally applicable. Blue-dollar is not applicable as a modifier at all, for it refers to a *something else* besides the bird, a something which occupies the same ontological status as the bird. Blue darter tells us something about the bird, what it does, what its color is; blue-dollar tells, or the boy hopes it will tell, what the bird *is*. For *this ontological pairing, or, if you prefer, "error" of identification of word and thing, is the only possible way in which the apprehended nature of the bird, its inscape, can be validated as being what it is.* This inscape is, after all, otherwise ineffable. I can describe it, make crude approximations by such words as *darting, oaring, speed, dive,* etc., but none of these will suffice to affirm this so distinctive something which I have seen. (71–72)

Percy acknowledges the logical necessity of mediation by showing that metaphor is necessary if the act of naming is to reach beyond mere indication. "Ontological pairing" characterizes the way analogy works, which is not by a correspondence of primary and secondary terms but by reason of the fact that something and something else both occupy "the same ontological status." This is a triadic conception of analogy.

And conception, not terminology, is crucial. By *analogy* Walker Percy means metaphor, but for Robert Oppenheimer, though he is arguing the same position, the terms are antithetical:

[By analogy] I do not mean metaphor; I do not mean allegory; I do not even mean similarity; but I mean a special kind of similarity which is the similarity of structure, the similarity of form, a similarity of constellation between two sets of structures, two sets of particulars, that are manifestly very different but have structural parallels. It has to do with relation and interconnection. I would like to quote you a scholastic comment on analogy. It is a translation of Penido. "In a very general sense every analogy presupposes two ontological conditions; one a plurality of real beings and thus among them an essential diversity. Monism is the born enemy of analogy. And, two, at the very heart of this multiplicity, of this inequality, a certain unity."[75]

Oppenheimer is, perhaps, more skillful in deploying the concept of ontology, but it is remarkable that in each case a scientist-poet defines analogy triadically, which is to say that both Percy and Oppenheimer recognize that it is by means of its ontologically conditioned form that analogy represents.

In contrast, table-leg philosophers are satisfied with a substitution theory of metaphor, an easy sidestep whereby one element of one act, situation, configuration, or composition – "domain" is a favored term – replaces an element corresponding to it in another. Each element has been apprehended separately and then brought together in a dyadic sign. The questions Percy raises about metaphor work to shift the focus from linguistic elements to the representation of articulated relationships. Unabashedly, he begins with the idea that metaphors represent acts of knowing:

It is the cognitive dimension of metaphor which is usually overlooked, because cognition is apt to be identified with conceptual and discursive knowing. Likeness and difference are canons of discursive thought but analogy, the mode of poetic knowing, is also cognitive. Failure to recognize the discovering power of analogy can only eventuate in a non-cognitive psychologistic theory of metaphor. (77)

Along with the ontological and cognitive dimension of metaphor, Percy identifies that creative energy which Cassirer saw as typifying "metaphorical thought"; he saw that "the discovering power of analogy" is crucial to claiming a cognitive role for metaphor. This claim depends on recognizing two modes of abstraction. In "conceptual and discursive knowing," abstraction is accomplished by means of generalization; in "the poetic mode of knowing," abstraction depends on apprehending particulars as participating in wholes, on images which bespeak more than the particular moment. Percy saw that the analogical structure of metaphor exemplifies abstraction without generalization, and in this passage he proceeds by waking up the dead metaphor of *juxtaposition*:

The modern semiotist is scandalized by the metaphor *Flesh is grass*; but he is also scandalized by the naming sentence *This is flesh*. As Professor Veatch has pointed out, he is confusing an instrument of knowing with what is known. The word *flesh* is not this solid flesh, and this solid flesh is not grass. But unless we name it *flesh* we shall not know it at all, and unless we call flesh grass we shall not know how it is with flesh. The semiotist leaves unexplained the act of knowing. He imagines naively that I know what this is and then give it a label, whereas the truth is, as Cassirer has shown so impressively, that I cannot know anything at all unless I symbolize it. We can only *con*ceive being, sidle up to it by laying something else alongside. We approach the thing not directly but by pairing, by opposing symbol and thing. (72)

For "semiotist," read "dyadicist," since it is not really semiotics which Percy is rejecting but the attitude of those guided by a view of language as a two-valued relationship. The positivist insists that particulars come first and that abstraction is accomplished only by generalizing about them. Thus some literary critics when faced with such a mythic metaphor as *all flesh is grass* believe that they can show how the words work by historicizing the image allegedly represented. But this positivist hunger for an unmediated actuality – we must have a particular reality, preferably a "behavior" first, before we can assign to it a figurative meaning – prevents an appreciation of that other mode of abstraction which Percy calls *analogy*. The passage I have just quoted continues as follows:

Is it not premature to say with the mythist that when the primitive calls the lightning serpentine, he conceives it as a snake and is logically wrong? Both truth and error may be served here, error insofar as the lightning is held to participate magically in snakeness, truth insofar as the conception of snake may allow the privately apprehended inscape of the lightning to be formulated. I would have a horror of finding myself allied with those who in the name of instrumentality or inner warmth or what not would so attenuate and corrupt truth that it meant nothing. But an analysis of the symbol relation reveals aspects of truth which go far beyond the notion of structural similarity which the symbolic logicians speak of. Two other traits of the thing are discovered and affirmed: one that it *is*; two that it is *something*.

The dialectic Oppenheimer finds in the "relation and interconnection" of structural parallels contradicts Percy's belittling characterization, but the central contention is sound: to name is simultaneously to see an identity and the representation of a kind. Seeing is always *seeing as*.

Sir Thomas Browne called Man "that great Amphibium, whose nature is disposed to live not only like other creatures in diverse elements, but in divided and distinguished worlds." Walker Percy, in his *religio medici*, acknowledged the difference between the environment and the world Man lives in, stressing not an adaptability to either but alienation from both. Man lives in Nature and in History and from either perspective the other appears alien. Percy understood the logic of analogy: the metaphor he chose was thus not amphibian creation but the castaway. Man lives in two worlds, yes, but he is at home in neither. The figure of the castaway on his island is an allegorical extension of the radical metaphor of life as a journey.[76] The shift from pilgrim to shipwreck is emblematic of an era in the history of ideas – and of sensibility, for to make the journey a sea voyage is already a step away from the social and political towards the metaphysical and ontological. Man is at odds not just with his fellow man and the institutions of communal life; he is at odds with himself. He is not just burdened with Sin and sins; he is alienated, lost in the cosmos. Percy sees Kierkegaard's allegorical metaphor of the gospel as "news from across the seas" in the light of "the Jasperian notion of shipwrecked man, Heidegger's notion of man's existence as a Geworfenheit" (146). Percy's contribution to the complex figure is to conceive of the island on which the castaway finds himself as language itself – "a forbidden island, a terra incognita" (33). Island knowledge is know-how; it is creaturely and time-bound, and even though triadic, it is not enough for the shipwreck who is doomed to walk the shore searching for the bottle with a message: "No knowledge which can be gained on the island ... can be relevant to his predicament as a castaway. The castaway is he who waits for news from across the seas" (146).

Castaway is the radical metaphor from which Heidegger derives *Geworfenheit*, which was a concept abhorrent to Cassirer.[77] It is, perhaps, symptomatic of an unresolved ambivalence that Walker Percy can accommodate both Cassirer's genial and hopeful humanism and the dark violence of Heidegger's irrationalism. In any case, Percy's castaway does not represent what Kierkegaard calls the *commune naufragium*, that "worthless consolation" which is the polar opposite of the solipsism in which "everything historical vanishes." The shipwreck is common to all, certainly: it is the Fall of Man. But in Percy's allegory it is a Fortunate Fall. The rationale for the doctrine of *felix culpa* is that although in Adam's sin we sinnéd all, it was a happy fault because it meant that the Lord God could exercise His beneficence towards us by sending His Son. The common shipwreck, on this view, is not a worthless consolation because it occasions the possiblility of hope: "The castaway is he who waits for news from across the seas." We read, we hear, we apprehend by means of the symbols language provides – and for Percy that symbolism is neither conflated with its graphic representation nor reduced to dyadic terms. Literacy is not entailed in receiving the Gospel, but language is: I know that my Redeemer liveth because I am the language animal. I can name the world; my knowledge arises from this power of naming, which transforms the environment into a world. The "middle course" is for Kierkegaard provided by "the doctrine of an *ecclesia*"; Percy's *ecclesia*, his third way, is his own amalgam of Christian existentialism and triadic semiotics, in which ontological pairing, intersubjectivity, the coupler, and the Delta factor are at once versions of Peirce's philosophy of signs and analogues of elements of Christian doctrine. It turns out that the good news is that the castaway will be able to recognize the good news when it arrives: he can construe the message in the bottle: he is free to be saved. *Felix culpa!*

For Walker Percy, polar oppositions are, as Coleridge puts it, expressions of a single force. Thus for Percy, the Fall and the consolation of language must be apprehended at one and the same time. Just so, the one awaiting the message in the bottle and the homebody are polar opposites; the one who feels lost in the cosmos, and the one who can be happy in the ordinariness of a Wednesday afternoon; the castaway and Eudora Welty at home in Jackson, Mississippi; the visiting Martian and Herman Melville (whom Percy proclaims an honorary Southerner) – all are linked indissolubly. These polarities are interdependent and dialectical; *interinanimated* is the word I.A. Richards borrowed from Donne.

Paradoxically, polar opposition is a triadic concept. The function of an axle is to turn, and that rotation is dependent on the polarity the axle makes possible. This dialectical activity is paradigmatic for all nonlinear processes, from Nicholas of Cusa's *docta ignorantia*, which depends on a *coincidentia oppositorum*, to cell biologists' description of the cell and its surround as a "dynamic reciprocity." Perhaps the most telling analogue for Percy's polar opposition of being lost in the cosmos and at home on the verandah with friends is found in the relationship which Schleiermacher saw between the sense of loss and the feeling of dependency, the polarity which would be the motive force of a revitalized church, a community discovering its history and its humanity. This Protestant minister, a contemporary of Kierkegaard, entertained a vision of the *ecclesia* which was entirely consonant with his hermeneutics. The relationship of the individual and the community is echoed by the two motives of the process of interpretation: careful grammatical construing of the text, with attention to all identifiable contexts; in dialectic with the divinatory insight. Schleiermacher insisted on their interdependence, for which his term was *Ineinandersein*. Walker Percy's diagnostic habit of mind, in combination with imaginative and risky insight, constitutes a hermeneutic in which acknowledgment of polar opposites is the informing power.

Walker Percy considered triadicity one of the two or three most important ideas in the history of Western thought. He knew that it provided ways of entertaining a question which Peirce was always meditating on, "What is Man to become?" It is the same sort of question which guides Percy in his meditations on "how queer man is and how queer language is, and what one has to do with the other." Philosophy is said by some to be extinct, which may or may not be true; what is indisputable is that the kind of philosopher Walker Percy was is near extinction. He was not a guru, like Joseph Campbell or Jacques Derrida; or an academic "bad boy," like Richard Rorty; he was neither a droning ideologue nor a cheapener. The key to the kind of philosopher he was may be found in his admiration for Peirce. He took seriously questions of meaning and purpose. He understood indeterminacy triadically, which is to say not as an invitation to solipsism but as a post-lapsarian necessity which it is the function of semiosis – Peirce's endless process of learning from signs – to accommodate. We interpret our interpretations; we arrange our techniques for arranging (I.A. Richards); we seek, as Coleridge recommended, to know our knowledge. We learn to bring the endless regression of one sign interpreting another to a temporary halt by asking, "If we put it this way, what difference would it make to our practice?" Walker Percy understood that pragmaticism is entailed by triadicity; if we really confront the fact that there is no direct access to the world, then we must reclaim the imagination, learning to ask "What difference would it make if we put it this way?" That is what finding a logical role for interpretation means. Walker Percy's castaway has this species-specific capacity both to learn by finding out (island knowledge) and to recognize the good news when it comes: he has been shipwrecked on the blessed isle of language.

III. KLEIST'S PARABLES AND
THE FALL INTO LANGUAGE

12

Marionettes and Automatons

> A Fall of some sort or other – the creation, as it were, of the non-absolute – is the fundamental postulate of the moral history of man. Without this hypothesis, man is unintelligible; with it, every phenomenon is explicable. The mystery itself is too profound for human insight.
>
> – Samuel Taylor Coleridge

Kleist's essay on the marionette theatre has long been regarded as one of the most important philosophical discourses in modern German literature and has been read – by Cassirer, among others – as emblematic of certain problems of Kantian epistemology. When an English translation appeared in *Partisan Review* in 1947, it found an audience ready for the fascinating argument that grace and consciousness are mutually exclusive. The dancer who attends performances at the marionette theatre in order to learn the secret of the puppets' graceful movement argues his case in a tone and style found familiar from reading modern writers whom Kleist had influenced – Isak Dinesen, for instance, in *Seven Gothic Tales* or Rilke in *Malte Laurids Brigge* and certain of the *Duino Elegies*. He was a culture hero for poets and students: "And David Hume stood high with me that year / & Kleist, for the 'Puppet-theatre'."[1] Kleist's essay was in some quarters considered one of the charters of modernist aesthetics. It was read with great interest both by those who took it as subversive of the tenets of modern dance and those who thought that Kleist was a previous incarnation of Martha Graham.

But there were other contexts. "On the Marionette Theatre" appeared in translation when Kafka was the center of critical attention; the fact that Kafka had given a public reading of Kleist's "Michael Kohlhaas" was taken as evidence of a shared spirit and attitude. Eugene Jolas, in an introductory note to the aforementioned translation, quoted Nietzsche's comment that Kleist dealt with "the uncurable part of nature," an appreciation which by highlighting the violence and strangeness of his art and mind recreated Kleist as a forerunner of modern literature. Kierkegaard was another man of the hour with whom Kleist seemed to have an affinity. Kierkegaard's penchant for self-humiliation and his sardonic castigations of the motives and attitudes of others; his uncanny ability to make metaphysical issues as compelling as the emblematic acts of the existentialists; his spirit of relentless, if profitless, inquiry, all provided a dramatic context in which to read "On the Marionette Theatre."

Each generation must, of course, read such works anew. I hope to show here that the idea of enabling limits is illuminated by a study of Kleist's parables. They were impelled by his "Kant-Crisis," one of the legendary events of his short life. His despair is thought to have led him to abandon plans for an academic career and to begin writing – a fortunate fall indeed – but it also precipitated a sickness of mind, heart, and soul. If there was no stable, affirmable world to which our reason can directly lead us, no given for which we could hope to find an accurate, corresponding representational form, then chaos is come again. But Kleist's struggle to obliterate the logic of necessity as quickly, as peremptorily, as his anti-heroes smash their victims' skulls; his defiance of mediation and his suicidal despair, these attitudes and convictions are not merely idiosyncratic symptoms, the signs of the suffering of a peculiarly afflicted soul. Kleist's experience can serve emblematically to represent an episode in the history of ideas which recurs, with more or less intensity, as one way of looking at the world of meanings succeeds to another.

"Über das Marionettentheater" takes the form of a dialogue – or, rather, a very one-sided conversation.[2] The narrator seems an unpracticed straight man, failing to press the points he does make or to articulate his exasperation, but his failure to understand and his slow reckonings provoke his dialogue partner to explanations which are somewhat more dramatic and extreme than those he might otherwise have settled for. Here in brief outline is the shape of the essay:

The narrator has noticed that Herr C., the leading dancer of the town's opera company, frequents the marionette theatre in the public gardens. One evening he accosts the dancer and asks what his interest in such a lowly art could possibly be. There follows a discussion in which the dancer explains to a puzzled and perplexed interlocutor that he goes to the puppet theatre to study the graceful movement of the puppets, not only to improve his own performance but also to guide his effort to develop specifications for designing a mechanical puppet, one which would not require an operator to do anything more than turn a crank. The claims made for the automaton are so extravagant that the narrator rejects them with something akin to indignation. But just as the conversation seems to have come to an end, the narrator remarks that he does indeed understand one thing Herr C. has told him – the power of consciousness to destroy natural grace – and he offers an anecdote which represents this understanding. The dancer tells a matching story and then says that his pupil is now ready to follow his argument about the nature of the automaton, about the character of knowledge and innocence. The essay ends with a dazzling restatement of the dancer's ideas.

In response to the assertion that the dancing of the puppets could instruct any dancer, the narrator asks how the gracefulness of a puppet's movement is assured: Is each limb carefully controlled by its own string? By no means, the dancer explains: the beautiful curves described by the puppet's limbs are the entirely natural consequence of the operator's skill in maintaining a clear and unobstructed straight line (*Linie*) between his fingers and the center of gravity (*Schwerpunkt*) of each movement (*Bewegung*). But must not the puppeteer have a sense of the beautiful to maintain this control? The answer is two-fold: In a sense the operation of a puppet is simple, but it is also mysterious (*geheimnisvoll*). Establishing the polarity of fingers and the center of gravity is a simple mechanical operation, but the line between the puppetmaster's fingers and the *Schwerpunkt* mysteriously becomes the path of the dancer's soul (*der Weg der Seele des Tänzers*): the puppeteer himself *dances*. When the narrator says that he had always been told that the operator's role was neutral (*ziemlich Geistloses*), the dancer again insists on the artful relationship (*ziemlich künstlich*) of the movement of the puppetmaster's fingers and the movement of the puppet, and claims that the one *Bewegung* bears the same relationship to the other as numbers do to their logarithms or hyperbolas to their asymptotes.

But having carefully established the dialectic, the dancer then sets all that aside with the comment that it should be possible to dispense with this last vestige of mind (*dieser letzte Bruch von Geist*), to free the puppet altogether so that its movement would indeed be subject only to a mechanical operation, as the narrator had thought was the case, like turning the crank of a hand organ. He continues with a description of how an English craftsman has made false limbs for amputees and that these unfortunates move with the grace of dancers. He then sketches his plan to design a puppet that would be, as it were, all limbs and joints (*Gliedermann*). This automaton would have the same qualities discernible in the puppets, but in a higher degree. The sceptical narrator still wants to know what advantage the *Gliedermann* would have over real, live dancers. The question leads the dancer to elaborate on the theme for which the essay is best known. The mechanical puppet would be free of that affectation which supplants grace when consciousness is present:

Such misconceptions [as represented in the affectations of dancers and actors] are inescapable ever since we ate of the Tree of Knowledge. Now Paradise is bolted and barred and the Cherub stands behind us; we must make a journey around the world and see if perhaps it is open somehow around at the back.

The dancer continues with further explanation of how the *Gliedermann* will exploit the fact that puppets are virtually weightless; they need only to touch the ground in order to renew their dance, instantaneously. Still the narrator resists, remarking that he would never be persuaded that a mechanical puppet could be more graceful than a human dancer. The dancer's is an absolute pronouncement: no human being could equal the mechanical puppet (*Gliedermann*):

Only a god could equal inanimate matter in this regard: it is at this point that the two ends of the circular world meet and are interlocked. (*Nur ein Gott könne sich, auf diesem Felde, mit der Materie messen; und hier sei der Punkt, wo die beiden Enden der ringformigen Welt ineinandergriffen.*)

When the narrator is speechless, the dancer seems ready to break off the conversation with the scolding remark that the narrator has not read the third chapter of Genesis attentively; that whoever does not understand the first stage of human history has no authority to comment on further developments, to say nothing of the ultimate situation. The narrator quickly moves to fill the breach by saying that he certainly has understood how consciousness can create confusion in the matter of human grace (*welche Unordnungen in der natürlichen Grazie des Menschen, das Bewusztsein anrichtet*). And he forthwith offers an anecdote, the story of a boy who catches sight of himself in the graceful pose of the boy removing a thorn from his foot and simultaneously loses the ability to resume the stance or to srike other graceful poses.[3] The dancer delightedly responds with an account of an experience he once had of fencing with a captive bear whose composure so entirely unsettled him that he was defeated. The boy in his childish innocence and the bear displaying its faultless instinct exemplify that same grace, the same freedom from consciousness which characterizes the marionette and its variants.

The story of the fencer (who is Herr C.) and the bear ends with Herr C.'s "Do you believe this?," which seems at once a story-teller's plea for trusting the tale and a tentative disclaimer. The narrator's joyful approval seems to end the litany which has initiated him into the mysteries, but the on-again/off-again exchange continues. Herr C. solemnly recapitulates his argument that Grace belongs either to the puppet or to the god:

We see that on a reduced scale as in the organic world, as thought grows dimmer and weaker, grace emerges more brilliantly ... Grace itself returns when knowledge has, as it were, gone through an infinity. Grace appears most purely in that human form which either has no consciousness or an infinite consciousness; that is, in the puppet (automaton: *Gliedermann*) or in the god.

The philosopher's pupil then asks, "Must we eat again of the Tree of Knowledge in order to fall back into (*zurückzufallen*) our original state of innocence?" And the dancer replies: "Of course! That is the last chapter in the history of the world." The metaphor insists on that being the final word, but the dialogue is not a syllogistic argument and it could logically go on forever.

It has been observed (by one who should know: Wolfgang Kurock, Marionettist and Instructor at the *Figurentheaterkolleg des Deutschen Instituts für Puppenspiel in Bochum*) that Kleist was wrong in the particulars of his description of the mechanics of marionettes, wrong in his explanations of design and function, but that he profoundly understood the effects, the mysterious beauty characteristic of string puppets. Kurock cites Freud on how there can be simultaneously a faulty understanding and an insight which goes to the heart of the matter.[4]

The first difficulty arises when we consider the line (*Linie*) which is said to go from the operator to the center of gravity (*Schwerpunkt*), not of the puppet but of each movement. When this line is established, the limbs of the puppet move according to natural laws. The mechanics are simple, but the line itself is mysterious (*Geheimnisvoll*) and is maintained only with skill. Uncannily, the line becomes the path by which the operator transports himself to the puppet: *der Weg der Seele des Tänzers*.[5] But it is never explained how this line is found or maintained, nor is its relationship to the strings or wires ever identified. Herr C. simply declares that the movement of the limbs depends not on individual strings but on the line. It is as if the straight line became in Kleist's imagination identical with a single wire (*Draht*).

Now the fact is that Kleist's references to graceful curves which come into being automatically by means of a single controlling "line" do indeed fit one kind of puppet – a wooden or cardboard figure called a "jumping jack" or *pantin* (Fr.). This puppet's arms and legs are attached to the torso by clips allowing free movement and are controlled by several strings which are all tied invisibly at the back to a single string issuing from between the legs. The *pantin* is held in one hand by the head or by a brace on the back while the other pulls the string in a single vigorous yank, upon which the limbs fly out and up and then return to their original resting point, having just described those arcs Kleist notes. There is a further characteristic shared by the marionette and the *pantin*, namely, manipulability. It is reflected in the fact that a secondary meaning for *pantin* is of a person who is at the beck and call of another.

Walter Silz who remains, I think, the most astute observer of the ways of Kleist's imagination, remarks in discussing Kleist's descriptions of paintings he had seen that he immediately begins to transform what had been seen.[6] In the very process of recounting, Kleist invents. This habit of mind can explain his puzzling description of the single "line" by which the operator controls the puppet. Kleist seems to have conflated the operation of the *pantin* and the multiple-stringed marionettes: as he visited the marionette theatre, he transformed what he saw to match what he knew.

Two further images are adduced by Kleist in characterizing the uncanny grace of the marionettes. When he describes a group of puppet peasants dancing the rondo in quick time so charmingly as to challenge the art of Teniers, Kleist may well have reversed the terms of the comparison; that is to say, the painting may have come first. In the Rijksmuseum (Amsterdam) is a painting by Teniers of peasants dancing in a circle outside an inn. The dancers are, as it were, rushing towards a central point, as if caught up in a single movement, as if pulled to the center of their circle by the yank of a single string.[7] It could be that this image provided the anterior example of a seeming inevitability which Kleist then ascribed to the movement of marionettes. The other analog for the *pantin*'s limbs moving effortlessly in rhythmic arcs is Kleist's grotesque image of the amputees who have been fitted with limbs made by English craftsmen. They can't really be said to dance, says Herr C., but they move with simplicity and grace. Nevertheless, they do not measure up to the ideal which the dancer has in mind, the puppet he wants to construct whose limbs would move freely and gracefully with the inevitability of a pendulum.

This brings us to the other chief difficulty, the matter of the ground (*Boden*). Herr C. will be guided in his design of the *Gliedermann* by what he has discovered in his attendance at the marionette theatre, namely, that "puppets need the ground only so they can touch it ... to renew the swing of their limbs through this momentary check" (*augenblickliche Hemmung*). The recalcitrance of the ground is recognized here as providing the necessary impetus, a relationship of check and action which, by the way, can be observed in the movement of Sicilian puppets, which are controlled by an iron rod set in the head. Once Orlando (forty pounds) strikes the boards and is hoisted from that encounter, he hits his stride. The dialectic of gravity and what Kleist calls "anti-gravity" creates that magical instant which entrances him, the Kleistian moment when the puppets rebound from the floor, their legs becoming pendulums, moving with that lifeless (*tot*) grace, unwilled and unconscious, which no human dancer can replicate.

But Kleist never rests for long in the knowledge that freedom is the knowledge of necessity. When Herr C. declares that the beautiful arcs are controlled by the law of gravity, he forgets the agency whereby this law is brought to bear. He contradicts what he has just explained, namely, that the graceful movement is the effect of the fall, the downward thrust, in dialectic with the rebound, the upward counterthrust. It is the heuristic power of the momentary check which is the necessary condition for the admirable freedom of movement. But the dancer is not content with puppets which must touch the ground. The momentary check is now dismissed as not being part of the dance, scorned as the last vestige of mind. In designing his ideal puppet, Herr C. will seek to eliminate that dependency which is no longer seen as enabling but as the sign of manipulation. The *Gliedermann* will be independent of an operator's mind and will. Kleist thus denies the very logic of necessity which he has so subtly identified in describing the motivating recalcitrance, the heuristic limit which touching the ground provides. That contact is no longer recognized as the ground of grace. (The pun is implicit in Kleist's terms.) It is, rather, a tie which must be dissolved. Never mind that the mechanical action which will supplant it will necessitate having someone to turn the crank! Kleist is building a clean machine and does not concern himself with the problem of any and all automatons, which is how the activity is to be initiated and sustained.

Illogicalities abound in Herr C.'s description of the *Gliedermann*. He shows no sign of recognizing that it is not simply better than the regular puppet, that it would work according to a radically different principle. This neglect is of course crucial if the argument is to be developed, and to question it is something like an unwillingness to suspend disbelief when we read a story. By its dramatic form, the essay requires that we forebear, as we must in order to enjoy any fiction, and it invites us to do so by its form. The pace of the dialogue – that pell-mell style which is so characteristic of Kleist's fictions – distracts us from the muddle of bigger-and-better with different-in-principle-of-operation, which is fundamentally a confusion of difference of degree and difference in kind.

But whether or not it occurs to us readers to question the dream of dispensing with the last vestige of mind – the minimal but essential point of control constituted by the puppetmaster's fingers – our surrogate, the narrator, does not question the idea of a world devoid of human purpose. Later, after hearing a fuller explanation, he reflects that "certainly the human spirit cannot err when there is no human spirit" (*Allerdings kann der Geist nicht irren, da, wo keiner vorhanden ist*). But he keeps this thought to himself, nor does he here ask what kind of dance it would be, this aimless movement which would represent no intention, no consciousness (or, indeed, an antithetical infinite consciousness, equally inaccessible); displaying ease, lightness, and grace to no end. What would this soulless dance be like?

Thomas Mann, who loved and admired Kleist, did ask that question and answered with a peculiarly horrible image in "Mario and the Magician."[8] Those who have volunteered to be subjects for the magician's demonstrations are hypnotized and set to dancing in just such an aimless fashion: there is no grace or sign of formal elegance. Here is the description of a willing victim:

He seemed quite content in his abject state, quite pleased to be relieved of the burden of voluntary choice. Again and again he offered himself and gloried in the model facility he had in losing consciousness. So now he mounted the platform, and a single cut of the whip was enough to make him dance to the Cavaliere's orders, in a kind of complacent ecstasy, eyes closed, head nodding, lank limbs flying in all directions.

And here is a description of how a young man who has claimed to be immune to the hypnotist's suggestion, finally succumbs:

The jerking and twitching of the refractory youth's limbs had at last got the upper hand; he lifted his arms, then his knees, his joints quite suddenly relaxed, he flung his legs and danced, and amid bursts of applause the Cavaliere led him to join the row of puppets on stage.

It is notable that Mann's magician declares to the audience that they should not think that those in the line of eight or ten jerking, jumping puppets will be exhausted by this strenuous exertion, because it is not they who dance but *he*. Kleist's dancer-philosopher would surely have been amused at this transition to a final "freedom," for Mann has invented a third *modus operandi*. The tight line of control from fingers to *Schwerpunkt* has been transformed not into a mechanical operation but into thought control: the last vestige of mind is still exercised, but at a distance.

Automatons serve as metaphors by which mechanical operations represent metaphysical problems. When the metaphor is extended, the relationship of the automaton to its creator becomes an allegory of philosophical questions of the relationship of body and soul, language and thought, necessity and freedom, etc. In Kleist's parable, there is a reversal of the significance of the automaton which from Golem and Frankenstein's monster to Mr. Spock has been the fascination of a body without a soul. Automatons, capable of locomotion and endowed with animal spirits, come to life without a soul and hence without the capacity to love. Kleist sees in this state of affairs – the absence of consciousness – not a terrifying lack but the guarantee of grace, a term which functions in both its senses: the beauty of the puppet's movement is the sign of spiritual favor or, rather, the state of grace, which is identified with lack of consciousness and is subject only to natural law, is signified aesthetically. Kleist's parable is thus the anti-type of such stories as Heine tells in his essay on Kant. His claim there is that in the *Critique of Pure Reason*, Kant wielded a sword which slew Deism. Heine begins with a fable which concerns a body of doctrine without a soul.

It is related that an English mechanician, who had already invented the most ingenious machines, at last took it into his head to construct a man. His creation even contained within its leathern breast a sort of apparatus of human sentiment differing not greatly from the habitual sentiments of Englishmen; it could communicate its emotions by articulate sounds, and the noise of the wheels in its interior, of springs and escapements which was distinctly audible, reproduced the genuine English pronunciation. This automaton was an accomplished gentleman, and nothing was wanting to render it completely except a soul.

The English craftsman is unable to provide a soul, but the automaton never gives him a moment's rest, always begging for a soul. The Englishman runs away, but the automaton follows in a mail coach, pursuing him all over Europe. Heine concludes with the comment that we discover in these two a somewhat more general condition: "We see how one portion of the English people is becoming weary of its mechanical existence, and is demanding a soul, whilst the other portion, tormented by such a request, is driven about in all directions, and that neither of them can endure matters at home any longer."[9] In his explication of the fable, Heine declares that a body demanding a soul is not so fearsome as a soul demanding a body.

In Kleist's parable, explication takes the form of further images, each a gloss for all the others, until by the end we have a kind of memory theatre of representations of the Fall into consciousness and the subsequent attempt to reclaim Grace. In recent criticism, a certain literal-mindedness, which is the converse of a fascination for the indeterminate, has mistaken the tone of these representations. Thus critics who ask if we are meant to take the story of the bear and the fencer "seriously" have forgotten how to suspend disbelief; they are the kind of readers who can recognize wit but who don't get the jokes. In this instance, they muddle the "indeterminate" with the uncanny, which is quite a different matter. The images and narratives of "Über das Marionettentheater" succeed one another like ghost stories told by a company of tale-tellers who are vying with one another: "Can you believe *this*?" "You *won't* believe this, but ..." "Wait 'til you hear what happened to a friend of mine in Rhode Island!" E.T.A. Hoffmann's "Automata" provides an example of what I think Kleist is doing.

In that tale, six or seven images and stories jockey for first place in suggesting the uncanny nature of automata. These accounts are gruesome and absurd, comic and chilling, each with one or another degree of implausibility. The sequence is as conventional as the boasting contest in *Beowulf* or shepherds' singing contests in classical and Renaissance pastoral. Certainly, a reader coming to Kleist from Hoffmann's "The Sandman" would be less likely to *worry* about plausibility. In this story, there is an episode featuring the beautiful Olimpia, supposedly the daughter of a sinister professor but revealed in time (in no time at all, to a reader familiar with Hoffmann) to be a wooden automaton. The descriptions are at once ludicrous and macabre. She dances beautifully – but too perfectly. It turns out that Olimpia's frequent sneezing masks the activation of a clockwork mechanism. Because of the brilliant eyes, which come to life as poor Nathanael gazes into them, this puppet seems to be responding with profound understanding, though all she ever says is "Ah! Ah! Ah!"

Beyond the failure to recognize generic conventions, there are other symptoms of literal-mindedness in recent criticism, principally a disregard for the interdependence of themes and images and an habitual muddling of token and type, vehicle and tenor, etc. Practical criticism would require that we read the text as if it made sense, assuming a central guiding purpose. I have tried to do that by assuming that the description of the puppets, the mathematical and Biblical allusions, and the subsidiary narratives all help to substantiate an answer to the question which the narrator poses to Herr C.: *Why do you so frequently visit the marionette theatre?* All the images, the explanations, the allusions are accounted for if we assume that the short answer to the question posed is that Herr C. seeks to discover how grace can be recovered. Since he insists that the key to everything is to be found in Genesis 3, we know that the Grace which comes as recompense after the Fall is what is meant; the grace which belongs to dancers who come close to the mechanical, unconscious, and natural action of the puppets is thus the metaphor of Grace taken as the successor to Innocence. Each of the metaphors and the narratives – which are extended metaphors – provides a gloss for the others, because all are analogs of the recovery of grace/ Grace.

None of this has any appeal for Paul de Man who takes dance as tenor, not vehicle – as theme rather than figure and image.[10] And, deploying a passage from Schiller in which dance is set forth as a metaphor of civilization, he undertakes to show that Kleist's essay documents the idea that dance is necessarily violent and thus metaphoric in ways which the Romantics could not apprehend.

What is allegedly revealed by this labor of deconstruction is the authoritarian violence of humanist values. No evidence is offered that

Kleist's purpose (conscious or not) was to reveal the secret horror of the dance-as-civilization metaphor; indeed, in order to match Kleist's images and stories to his reading, de Man continually perverts the text. For instance, he takes the Hoffmannesque hyperbole of the "dancing" amputees – those whom Kleist call *Unglückliche* – as an image of the violence inherent in all formalization as it is in language and, *a fortiori*, in art. De Man, as we should expect, speaks of the *Unglückliche* as being *mutilated*.

De Man considers the mathematical figures as meaningless and pays no attention to the role of Biblical allusion. He concludes that the essay is full of gaps and abysses, but his micro-managed decoding never could yield a sense of the whole. He proceeds to his pronouncements by way of chiasmus and unsupported identifications and analogies, by ellipsis and conflation. His treatment of Herr C.'s story of the fencer and the bear can stand as an example of his method.

De Man believes that Kleist's *Aufsatz* is "a text about teaching" (269). He claims that what the narrator learns is that "the increased formalization of consciousness" "enhances" "aesthetic effect," observing that "this loss of hermeneutic control is itself staged as a scene of hermeneutic persuasion." Kleist nowhere describes Herr C.'s project as a matter of formalizing consciousness; his aim is not loss of control – hermeneutic or otherwise – but the obviation of any need for control, since the *Gliedermann*, like the pendulum, is subject only to *das Gesetz der Schwere*. The "aesthetic education," which de Man sees as central to both the account of the puppets and the subsidiary narratives, is discussed in terms of various "scenes of instruction." "The third anecdote (that of the bear) [is] a scene of reading" (271). Before considering what de Man has to say about the bear, let us recall what Kleist says.

Herr C. is very successful as a fencer, but the Baltic nobleman whom he has bested tells him there is a master for everyone and leads him to a shed on the estate where there is a bear his father is training: "I was astounded to see the bear standing upright on his hind legs, with his back against the post to which he was chained, his right paw raised for battle." The fencer is entirely unsuccessful in his attack:

It wasn't merely that he parried my thrusts like the finest fencer in the world; when I feinted to deceive him he made no move at all, and no human fencer could equal his perception in this respect. He stood upright, his paw ready for battle, his eye fixed on mine as if he could read my soul there, and when my thrusts were not meant seriously he did not move.

Herr C. is himself like his colleagues, those conscious, deliberate, awkward ballet dancers whom he has earlier ridiculed. And the bear? "Dancing" bears were commonplace all over Europe for centuries: I think we could claim that Kleist has been up to his hyperbolical tricks, pushing *dancing* over to *fencing*, just as he had had Herr C., in describing the amputees, extend easy, graceful movement to dance. But it is also true, of course, that the bear is representative of all beasts who by definition live in an eternal Now, universally taken as an analog of Man's first estate. The instinctively acting bear stands in relationship to the deliberate, skilled fencer as the *Gliedermann* does to the mortal dancer. The ground of the analogy is the idea that unconscious, instinctual acts, responsive only to natural law, are superior to willed, conscious, deliberate acts because their grace is assured by the innocence of the agents. In this delightful algebra, the natural becomes an emblem of Grace: the pleasure comes in appreciating Kleist's zany ability to bring about the mysterious collapse of this mythical antithesis of Nature and Grace.

Paul de Man does not find this delightful; indeed, he does not find the analogical structure at all. He needs to accommodate the story of the fencer and the bear under the rubric he has devised for the essay, namely, the principle that "promises increased aesthetic pleasure as a reward for increased formalization," a principle which is inherent in the linguistic medium, which entails violence, etc., etc. How does he make sense of the story of the bear and the fencer in these terms? He takes *lesen* literally: the bear who looks Herr C. in the eye, "as if he could read my soul there" (*als ob er meine Seele darin lesen konnte*) becomes a *reading* bear: "The superiority of reading over writing as represented by the superiority of the reading bear over the fencing author, reflects the shift in the concept of text from an imitative to a hermeneutic model" (281). Where does this reading bear come from? From the toy shop of Paul de Man's obsessions. If we remain unpersuaded that the act of reading can be represented as meaningless, mindless, will-less, mechanical, and inhuman, at least we know where we stand with this critic.

Short as it is, *Über das Marionettentheater* appeared in three installments, which is reason enough, as Silz points out, for discontinuities, contradictions, and spurious reasoning.[11] But there are deeper reasons, I believe, which have to do with Kleist's attitudes towards language and life, and although this essay might not offer a key to Kleist's oeuvre, the paradoxes for which it is famous do illuminate a theme of central importance in his mind and art. Kleist understood the role of mediation, the dialectic of form and projection, the heuristic power of limits: he understood the conditions of making meaning, but he would not – could not – accept the consequences. He could and did represent the logic of necessity: his images bear the very stamp of a recognition of recalcitrance, polarity, interdependence and interinanimation, of process and dialectic. But he rejects both the principle and it representations in the essay on the marionette theatre.

13

The Journey to the Back Door of Paradise

In the actual use of expressions we make detours, we go by side roads. We see the straight highroad before us, but of course we cannot use it, because it is permanently closed.

– Ludwig Wittgenstein

When Kleist has the dancer-philosopher (Herr C.) claim that his argument cannot be grasped without an attentive reading of the third chapter of Genesis, I think we must take this seriously, but the guidance it offers does not suffice. "On the Marionette Theatre" does, certainly, concern the consequences of the Fall, but the radical ambiguities in Kleist's images and in the explications he offers are not those familiar in the idea of salvation and redemption. The circular journey, whatever else it might be said to represent, is not an image of eternal life for the soul.

When the dancer declares that understanding the first period of man's history is necessary in order to grasp the significance of what follows, as well as of the ending, he seems to offer a sequence, but it is a quite illogical one. The second period – what follows the Fall – is life as we lead it and the final stage is synonymous with the end of man's history. Neither the end nor the beginning is part of the world we live in, though both these mythical times determine our life by constituting its boundaries. The sequence thus pretends to a logic it does not have; for the two non-temporal periods are made to seem of a sort with our life in time, to be measurable on the same scale.

There are comparable ambiguities in the dancer's musing suggestion that we undertake a journey around the world to see if Paradise is still somewhere open at the back. The spatial imagery of a circular journey is confusing, since the back door would be half way around the walled garden; whereas the journey we are invited to make is around the *world*, not the garden. Nor does the dancer acknowledge that if the Cherub stands behind us at the start of the circular journey, he will be there at the finish, confronting us; in Genesis 3, the fiery sword turns every way. On the other hand, simply to undertake such an exploration could be said to preclude returning to the front gate: the journey, if we ignore the spatial ambiguities, could be construed as a witty characterization of learning to live in the fallen world. But insofar as it is entertained in spatio-temporal terms, the point of departure for a circular journey will, by the laws of geometry, be the same as the point of return. And is that point – we must further ask – identical with the one at which the dancer says the two ends of the circular world meet? What is brought together at this point – which Kleist also calls a *field* – are the two ends of a scale, namely, infinite consciousness and absence of consciousness, as represented by a god or by a puppet. It is all or nothing; it is not a human world, this point: and of course that is precisely the dancer's contention. But how could we apprehend this perfection? There can indeed be a scale of consciousness – and it can be brought into circular form – but neither no-consciousness nor infinite consciousness (*entweder gar keins, oder ein unendliches Bewusztsein*) will be registered; they are off the scale and cannot be measured by it.[12] This is a logical muddle comparable to the confusion of difference by degree and difference in kind.

The dancer explains in a final geometrical image that, just as a section drawn through two lines on one side of a point suddenly reappears on the other side after passing through infinity (*Doch so, wie sich der Durchschnitt zweier Linien, auf der einen Seite eines Punkts nach dem Durchgang durch das Unendliche, plötzlich wieder auf der anderen Seite einfindet*) so knowledge must pass through infinity before it can return to us as grace (*Wenn die Erkenntnis gleichsam durch ein Unendliches gegangen ist, die Grazie wieder ein*). The idea of a return from infinity is analogous to finding the backdoor of Paradise. Kleist's obsessive concern with defining that point at which beginning and end meet – not the ends of a scale but what lies beyond the extremes – this obsession is perhaps better represented in the second figure, that of the fun house mirror where the concave image dwindles to nothing and then suddenly reappears as convex (*das Bild des Hohlspiegels, nachdem es dich in das Unendliche entfernt hat, plötzlich wieder dicht vor uns tritt*).

When the narrator finally expresses openly his astonishment – "Must we eat again of the Tree of Knowledge? Must we fall back into Innocence?" – he comes close to the Christian metaphor of rebirth, but the born-again moment is shortlived. It explodes with a Kleistian violence: "Of course! That is obviously the final stage of man's development, but it is as well, the last chapter in the history of the world." Is the dancer exhilarated, making this point? Is he despairing, sardonic, amused, bemused? How we read his response will, of course, depend on how we take the paradoxes here and throughout the essay.

In one perspective, the paradoxes of Kleist's essay suggest a profound confusion. It is arguable that the very illogicality of the argument Kleist has the dancer set forth is symptomatic of suicidal despair; within a year of the publication of "Über das Marionettentheater," Kleist was dead by his own hand. In any case, the illogicalities do suggest a disconcerting obsession: to plot and plan how to get rid of the last vestige of mind (the operator's intention and control); to design an automaton, free of human purpose; to deride all accommodation to the human world in favor of a hypnotic vision of a point outside human consciousness, will, or desire – this is indeed the last chapter of the history of the world. In this reading, the circular journey represents the promise that direct access to reality is possible. It will be momentary – even a single flash – this knowledge that returns as grace, but it is a plausible vocation for us to prepare ourselves to experience it.

But what happens if we decide that the illogicalities are deliberate? Are we meant to realize that the entire argument is spurious? In this perspective, the plan to design the *Gliedermann*; the search for the backdoor of Paradise; waiting for knowledge to return as grace, by way of passing through infinity – all are witty emblems of impossibility, in recognition of which lies the only chance of creating new worlds. To be conscious always of the Fall of Man in order to learn the limits of knowledge and action is to accept mediation and its consequences. In this perspective, the paradoxes of Kleist's essay are unresolvable because it is only by their means that the relationship of freedom and necessity can be formulated.

A difficulty in justifying this reading is that Kleist offers no framework in which his quasi-theological metaphors could be so construed; outside a belief structure which defines the conditions of salvation and the costs of redemption, there are no grounds for casuistry. (The fact that casuistry, as its modern meaning testifies, can be the instrument of bad faith, does not gainsay the fact that it empowers all religious paradoxes by which tenets of faith are formulated.) The paradoxes and contradictions which are alternately hidden and revealed in the puppet and journey images and the mathematical figures are *not* of a sort with those by which the Christian faith is represented. In such a declaration as *You must lose your life to save it*, contradiction is deliberate; a logical game is played in which cogency is seemingly sacrificed, but then as it turns out that meanings have shifted, the contradiction vanishes. Casuistry is a rhetorical strategy by which meanings are flushed, driven out into open country. Kleist does not deploy the ambiguities of his figures and images for this kind of rhetorical effect: his spurious reasoning forces deeper significances to remain hidden – with the exception of the single, unspoken observation of the narrator: "Certainly, the human spirit cannot err when it is not present." The narrator here notes the logical error – sufficient reasons are supererogatory when no necessary reason has been adduced – but none of the others is acknowledged: the conflation of difference by degree and difference in kind; the sequences in which things alleged to be of a kind are weighted and located on a scale by which they cannot actually be measured; the surreptitious substitution of one kind of opposition for another and the consequent muddle of continuous and discrete degrees. These illogicalities may or may not be deliberate, but they are not simply tropes and they are not in the service of eschatology. "Über das Marionettentheater" is neither a pocket *Paradise Regained* nor a version of *Pilgrim's Progress*.

But if the possibility of casuistry is foreclosed, there are other modes of irony. I suggest that Kleist's puppets and his mathematical figures are presented as if they were models, but that they function as images. I take that distinction from Susanne K. Langer who notes that models show us modes of operation, whereas images represent appearance, in one or another perspective.[13] Kleist is a master of what we might call *virtual* logic: his propositions and inferences sound exact and formally correct, but upon examination they are shown to be radically faulty. As we read, however, we do not stop to examine. Kleist could have had the narrator stop the dancer to question his argument by attending to the figures, but he decided to leave that to us – or, rather, he assured that the charm of the rhetoric, the pace of the dialogue, the wit and extravagance of the images and anecdotes would all work to divert us. The logic of the *essay* is, so to speak, to ignore the illogical inferences of the *argument*. Having it both ways is certainly one mode of representing the antinomies associated with *what follows the Fall*, as Kleist insouciantly puts it.[14]

The ambiguities of the circular journey and the puppet imagery suggest that Kleist did indeed learn from Kant the logic of necessity, but that his grasp of the dialectic was fitful and insecure. His sardonic acceptance of the conditions of knowing as articulated in the critical philosophy was continually checked by an obsessive search for unmediated encounter with Truth or Being.

The conflict of a dialectical understanding and fantasies of direct access or transcendence is reflected in the novellas. It could be claimed that all of Kleist's stories are concerned with this conflict of two orders, the sublunary and the heavenly, but that is generally true of the novella, a form which typically concerns extraordinary events and pushes characters to extremes so that they function as types and are not meant as psychologically authentic portraits. In any case, Kleist pushes the generic constraints to an extreme, but what determines his characteristic style is not so much the extremity as it is the co-existence of the violent and obsessive with the coolness of the telling.

Recognition of impossibility and the consequent horror of resting for even a moment in this knowledge impels Kleist forward. The search is for a pure moment beyond the rushing of consequence, but it never comes. This may account for the very strong endings in the stories and tales; the only surcease, it turns out, is when the story is over and done. While it is in progress, there is a passionate, obsessive drive to define the very instant which marks a radical transformation, as if identifying this single transfiguring moment would make revelation of deeper truths inevitable. This very search would seem a symptom of the loss of dialectic, but the actual moment functions as a momentary check from which the narrative will spring forward. The Kleistian moment is not a liberation from the last vestige of mind; it is to the story line what the Kleistian figures are to the argument of the essay on the marionette theatre – points of departure for continuing discourse. The Kleistian moments are emblematic, summing in themselves the significance of the tale and illuminating its course as they explode. The dialectic of point and line depends on speed and a lack of deliberation and, most of all, on suddenness.[15] In a trice it happens; the world slows down and irreversible changes take place. People are suddenly not what they were: the unconscious Marquise is raped; Gustav awakens to find himself bound; the Protestant brothers, intent on the ruination of the chapel, are entranced; Elvire falls from the ladder; Jeronimo, the rope around his neck, is interrupted in his suicide attempt by an earthquake.

There is sudden conviction, instant decision, loss of consciousness with knowledge going away and coming back, with innocence lost again. This suddenness is an image of timelessness, a way of splitting a second until it is no longer a quantum of time but appears to us in a new dimension. Each Kleistian moment creates a new space in which energies are gathered and transforming decisions can be made. Conscious, deliberate argument, questioning and analysis bring anguish, but the extraordinary moments propel the narrative, driving it forward and thus forestalling such contemplations. Kleist's storytelling is not a fall back into innocence, but a fall into language. It is of course a fortunate fall and, we might say, it is the means of discovering the back door of Paradise.

14

Green Glasses, the Figured Bass, and the Brakeshoe

> No true meaning is perfectly simple; it is both one and twofold; and this inherent polarity does not divide and destroy it but rather represents its actual fulfillment.
>
> – Ernst Cassirer

In an essay entitled "Über die allmähliche Verfertigung der Gedanken beim Reden" (On the Gradual Fabrication of Thought while Speaking), Kleist invents a figure by which to represent the relationship of language and thought, a figure which illuminates both the narrative style I have been describing and the logic of the figures in his essay on marionettes. The dialectic of control and response is represented there, it will be remembered, by the polarity of the *Bewegung* of the operator's fingers and the *Bewegung* of the dancing puppet. And the heuristic character of limits is represented by the momentary check (*augenblickliche Hemmung*) the floor provides when the puppets touch down. In "Gradual Fabrication," we are given another dialectical figure: the wheel of thought (*Geist*) and the brakeshoe of speech (*Sprache*) both turn on or engage the same axle which, by metaphoric extension, represents discourse. Kleist describes the unconscious, undeliberate, unpremeditated utterance in which speech is absolutely congruent with thought, whose shaping is made possible by the limits which language provides. Speech, he writes, is at such times not a shackle (*Fessel*) but a brakeshoe, not a constraint which impedes but a limiting form which enables: a mysterious barricade.[16] A brake is required to control speed: a certain energy and rapid forwardness, then, is necessary if the heuristic power of discourse is to be exploited. It seems to me that this is precisely exemplified by Kleist's narrative style – very fast, but beautifully paced and steadily driving forward.

The impetus for the gradual fabrication comes from utterance, from speech, from talking out loud – no matter to whom. Kleist explains that talking helps him find his meaning when his writing is blocked; that he often talks to his sister when he catches her eye as she sits sewing across the room. He urges the reader to start talking to the first acquaintance he meets; no intelligence or wit is required since the point is not an exchange. What the other person is needed for is to provide an occasion to start talking; the function of this second person is, as it were, to give the wagon a push, to get the axle turning.[17] It is thus not Bakhtin who provides the appropriate gloss but Vygotsky; for what Kleist describes in his figure of the wheel and the brakeshoe is the way in which we represent for ourselves and others what Vygotsky calls "inner speech." Of course, all speech (and all thought) presupposes a social context, but that is not to say that Kleist is making a plea for the central importance of the concept of "audience." His point is, rather, a matter not of rhetoric but of logic: the analysis appropriate to the relationship of language and thought must begin not with one or the other but (as Vygotsky has it) with "the unit of meaning," with what language and thought create in their peculiar interdependence.

And this is the significance of *Verfertigung*: although it is not mistranslated as *fabrication* or *completion*, the core of the word, *fertig*, means *ready* – and *ready* means *prepared to start* as well as *completed, finished*. The radical ambiguity characteristic of all spatial and temporal linguistic forms is crucial to this representation of the dialectic. In Kleist's metaphor, there is figured the idea of readiness as both end and means: the readiness is all. The relationship between *Geist* and *Sprache* and the revolving axle of discourse is that same dialectical cause/effect which Vico called *eloquence*. If the Fall is into language, then rhetoric succeeds to innocence and eloquence is the analog of grace. The fact that Kleist suffered from a severe stammer which made expression a trial, occasioning rage and humiliation, adds a psychological intensity to the logic by which thought is seen not as waiting on speech but as being readied for it and by it.

But the triadic conception of readiness is probably not what Kleist had in mind. In the light of his explanation of the function of the momentary check when the puppets touch the ground, we could see the revolving axle with wheel and brakeshoe working interdependently as an emblem of purposeful discourse, of a healthy recognition that the heuristic power of language depends on an unconscious recognition of constraining limits. But when we remember what happens to the dialectic in Herr C.'s account, how he dissociates the *augenblickliche Hemmung* from any role in controlling intention, how touching the ground is denied any role in the dance, then the significance of the wheel and brakeshoe becomes problematic. Though logically sound and psychologically authentic, the metaphor from "Gradual Fabrication" probably did not mean dialectic to Kleist but the identity of language and thought. Does not fluent, unpremeditated speech suggest a direct access to the world? And is not the emphasis on the unconscious character of the *Verfertigung* a way of saying that in artful storytelling knowledge returns as grace? Is not art thus the means of falling back into innocence? The wheel and the brakeshoe working together probably signified to Kleist not mediation but *immediacy.*

Kleist apparently found no satisfaction in his understanding of the psychology of speech, so far in advance of his time. What *we* might read as an emblem of the sign triadically conceived was probably not so intended; or, rather, if Kleist did intend by it the subtle understanding it certainly conveys, he seems to have lacked conviction. Kleist apprehended no analogy between linguistic necessity and the generative power of the constraints of our life in time and space. Cassirer realized this and in the following passage seems to be writing in a fatherly tone to Kleist himself:

The word is one of the most important instruments for the concept's actualization, its liberation from immediate perception and intuition. This liberation may seem like a kind of fall from grace, whereby knowledge is driven from the paradise of the concrete and the individual; still, by this very token, it is also the beginning of that boundless endeavor of the spirit by which it conquers and gives form to its world.[18]

The Fall is into language and though Kleist knew that, in a sense, he felt its significance only fleetingly and the knowledge brought him no comfort beyond the pleasure of actual composition. Just as for Kleist the fall into innocence is simultaneously the last stage of man's development and the last chapter of the history of the world, so the end of the story – a pure transcendental moment – brings surcease of eloquence. With the gradual fabrication of thought at an end, there is no more meaning to be made and Kleist relapses again into despair.

Kleist's imagination continually provides images which bespeak recognition of the process of determination and the logic of necessity. When he declares that an understanding of the figured bass would yield an understanding of life,[19] we might assume that, as with the wheel of thought and the brake of speech, he recognized the heuristic power of limits, the concept of form as a mysterious barricade. As the bass – given and determining – is realized, the harmony is expressed or, rather, the soul of the music comes into being, expressed in harmony. The relationship of ground (*Grund*) and harmony is analogous to that of ground (*Boden*) and graceful movement in the puppets. But Kleist found no comfort in such images of mediation and, as I have argued, probably did not see them as such. His obsessive search for a direct access to reality; his fascination with fact and scientific evidence, without a balancing concern for the logic of inquiry; his frantic struggle to be free of all forms of mediation – these attitudes mark him as a naïve realist. It is not, of course, for us to regret this fact, since attitudes which are crippling may nevertheless inspirit the activity by which works of art are brought into being. Kleist's disquieting and fascinating oeuvre can be examined in the light of what can be known of his "Kant-Crisis," of the psychopathology of his relations with women, his attitudes towards his family and the Prussian state, but it is a fact of literary history that his metaphysical and psychological anguish was transformed by the power of his imagination.

In his early twenties – he shot himself at the age of thirty-four – Kleist drew up his *Lebensplan* which specified what he was to learn and what he was to do. To proceed without such an explicit guide, Kleist wrote his sister Ulrike, would be to be always unsure, at the mercy of chance, like a puppet on the wire of fortune (*eine Puppe am Drähte des Schicksals*). To be without a *Lebensplan* seems to him so contemptible, and would make him so unhappy, that death would be preferable.[20] His *Lebensplan* (which he found it difficult to draw up) served to quell anxiety arising from uncertainty, but at a cost: its very rigidity left him helpless in the face of the unforeseen.

The story of the "Kant-Crisis" has often been told, but the character of Kleist's understanding should be seen for what it surely was – inaccurate and sophomoric. Here he explains to his fiancée the principles of the critical philosophy:

If everybody had, instead of eyes, green glasses, they would have to judge that the objects they saw through them *are* green, and they would not be able to decide whether their eyes showed them things as they are or if they didn't present that which except for their eyes would not be there. So it is with understanding. We cannot decide whether that which we call truth is really truth or if it simply appears to us so.[21]

Kleist's figure presupposes a reality accessible without mediation. Kleist has muddled *seeing* and *seeing as*, holding out for unmediated vision. He does not suggest that it is by means of the green glasses that we see at all; there is nothing here of the logic of necessity. The green glasses represent only the constraining aspect of imposed – and implicitly optional – limitations. The heuristic power of limits is not recognized; the green glasses do not represent a gradual fabrication in the very process of seeing.

It is probably an exercise in another kind of naïvety to speculate about what could have saved Kleist, but he does not seem to have read any other philosopher, no one whose arguments could have offset what he thought he had found in Kant – Fichte, for instance, or Schleiermacher, who was writing at exactly the time Kleist needed him most. It is tempting, if we are going to play this game, to think that he could have found in the concatenation of theories of language and programs for instilling a sense of national unity a motive he could have made his own. Still, it is unimaginable that Kleist could have worked in any kind of community, religious or academic. He could no more have espoused Schleiermacher's cause than he could have become a kindergarten teacher. Driven as he was by ill fortune, so unrelenting as to seem conspiratorial or, to a metaphysical imagination, indistinguishable from destiny; burdened with ill health, physical and mental, there is nothing he could have read which would have offered balm: only his writing could do that – including, surely, the expressions of despair in letters to family and friends.

I have argued that Kleist was capable of enjoying the comforting doctrine of the happy Fall only as he enacted its consequences in his art; philosophically, *felix culpa* brought him no consolation. The figure who can stand as his anti-type is Nicholas of Cusa, "the learned and witty Cardinal Cusanus" as Andrew Marvell called him.[22] By juxtaposing Kleist and Cusanus – each a type-specimen of his era – my aim is not to compare the world views of the Romantic poet, incapable of immersion or submission or transcendence, and the Renaissance man, able to articulate the dialectic of individual and cosmos, freedom and necessity. But the juxtaposition can illuminate the consequences of triadicity.

Cusanus discovered how the limits of knowledge were themselves the means of knowing: his doctrine of learned ignorance (*docta ignorantia*) has more in common with modern science than it does with *credo quia impossibile*. The central principle of this doctrine was the coincidence of opposites (*coincidentia oppositorum*). It is surely a member of the family of interinanimations to which Kleist's axle of discourse also belongs. Polarity is, of course, the archetypal metaphor of a coincidence of opposites. In the dyadic perspective, however, opposites are simply at odds; triadically, we can see them as interdependent, necessary to one another, fulfilling the double function of dividing and uniting. It is by their being poles apart that the ends can effect unified activity. But this dialectic is emergent and can properly be represented only in terms of a process of determination. Thus it is the function of the axle to rotate, to transform position to movement, point to line, to allow a world to wheel, to enable the gradual fabrication of thought.

Cusanus found chiefly in mathematics the images (and the proof, he thought) which allowed him to move from the recognition of *finiti et infiniti nulla proportio* to *coincidentia oppositorum*. There is a difference between the contradictories we confront on this side of infinity and what they become when they pass through infinity: they return to us as grace and redemption, not as portents of the last chapter in the history of mankind. Cusanus finds God only as he confronts impossibility and the recognition of necessity is at that very point. His imagery derives, like Kleist's, from Genesis 3:

> Wherefore I give thee thanks, my God, because Thou makest plain to me that there is none other way of approaching Thee than that which to all men, even the most learned philosophers, seemeth utterly inaccessible and impossible. For Thou hast shown me that Thou canst not be seen elsewhere than where impossibility meeteth and faceth me. Thou hast inspired me, Lord, who art the Food of the strong, to do violence to myself, because impossibility coincideth with necessity, and I have learnt that the place wherein Thou art found unveiled is girt round with the coincidence of contradictories, and this is the wall of Paradise wherein Thou dost abide. The door whereof is guarded by the most proud spirit of Reason, and, unless he be vanquished, the way in will not lie open. Thus 'tis beyond the coincidence of contradictories that Thou mayest be seen, and no where this side thereof.[23]

For Cusanus, the Wall of Paradise is a mysterious barricade, symbolic of the truth that when impossibility is confronted, necessity becomes the ground of choice. The contingency of the exercise of freedom and the knowledge of necessity is an idea as old as philosophy and as up-to-date as complementarity. As Cassirer continually argued, the logic of necessity informs any philosophy of representation which recognizes the heuristic power of form. It was for his profound understanding of the consequences of mediation that Cassirer chose Cusanus as a representative man, representative of the newly apprehended relationship of the individual and the cosmos.[24]

In an essay written upon completion of *The Philosophy of Symbolic Forms*, Cassirer sounds once more his great theme of man's destiny – his Fortunate Fall into language, escaping the prison of the momentary by way of becoming the *animal symbolicum*. He calls again on Kleist's imagery:

For man, once driven from the paradise of immediacy – man who has once partaken of the tree of knowledge and therewith has forever left behind the limits of merely natural existence, of life which is unconscious of itself – for man it follows that he must traverse his appointed orbit, in order at the end of his road to find his way back again to its beginning.[25]

All images of the paradox of enabling limits – all mysterious barricades – deserve our most careful consideration: Kleist's parables provide speculative instruments in such an endeavor.

Notes

Introduction

1 *Times Literary Supplement*, February 18, 1983, p. 159.
2 *Times Literary Supplement*, August 28, 1992, p. 19.
3 Peirce's spelling is *semeiotic*. He changed *pragmatism* to *pragmaticism* when William James popularized what Peirce considered a misconception. I will use the usual spelling, *semiosis*, but will keep *pragmaticism*, which is not simply a matter of orthography.
4 "Powers and Limits of Signs," in *Poetries: Their Media and Ends*, ed. Trevor Eaton (The Hague, 1974), p. 1.
   This and most other citations from Richards' work can be found in *Richards on Rhetoric: I.A. Richards Selected Essays 1929–1974*, ed. Ann E. Berthoff (New York, 1991).

Part I

1 "Gangster theories" make their appearance in the Preface to *The Screens* (1960), reprinted in *Internal Colloquies* (1971).
2 See John R. Platt, "Strong Inference," *Science*, 145 (16 October 1964), 347–352.
3 *An Introduction to Symbolic Logic* (1937; New York, 1953), p.142.
4 The French lack a Veblen, which is perhaps why they needed a Barthes. The best account I have seen of Barthes's studied rejection of representation – of the symbolic function of language – comes from his countryman, Robert Marty:

> Most existing semiologies have neglected this element [of the Third, the mediating thought] by making it universal, as though the correspond-

ence were a datum entitled to universal approval. At the very most, such systems admit of a few secondary variations (e.g. in passing from one language to another), but the universal character of the signified in particular was for a long time ... a widespread a priori. Such universalistic assumptions exclude all ideo-systems, and indeed all particularities far removed from the dominant systems, from the theory. The universal character of the *signifiant/signifié* correspondence has, in a way, turned Saussurian semiotics into the semiology of the dominant sign-systems of a given society, and semiologists into the guardians of a kind of semiotic orthodoxy. Thus Barthes's reaction when he called for a semioclasm (*semioclastie*) can be considered a political denunciation of institutionalized signs.

("Peirce's phaneroscopy and semiotics," *Semiotica*, 41–1/4 [1982], 169–81.)

5 "A Conversation with Shirley Sugerman," in *Evolution of Consciousness: Studies in Polarity*, ed. Shirley Sugerman (Middletown, 1976), p. 14.
6 *Reflections*, pp. 314–332.
7 Foreword, *The Poetics of Prose*, Tzvetan Todorov (Ithaca, 1977), p. 8.
8 *The Classic* (Cambridge, Mass., 1983), p. 135.
9 "Functions of and Factors in Language," in *Poetries*, p. 14
10 Max Black and I.A. Richards disagreed about some things, but not about the hazards of information theory. See Black's discussion in *The Labyrinth of Language* (New York, 1968), pp. 22–24.
11 *The Right to Dream* (New York, 1970), pp. 3–7; 32. Jacques Derrida, writing on the tain of the mirror, typically creates a false paradox. He comments that it is the "dull surface" of the back of the mirror which enables reflection to occur but which "cannot itself take part in reflection's scintillating play." But the back of the mirror does not function as a surface and the fact that it is dull is immaterial to the function it does serve. The logic of necessity is that each opposition is made up of pairs which are mutually entailed: every top must have a bottom; every front, a back. But the dull non-surface is not itself a dialectical structure, nor does it function dialectically with a scintillating non-side.
12 *The Philosophy of Rhetoric* (1936; New York, 1965), p. 36.
13 *In Defense of the Imagination* (Cambridge, Mass. 1982), p. 88.
14 *The Philosophy of Composition* (Chicago, 1977), pp. 150–51.
15 *Visual Thinking* (Berkeley, 1969), p. 186.
16 *Mind: An Essay on Human Feeling*, (Baltimore, 1967), I, pp. 33–54.
17 Explanations of this method, including Husserl's own, are often confusing and vague. The clearest exposition I have found comes from Edgar Wind in a

review article written over seventy years ago. I quote at length, first the explanation of "phenomenological reduction" and then the critique:

> Husserl tried to approach the field of essences by seeking a field of immediately evident statements ... When we see a man, we may doubt whether he really exists. But what we cannot doubt is that we see him [or] that this "seeing" presents certain visual qualities which we interpret as representing a thing. So, if we eliminate the question, whether this thing exists or not, there still remains 1) the act of seeing which presents the phenomenon, 2) the hypothetic relation of this phenomenon to the thing, which relation itself contains the phenomenon of representation. All that we notice in this way can not be doubted. A field is open for evident statements as soon as we eliminate the problem of reality. And to this elimination Husserl gave the name of "phenomenological reduction. "... He believed that by [it] he had extracted essences from facts. But he really had only transformed a problematic fact into an unproblematic phenomenon. The phenomenon remained a single phenomenon and just as complex as a fact. ...
>
> Husserl saw two things very clearly, that the essences were inherent in facts, and that in order to grasp them as essences, the facts had to be free from their individuality. But what he did not see was that this individuality was based on complexity. He knew that some reduction had to be made; but he failed to notice that the process of reduction had to be a process of simplification. He thought the fact could remain as complex as it was and be transposed into the essential order simply by declaring that the relations which it presented were not meant to be individual and real relations. ...
>
> Every fact presents an aggregation of different phenomena, each of which belongs to another essential order; so that very various orders of essences meet in the complexity of a single fact. None of these orders simply *corresponds* to the order of facts. Each of them must be extracted by means of reduction and construction. (*Journal of Philosophy*, 22 (1925), 524–25)

When Husserl sought to make evident statements representative of universals, he did not change his logic.

18 "Some Principles of Literary Criticism," *Times (London) Literary Supplement*), July 26, 1963.
19 "Kenneth Burke and Literary Criticism," in *The Sewanee Review*, LXXIX (1971), 177–88.

20 *TLS*, July 26, 1963.
21 Susanne K. Langer, *Feeling and Form* (New York, 1953), p. 378.
22 In *Textual Strategies*, ed. Josué V. Harari (Ithaca, 1979), pp. 121–40. The contrast with Kenneth Burke is instructive: *The Rhetoric of Motives* suggests the conception of rhetoric needed if dialectical purposes are to be served.
23 Here is Scott-Moncrieff's translation, followed by the original:

> This dim freshness of my room was to the broad daylight of the street what the shadow is to the sunbeam, that is to say, equally luminous, and presented to my imagination the entire panorama of summer, which my senses, if I had been out walking, could have tasted and enjoyed in fragments only; and so was quite in harmony with my state of repose, which (thanks to the adventures related in my books, which had just excited it) bore, like a hand reposing motionless in a stream of running water, the shock and animation of a torrent of activity and life.
> Cette obscure fraîcheur de ma chambre était au plein soleil de la rue ce que l'ombre est au rayon, c'est-à-dire aussi lumineuse que lui et offrait à mon imagination le spectacle total de l'été dont mes sens, si j'avais été en promenade, n'auraient pu jouir que par morceaux; et ainsi elle s'accordait bien à mon repos qui (grâce aux aventures racontées par mes livres et qui venaient l'émouvoir) supportait, pareil au repos d'une main immobile au milieu d'une eau courante, le choc et l'animation d'un torrent d'activité.

24 The old misconceptions of nineteenth-century philology reappear when some literary critics turn to certain sources in linguistics for guidance. Max Müller's theory of language as a faded mythology may have to be disproved all over again. Michael Ferber has an instructive note in his essay on Blake's "London" in *ELH*, 48 (1981): "An amusing essay could be written on the impact of *The American Heritage Dictionary* (1969) on the Yale English Department." Ferber's very brief comment substantiates the claim that Whorfism is alive and well.
25 Fredric Jameson, *The Prison-House of Language* (Princeton, 1972), pp. 30ff.
26 *Ferdinand de Saussure* (New York, 1977), p. 15.
27 See the unsatisfactory exchange with his critics, *Critical Inquiry*, 12 (1985), 290–99.
28 The point was made in personal correspondence by Phoebe C. Ellsworth.
29 *Writings of Charles S. Peirce* (Bloomington, 1982–), III, p. 84.
30 Michael Riffaterre "Interpretation and Undecidability," *New Literary History*, XII [1981], 227–242.) refers to the "hoary concept" of ambiguity, urging instead the notion of intertextuality, an example of the kind of pseudo-

concept which proliferates as the dyadic sign begins to suffer semiotic fatigue.
31 *Patterns of Intention* (New Haven, 1985), p. 11.
32 R. B. Onians, cited in *The Image and the Past*, Bertram Lewin (New York, 1968), p. 21. Max Müller makes the observation in *The Science of Language* (1887).
33 Derrida's knowledge of anatomy and physiology, faulty and incomplete as it is, is set forth with a textbook sort of particularity and made to sound fundamentally serious and straightforward, no matter how wrong-headed the inferences drawn might be. Derrida aims, occasionally, at a deconstruction of the dichotomy of inner/outer in favor of dialectical definition. If he understood the physiology of skin, he would find its structure and function a model of language as a mysterious barricade, but I know of no such instance. Instead, he deploys his own fanciful conceptions of the physiology of vision and of organic structures, notably the hymen and the tympanum.

The following is from "Tympanum," a foreword to *Margins of Philosophy*:

> Can one violently penetrate philosophy's field of listening without its immediately ... making the penetration resonate within itself, appropriating the emission for itself, familiarly communicating it to itself between the inner and middle ear? In other words, can one puncture the tympanum of a philosopher and still be heard and understand him?

The tympanum (eardrum) does not function by resonating within the body. There is no communication between inner and outer ear in the transmission of sound; there is thus no basis for the pun on inner ear, nor is there any logical justification for the play with transmission and emission. This comment exemplifies the construction of a strong theory: penetration becomes puncturing; transmission becomes emission; reception becomes rape.

In several places, Derrida pursues his notions about what his translator and disciple lovingly calls his "hymeneal fable." Her description, written in the mode of primary process, can be found in her Introduction to *Of Grammatology*. She writes: "The hymen is always folded (therefore never single or simple) space in which the pen writes its dissemination." Female anatomy (or male anatomy, for that matter) is rather more complex than Derrida's anatomical allegory, as explicated by Ms Spivak, suggests. For starters, we might note that the hymen is a fold but is itself not folded; it is a membrane, not a space and, leaving aside the non-Euclidean assumptions of its folding when it is described as a space, its being a fold is irrelevant to its being a membrane. The hymen is not permeable: there is no *dissemination into* the hymen. That is a contradiction in terms, since if the semen were stopped by the hymen there would be no dissemination; *ejaculation* is what is meant.

In *Éperons* (Spurs), Derrida speaks of a "deflowered abyss;" elsewhere, he speaks of a moat of risk surrounding language. The first figure remains a useless mixed metaphor, without cogency or interest; the second is undeveloped and the idea which it was meant to symbolize is re-stated in these terms:

> Does the general risk ... *surround* language like a moat, an external place of perdition into which speech could always not emerge [sic], which it could avoid by staying at home? ... Or on the contrary, is this risk its internal and positive condition of possibility? is this outside its inside? the very strength and the law of its coming into being?

The question cannot be entertained in a dyadic perspective, in terms of an inside-outside dichotomy, which here sounds like Hiawatha's mittens. The *condition of possibility* is a triadic conception, an expression of the logic of necessity which Peirce symbolizes by Shakespeare's "glassy essence" and Emerson's line, spoken by the Sphinx: "Of thine eye I am eyebeam."

Apparently, it was a deconstructionist who contributed information for a record liner to the effect that Couperin's title, "Les baricades mistérieuses," is a reference to the hymen. We must await further deconstruction of the anagrammatic names of the organists' guild, to say nothing of those bears and monkeys, the dominoes and clowns of Couperin's great suites, but meanwhile it should be noted that there is nothing mysterious about this barricade: the hymen is either intact or it is not, which is why determination of the evidence for virginity is a perennial motif in folk tale and Renaissance drama, in balladry and grade B Italian movies.

Couperin explained his titles in the preface to the first book of suites: "J'ai toujours eu un objet en composant toutes ces pièces; des occasion differentes me l'ont fourni. Ainsi les titres repondent aux idées que j'ai eues; on me dispensera d'en rendre compte ..." (Pierre Citron, *Couperin* [Editions du Seuil, 1956], 93–94). Pierre Citron comments on the title "Les baricades mistérieuses': "Mais le prétexte anecdotique traduit par le titre ne joue guere ici: la raison de cette restriction volontaire est musicale" (p. 107). Citron is doubtless referring to the fact that the entire piece is written in the bass clef. But we may take *voluntary restriction* in the larger sense as a description of the character of aesthetic form, a characterization of the heuristic power of limits. As Allen Tate once observed: "A poet is a man willing to come under the bondage of limitations, if he can find them."

34 *The Sense of Order* (Ithaca, 1979), p. 143.

Notes to pages 40–43   173

35 *Art and Illusion* (New York, 1960), pp. 5–6.
36 For an example, see Don Ihde, "Phenomenology and deconstructive strategy," *Semiotica*, 41–1/4 (1982), 8.
37 *The Structure of Scientific Revolutions* (Chicago, 1970), p. 85.
38 From *Schöpferische Konfession* which Klee published in 1920. Translation appears in the second edition (1945) of the Museum of Modern Art catalogue for the Paul Klee memorial exhibition of 1941.
39 "Analogy in Science," *The American Psychologist*, 11 (1956), 127–35.
40 *Art and Illusion*, p. 179–287. Gombrich, it must be noted, does not use the duck-rabbit to symbolize or represent the idea of "the beholder's share" which he firmly associates with the sense of order we must learn.
41 *Philosophical Investigations* (Oxford, 1953), pp. 196–99.
    Apparently, Wittgenstein thought the duck-rabbit exemplified figure-ground reversal since he goes on the discuss a Maltese cross, alternately black and white, as being of the same type. But the duck-rabbit does not involve a figure and a ground, nor is there a question of positive and negative spaces. Wittgenstein was writing at a time before the thorough philosophical and physiological investigation of vision had been undertaken, but it is surely odd when philosophers and art historians, ignoring Gibson, Hochberg, Arnheim, Gombrich, Gregory (*inter alios*), follow along Wittgenstein's meanders. Stanley Cavell, for instance, though he sees the duck-rabbit as having limited application, claims that the flip is one's own doing, that you know that "the change is in you" (*The Claim of Reason* [New York, 1979], p. 354), subject to your will, and that for some, the flip may not happen. This is all highly misleading since the brain is not acting here according to one's will and any normal brain will react so that anybody and everybody will see alternately a duck and a rabbit. Professor Cavell's disquisition on the significance of physiognomic perception and his further discussion of Wittgenstein's notion that "the human body is the best picture of the human soul" illustrates the mystic-positivist flip-flop, from veil to picture. If we take *Bild* as *form* or *image* rather than as *picture*, then to speak of the "allegorical" character of *Bild* is pleonastic.
42 Toulmin and Janik, citing F. Waismann, in *Wittgenstein's Vienna* (New York, 1973), pp. 65–67, 85–87.
43 Note the almost identical formulation in Whorf's version of this typically positivist "what if": "If a race of people had the physiological defect of being able to see only the color blue, they would hardly be able to formulate the rule that they saw only blue." (*Language, Thought and Reality* [Cambridge, 1956], p. 209.) Wittgenstein frequently made color the point of departure in his 1933–1934 lectures at Cambridge, notes for which are known as *The Blue*

Book. The set of aphorisms he was working on up until the time of his death have been edited by G.E.M. Anscombe and published as *Wittgenstein on Color* (Berkeley, 1978).
44 *Collected Papers of Charles Sanders Peirce* (Cambridge, 1931–1935; 1958), 1.387. Hereafter, Peirce is cited parenthetically in the text.
45 Noted by Thomas A. Sebeok and Jean Umiker Sebeok, "'You Know My Method': A juxtaposition of Charles S. Peirce and Sherlock Holmes," in *The Sign of Three: Dupin, Holmes, Peirce*, ed. Umberto Eco and Thomas A. Sebeok (Bloomington, 1983).
46 The *catalogue raisonée* prepared by Sarah Whitfield (*Magritte*, The South Bank Centre, London, 1992) notes that Geert van Bruaene, one of Magritte's early admirers, displayed in his gallery a sign reading: "Ceci n'est pas de l'Art," commenting that that inscription is "an adaptation, no doubt, of the title of a book by Diderot, 'Ceci n'est pas un conte.'" However that might be, Magritte came to feel possessive about the little phrase. When "rival Surrealists" pamphleted a retrospective show with a tract in which the phrase appeared in Belgian dialectal form, Magritte was "so infuriated that he walked out of the exhibition" (p. 149).
47 *This Is Not a Pipe* (Berkeley, 1983), p. 18.
Antonia Phillips (*TLS*, April 27, 1984) properly objects that "there is not a single configuration [as in the duck-rabbit] in Magritte's figure, which is both text and unmistakable pipe. The two cases are not assimilable in this way." They never are, but that awareness is impeded so long as the code and what is encoded are entertained in a dyadic perspective.
48 See Gombrich's essay, "On Physiognomic Perception," *Daedalus*, 89 (1960), 228–41.
49 The phrase is I.A. Richards.' He claimed he took it from Coleridge but had been unable to locate it ever again. My own opinion is that he heard in Othello's witty reference to his "speculative and officed instruments" something he could use – and promptly forgot its origin. See note in *Richards on Rhetoric*, p. 224.
50 *The Prison-House of Language*, p. 26
51 *The Meaning of Meaning* (1923; New York, 1946), p. 11.
52 Cited in *Wittgenstein's Vienna*, p. 128.
53 *The Labyrinth of Language* (New York, 1969), p. 152.
54 *Language and Myth* (1925; New York, 1946).
Here are two examples. Michel Benamou writes in *Wallace Stevens and the Symbolic Imagination* (Princeton, 1972): "As Cassirer suggestively wrote in *Language and Myth*, 'All symbolism harbors the curse of mediacy.' Symbols block man's access to reality" (p. xiii). And Geoffrey Hartman, in *Beyond For-*

malism (New Haven, 1970), provides this note: "I borrow the phrase 'the curse of mediacy' from Ernst Cassirer who says that language is bound to obscure what it seeks to reveal" (p. 108). Hartman refused the correction I offered and went on to compound the original error. See the exchange of letters, *Times Literary Supplement*, September 5, October 24, November 7, 1975.

Crediting (or borrowing) the phrase as expressive of Cassirer's own views suggests both a failure to understand the chief principle of Cassirer's philosophy of symbolic form and an unfamiliarity with his style and method. Cassirer generally offers very careful and extraordinarily generous recapitulations of an argument before showing how misconceived premises and faulty analysis yield invalid theories. Phrase-hunting readers must be alert to just where they are in the exposition; for some, of course, RUP makes it hard to know what they have, even if they do know where they are.

55 *Reflections*, ed. Peter Demetz (New York, 1978), p. 315.
56 *Reflections*, p. 316.
Benjamin calls the identity of language and thought "an incomprehensible paradox" if it is taken as a point of departure; if it is continuously examined, it is a "solution" to the problem of defining the relationship of what is said and what is meant. But his example of the ambiguity of *logos* and his image of suspension suggest that precisely the reverse is what he intended in his characterization: beginning with the identity of language and thought is an easy non-solution which is to be avoided since it closes off the compelling questions which can lead us to an apprehension of the relationship of language and thought as the kind of paradox which is necessary to the formulation of our answers. Benjamin means, I think, not that there is something unmediated which we might call an immediate form, but that mediation is not something we can dispense with, nor can it be reduced or set aside. The thrust of the argument in this essay would seem to make it impossible that he would mean to exempt anything from mediation.
57 *Thought and Language* (Cambridge, Mass., 1986), p. 10.
58 *Mind in Society* (Cambridge, Mass., 1978), p. 54.
59 *Modes of Thought* (1938; New York, 1958), p. 50.

Part II

1 The best short account of Peirce's life and his importance to philosophy is by Max Fisch, the leading Peirce scholar: "Peirce's General Theory of Signs," in *Sight, Sound, and Sense*, ed. Thomas A. Sebeok (Bloomington, 1978).
2 *Collected Papers of Charles Sanders Peirce* (Cambridge: Harvard University Press, 1931–1935; 1958), 8.378. Further citations are made parenthetically.

3 *Semiotic and Significs: The Correspondence between Charles S. Peirce and Victoria Lady Welby*, ed. Charles S. Hardwick (Bloomington, 1977), p. 84. Further citations are made parenthetically in the text as *S. and S.*
4 *Of Grammatology* (Baltimore, 1977), p. 48.
5 *Writings of Charles S. Peirce*, ed. Max H. Fisch (Bloomington: Indiana University Press, 1982), III, p. 84.
6 "Man: Sign or Algorithm? A Rhetorical Analysis of Peirce's Semiotics," *Transactions of the Charles Sanders Peirce Society*, XIV (1980), 279–92.
7 When Peirce rejects rhetoric, it is as a matter of eloquence or mere expression; rhetoric as the representation of logical articulations he calls "speculative Rhetoric" and it is the same as his *methodeutic*, the ways we have of making arguments more effective.
8 For a thorough examination of Habermas' misreadings of Peirce, see Roberta Kevelson, "C.S. Peirce's Speculative Rhetoric," *Philosophy and Rhetoric*, 17 (1984), 16–29.
9 *Consequences of Pragmatism* (Minneapolis, 1982), p. 161.
10 This motif has an importance for Coleridge too. He comments on Mrs. Barbauld's censure of "The Ancient Mariner" for two faults, "that it was improbable and had no moral." "As for the probability," Coleridge then goes on, "I owned that that might admit some question; but as to the moral, I told her that in my own judgment, the poem had too much. ... It ought to have had no more moral than the Arabian Nights' tale of the merchant's sitting down to eat dates by the side of the wall, and throwing the shells [sic] aside, and lo! a genie starts up, and says he *must* kill the aforesaid merchant, *because* one of the dates shells had, it seems, put out the eye of the genie's son." (See John Livingston Lowes, *The Road to Xanadu* [Boston, 1927], p. 302.) The compunction to avenge a meaningless act is the primitive, irrational core of "The Ancient Mariner," as it is of the tale from the Arabian Nights, and it is the reason that the boy Peirce wept and would not be comforted.
11 Since Peirce has just said *before* Adam was conscious and since consciousness he often describes as virtually the same as representation, I presume that *conscious* in this wonderful list is a slip and that *unconscious* was meant. However, Peirce is very quick to develop three stages or effects or aspects from one element of a triad so that it is conceivable that *conscious* Firstness would not be contradictory in a new set of terms.
12 I have found Joseph L. Esposito's discussion of synechism instructive and inspiring. See especially Chapters 4 and 5, *Evolutionary Metaphysics: The Development of Peirce's Theory of Categories* (Athens, Ohio, 1980).
13 *Philosophy and the Mirror of Nature* (Princeton, 1979), 42n. This statement is

inaccurate since the phrase appears much earlier in the lecture in which Peirce presents his argument for the claim that Man is a Sign, c. 1867.
14 *Complementarities* (Cambridge, Mass., 1976), p. 111.
15 *Design for Escape* (New York, 1968), p. 46.
16 "History as System," in *Philosophy and History: The Ernst Cassirer Festschrift*, ed. Raymond Klibansky and H.J. Paton (Oxford: Clarendon, 1936), p. 314.
17 *Practical Criticism* (New York, 1965), p. 315.
18 *Mencius on the Mind* (London, 1932), p. 90.
19 *How to Read a Page* (New York, 1942), p. 239.
20 *The Wrath of Achilles: The Iliad of Homer Shortened and in a New Translation* (New York, 1950), pp. 24–25.
21 *Poetries*, p. 9.
22 *How to Read a Page*, p. 24.
23 *Interpretation in Teaching* (New York, 1938), pp. 48–49.
24 This particular phrasing of a commonplace in the fatuous debates between "subjective" critics and their opponents comes from Norman Holland and is quoted by Charles Altieri in "The Hermeneutics of Literary Indeterminacy," *New Literary History*, 10 (Autumn 1978), 72.
25 *Poetries*, p. 14.
26 *So Much Nearer* (New York, 1968), pp. 171–72.
27 *Beyond*, (New York, 1973), p. 20.
28 *So Much Nearer* p. 197.
29 For an excellent analysis of this curious phenomenon, see Walter Benn Michaels, "The Interpreter's Self: Peirce on the Cartesian 'Subject,'" *The Georgia Review*, 31 (Summer 1977), 383–402. "The problem of the reader's subjectivity," Michaels writes, "is a false problem. ... What Abrams, Hirsch, Culler, et al. fear is a situation in which the reader will be allowed or encouraged to grant his unconstrained subjective responses the status of 'meaning.' Their model of interpretation is the nineteenth-century scientific model of the autonomous reader or observer confronting an autonomous text or data. If all doesn't go well, the reader suspends his prejudices and interprets the texts correctly. If all doesn't go well, the reader enforces his prejudices and makes the text over in their image. From Peirce's stand point, however, neither of these alternatives is feasible because the model they are derived from is mistaken. ... These two positions are simply the flip sides of the context-free self, active and passive: one generates any interpretation it pleases, the other denies that it interprets at all."
30 *How to Read a Page*, p. 14.
31 *Beyond*, p. 14.

32 *So Much Nearer*, p. 175.
33 Ronald Shusterman ("Blindness and Anxiety: I.A. Richards and Some Current Trends in Criticism," *Études anglaises*, 39 (1986), 411–23) makes a very good case for claiming that those who garble or reject Richards have read nothing he published after 1942 and what they have read, they misrepresent. (The date is too late, in my opinion; few cite anything after *Practical Criticism* [1929] and in some cases, after *Principles of Literary Criticism* [1924].) He carefully disentangles what Richards actually wrote from what Stanley Fish thinks he did, or says he did. Shusterman observes that whereas Jonathan Culler "systematically omits Richards from his accounts of Deconstruction, taking no notice of relevant connections," Paul de Man could be "convicted of assault and battery on Ricardian theory." He comments that there is something more than "faulty scholarship" in de Man's misrepresentations. Professor Shusterman is mistaken, I believe, in seeing a correspondence between *différence* and "the interinanimation of words," but in his discussion of complementarity – the chief speculative instrument of Richards' later writings – he writes "One cannot get beyond this complementarity." Precisely: it is this recognition of the logic of necessity which differentiates I.A. Richards' philosophy of rhetoric from what Shusterman properly calls the "willful paradoxes" of post-structuralist theory.
34 *Poetries*, p. 24.
35 The phrase is Claude Rawson's (*London Review of Books*, 6 February, 1986).
36 *Kant's Life and Thought* (New Haven, 1981), p. 55.
37 "Analogy in Science," *The American Psychologist*, 11 (1956).
38 *Wittgenstein's Vienna*, p. 219.
39 For this account of Schleiermacher's thought, I have drawn on the following: Richard B. Brandt, *The Philosophy of Schleiermacher* (New York, 1940); *Schleiermacher's Sololoquies*, tr. H.L. Friess (Chicago, 1926); Robert Munro, *Schleiermacher: Personal and Speculative* (Paisley, 1903); Andrew Osborn, *Schleiermacher and Religious Education* (London, 1934). Most important have been Karl Barth's essay on Schleiermacher in *Protestant Thought from Rousseau to Ritschel* (New York, 1959) and Richard R. Niebuhr, *Schleiermacher on Christ and Religion* (New York, 1964).
40 *Samm. Werke*, XIII, p. 23, quoted by Friess.
41 *SW*, XIII, p. 373, quoted in Osborne.
42 Friess, p. 31.
43 In explaining the role of iconology – the study of the contexts of iconography – Erwin Panofsky put it this way:

> To control the interpretation of an individual work of art by a "history of style," which in turn can only be built up by interpreting individual works

may look like a vicious circle. It is, indeed, a circle though not a vicious but a methodical one. Whether we deal with historical or natural phenomena, the individual observation assumes the character of a "fact" only when it can be related to other analogous observations in such a way that the whole series "makes sense." This "sense" is, therefore, fully capable of being applied, as a control, to the interpretation of a new individual observation within the same range of phenomena. If, however, this new individual observation definitely refuses to be interpreted according to the "sense" of the series, and if an error proves to be impossible, the "sense" of the series will have to be reformulated to include the new observation. (*Studies in Iconology* [New York, 1939], p. 11n.)

44 As an emblem of Schleiermacher's dogmatics, Karl Barth chose not a circle but an ellipse with two foci, named as follows:

faith	Christ
experience	history
psychological moment	historical moment
anthropological center	Christological center

Each focus is continually drawn to the other, though they never coincide: identification or dissolution or reduction or fusion is avoided because they are mediated by the Holy Spirit. The doctrine of the Trinity is emblematic of all third terms. For Schleiermacher, acts of interpretation, are acts of mind and spirit and thus share the trinitarian form, the triadic character of the sign assuring the role of mediation from the start.

45 "Über die Religion," quoted in Brandt, p. 91.
46 *Hermeneutics: The Handwritten Manuscripts*, ed. Heinz Kimmerle, tr. James Duke and Jack Forstman (Missoula, Montana, 1977), p. 98. Schleiermacher follows this statement with an explanation of the relative importance of the psychological and grammatical aspects: the psychological is of "higher" importance when one regards language as a means of communicating thought of a particular; insofar as one considers how language reveals meaning, the grammatical will be more important. For Schleiermacher the two tasks are completely equal. (*Aus dieser Duplizität folgt von selbst die vollkommene Gleichheit.*)
47 *Philosophy of Symbolic Forms*, III (Princeton, 1957), pp. 82–85.
48 *Selected Writings of Edward Sapir in Language, Culture, and Personality* (Berkeley, 1949), ed. David Mandelbaum, 15. Most of the references to Sapir's writings are to this volume and will be noted parenthetically in the text.
49 *Language* (1921; New York, 1949), p. 124. Cited hereafter in the text.

50 *The Freeman*, 7 (1923), 572–73. Sapir graciously does not chide Ogden and Richards for their wrong-headed and arrogant censures of his claims about the irrelevance of word order to meaning and his use of the term *concept* to cover both concrete and relational ideas (*Meaning of Meaning*). But to read the footnote references to Sapir is to feel an edge to Sapir's comment that the authors are short on understanding the complexity of the formal system of language. But that is not the same thing as muddling symbols and signals, which is what we have in contemporary theories of discourse.

It is instructive to juxtapose Sapir's reservation with Fredric Jameson's comment that Ogden and Richards, "as semanticists, are concerned with words as symbols," in contradistinction to Saussure's insistence on language as "a system of signs" (*Prison-House*, p. 29). Jameson's comment that it is "the dialectical quality of [Saussure's] thought "which Ogden and Richards object to is a comical demonstration of misreading. Rhetoric, as Richards noted (as if echoing Schleiermacher, unconsciously or not), is "a study of misunderstanding *and its remedies*" (my italics). In this case, the remedy is to be found in Appendix D of *The Meaning of Meaning*, in which C.S. Peirce makes his first appearance outside the philosophical journals.

51 For a discussion of Whorf's misunderstandings of Sapir, see the version of this essay published in *Semiotica*, 71 1/2 (1988), 1–47.

52 For appraisals of Sapir's career and influence, see *New Perspectives in Language, Culture, and Personality: Proceedings of the Edward Sapir Centenary Conference* (Ottawa, 1–3 October, 1984), ed. William Cowan, Michael K. Foster, and Konrad Koerner (Amsterdam/Philadelphia, 1986).

53 Many of those who have studied Whorf's principle of "linguistic relativity" have assumed that it is representative of an emphasis which can be traced to Humboldt. James H. Stam in a thoughtful analysis of 'linguistic relativity' in an historical perspective, offers a useful check to such claims. Though I believe that he misapprehends Sapir's argument about the relationship of language and "the 'real world,'" Stam's analysis of Whorf is fair-minded and he is fully alert to the logical issues posed in any consideration of the limits of language.

54 *An Essay on Man* (New Haven, 1944), p. 128.

55 Susanne K. Langer was married to the historian William Langer and apparently preferred "Mrs. Langer" to academic titles, even after they were divorced. This usage belongs to a different era, but "Langer" is unsatisfactory, as it is always in the case of a woman who has taken her husband's name, especially when his name is well known. Instead of repeating "Susanne Langer," I have chosen to refer to her by her full professional name in abbreviated form, "SKL."

56 *Introduction to Symbolic Logic* (1937; New York, 1953), p. 14. It is noteworthy that "popular" never meant "simplified" or "reduced" for SKL. She could speak of the *Bibliothek Warburg* as "a great venture in popular education."
57 "Form and Content: A Study in Paradox," *Journal of Philosophy*, 23 (1926), 435–38; "A Logical Study of Verbs," *Journal of Philosophy*, 24 (1927), 120–29.
58 The ugly word is Coleridge's invention. He held that "the whole process of human intellect is gradually to desynonymize terms." *Biographia Literaria*, I, iv, ed. W. Jackson Bate and James Engell (Princeton, 1983), p. 82n.
59 *Feeling and Form* (New York, 1953), p. 379.
60 *The Practice of Philosophy* (Cambridge, 1930), p. 170.
61 *Philosophical Sketches* (New York, 1962), p. 63.
62 Coleridge had himself carried out a desynonymizing exercise with abstraction and generalization.
63 *Mind*, I (Baltimore, 1967), p. 156.
64 *Feeling and Form*, p. 237.
65 "On Cassirer's Theory of Language and Myth," in *The Philosophy of Ernst Cassirer*, ed. Paul Arthur Schilpp (Evanston, 1949), 385.
66 *Philosophy in a New Key* (Cambridge, Mass., 1942), p. 142.
67 *Problems of Art* (New York, 1957), pp. 104–5.
68 SKL cultivated the habit of keeping her readers abreast of the latest development in her thought. Like Peirce, she believed in the architectonics of theory, but the effect was to sound self-important to those who were disinclined to credit her with other motives. She recognized the fact that not everybody would have read everything she had hitherto written on the subject at hand. On occasion, she publicly changed her mind, adjusting terminology and shifting emphases; to some ears, such self-correction was "self-lenience." At a time when the word is that all knowledge is socially constructed, would this kind of direct engagement with one's readership be acclaimed as a sign of self-effacement?

Claude Lévi-Strauss has recently remarked that if he had it all to do over again, he would have begun with music. We may note – I doubt that she would have – that this was the point of departure for SKL in 1942; indeed, she had raised a generative question twelve years before, in *The Practice of Philosophy*: "Could it be that the final object of musical expression is the endlessly intricate yet universal pattern of emotional life?" (152)
69 *Philosophy in a New Key*, p. 219.
70 *Feeling and Form*, p. 17. Since aesthetics has long been the home ice for slipshod thinking, it is no wonder that *Feeling and Form* drew some of the most vicious attacks of her career. A criticism she took seriously led to a disen-

tangling, "The Art Symbol and the Symbol in Art," reprinted in *Problems in Art*.
71 *Philosophical Sketches*, p. 69.
72 *Mind*, I, p. 152. It is more difficult to demonstrate the role of dozens of detailed discussions of patterns, structures, habits, organs, behavior, artifacts, architectural and sculptural elements, motifs, designs, etc. But I wish to emphasize the care with which SKL uses physiological structures as speculative instruments. This use provides an instructive contrast with the frivolous and illogical metaphors which Jacques Derrida derives from the body and its organs. (See note 33, Part I.) Here, for instance, is her comment on the mysterious barricade of the skin:

> In every animal, the external surface ... is at once the creature's permanent separation from its surroundings and its organ of contact with them; a means of division and of continuity. Here we find in nature the principle of composition by division that is fundamental in art, where it is universally recognized as one of the essential characteristics of "living form." Plastic space is made by divisions that are conjunctions; and plastic space is the image of vital space, the space of an agent's being and ambient. Nowhere in the inanimate world are cleavages organized to be connectives; but as every volume in pictorial, sculptural or architectural space serves to create the spatial unity in which it is defined, so every actual living form – every individual in its shell, hide, or containing membrane – creates its ambient, the world with which it has contact, through that same separating surface. (*Mind*, I, p. 421)

73 This observation comes from Beatrice Nelson, a philosopher whose forthcoming study of SKL will encourage an appreciation of her contributions. I have elsewhere discussed SKL's ideas of the evolution of mind and culture. See "Susanne K. Langer and 'the Odyssey of the Mind,'" forthcoming in *Semiotica*.
74 *The Message in the Bottle* (New York, 1975), p. 167. Further references to this book are made parenthetically.
75 See note 39, Part I.
76 Like virtually every other novelist who ever lived, Walker Percy denied that he wrote allegories, presupposing that that form only presents minimally animated personifications – "the naming game," as Rosemond Tuve called this misconception. Paul de Man's perverse defense of allegory – we are not misled by allegory into mistaking representation for identity, as we are with symbolism – has set back attempts to reclaim allegory as continued metaphor.

77 It was the only point on which Cassirer was explicit in his rejection of Heidegger's philosophy, but the two philosophers are antithetical in every way. Those who, like George Steiner, refuse to take into account Heidegger's Naziism as anything but an aberration, entirely irrelevant to his philosophy, should trouble to read the account of the debate on Kant at Davos in 1929, when Heidegger refused to shake the hand of the Jew Cassirer. (See *The Philosophy of Ernst Cassirer*, 1949.) Felix Gilbert's memoir, *A European Past* (1990), includes an account of meeting Heidegger after the war, which reveals the constitutional mendacity of this philosopher.

Part III

1 John Berryman, "Nowhere," *Love and Fame* (New York, 1972).
2 I have depended on two translations, by Eugene Jolas (*Partisan Review*, January–February, 1947, 67–72) and by Idris Parry (*Times Literary Supplement*, October 20, 1978). Following all important phrases in translation, whether Jolas's, Parry's, or my own, I add the German parenthetically. In some discussions of the essay, the narrator is referred to as "Kleist," whereas his dialogue partner is called "the dancer." This is entirely unwarranted: the dancer's arguments are as much Kleist's own as are the narrator's. In their various forms, *puppet* and *marionette* are interchangeable in all languages, but it should be noted that Kleist is throughout referring to string puppets, not to hand puppets. Thus Eugene Jolas is mistaken in translating *kleine dramatische Burlesken, mit Gesang und Tanz durchwebt* as a *Punch and Judy show*, since those figures are always hand-puppets.
3 Walter Silz (*Heinrich von Kleist: Studies in his works and literary character* (Philadelphia, 1961), p. 88. Silz is the only critic I have read who remarks the discrepancy between what Kleist describes and the actual pose of the boy in the famous statue known as the Spinario, which is a seated figure with one leg resting at the ankle on the other knee as the boy leans over to inspect the sole of his foot. There are two possibilities: one is that Kleist has another statue in mind (say, of a boy standing on one foot, the other caught up in his hand while he glances over his shoulder at it) and the other is that, as Silz suggests, Kleist's imagination began transforming what he saw the instant he saw it.
4 "Heinrich von Kleist und die Marionette," *Heinrich von Kleist Studies*, ed. Alexej Ugrinsky. Hofstra University Cultural and Intercultural Studies, 3 (New York: AMS Press Ltd., 1980), pp. 102–8.
5 The phrase *der Weg der Seele* appears in the Preface to Hegel's *Phänomenologie des Geistes* where it describes one way of considering phenomenal

knowledge. That can be seen as "the pathway of the natural consciousness which is pressing forward to true knowledge;" or, Hegel continues, it can be regarded as

> the path of the soul, which is traversing the series of its own forms of embodiment, like stages appointed for it by its own nature, that it may possess the clearness of spiritual life when, through the complete experience of its own self, it arrives at the knowledge of what it is in itself. (*The Phenomenology of Mind*, tr. J.B. Baillie [N.Y.: Macmillan, 1910], p. 78)

> (... *der Weg der Seele, welche die Reihe ihrer Gestaltungen, als durch ihre Natur ihr vorgesteckter Stationen, durchwandert, dasz sie sich zum Geiste lautere, indem sie durch die vollständige Ehrfahrung ihrer selbst zur Kenntnis desjenigen gelangt, was sie an sich selbst ist.*)

To find *der Weg der Seele* in both Kleist and Hegel is striking, but it must be noted that *paths* are mythically associated with the *Soul*, *roads* with *life*, etc. The phrase may well be as commonplace as "horizon" is in theoretical discussions of interpretation. In any case, theories of consciousness/knowledge in Romanticism are, like Platonism in the Renaissance, diffused throughout poetic discourse and lay philosophical writing alike. Kleist's fascination with the polarity of natural knowledge and Absolute Knowledge, with the dialectics of mediacy and immediacy, manifests the *Zeitgeist*.

The point is not at all to try to establish that Kleist "must have" read Hegel, but it might be worthwhile to explore to what extent Kleist's emblems and extended metaphors – his allegories – are illuminated by Hegel's themes and images. For example, the conflation of what is natural and what is logical is at the heart of Kleist's essay, but it is achieved only with the dissolution of consciousness. In Hegel's account, the progress of the soul is also a self-destroying progress, but what is destroyed is not natural consciousness but the conviction that it constitutes "real" knowledge. On the path of the soul, consciousness "loses its own Truth," it overthrows itself. In this light, Kleist's images are shown more clearly to be hyperbolic extensions of conventional figures, rather than idiosyncratic, perverse inventions.

6 Silz, p. 88.
7 Such mechanical effects are currently familiar from mime performances. In Kleist's "St. Cecilia or The Power of Music," the heretical young men who are under a punishing spell cast by St. Cecilia, are described as acting "as if in one motion" or "in a body," when they hear church music or church bells. Each of these uncanny moments comes *suddenly*.
8 *Stories of Three Decades*, (tr. H.T. Lowe-Porter (New York: Knopf, 1945), pp. 560–61.

9 "Kant and Deism," in *Religion and Philosophy in Germany*, tr. John Snodgrass (Boston: Houghton, Mifflin & Co., 1882).

  This motif of the incredible mechanical skills of the English in making artificial limbs appears in Gogol's *Dead Souls*. The postmaster claims that the mysterious Chichikov – the buyer of dead souls – is really one Captain Kopeikin. He tells a tale of how this captain, who had lost an arm and a leg, attempts to get a pension. One of his audience interrupts the tale, pointing out that Chichikov is not missing any limbs. Nothing daunted, the tale-teller decares that "he could not understand how a circumstance like that had not occurred to him at the beginning of the story ... However, a minute later he tried to be a little too clever and attempted to get round it by pointing out that mechanical devices had reached such a point of perfection in England that, as it would appear from the newspapers, some one had invented a pair of artificial legs which the moment a hidden spring was touched would carry off a man goodness only knows where, so that he could not be found anywhere afterwards." (*Dead Souls*, tr. David Magarshack [Penguin, 1961], p. 215)

10 De Man's fanciful essay, "Aesthetic Formalization: Kleist's 'Über das Marionettentheater,'" in *The Rhetoric of Romanticism*, 1984, is a type-specimen of unresponsive and irresponsible criticism.

11 Silz, p. 306.

12 What Kleist does is to supplant opposition by cut with opposition by scale. The terms are C.K. Ogden's in *Opposition* (1932; Bloomington, 1967). High/low, hot/cold, morning/night are all oppositions by scale with no discernible point at which one stops and the other starts. A left-hand glove and a right-hand glove, the banks of a river, identity and difference are all oppositions by cut. Many of the classical conundrums of logic – to say nothing of present day muddles – involve entangling the two kinds.

13 *Mind: An Essay on Human Feeling*, I, p. 59.

14 I agree with Silz who characterizes "Über das Marionettentheater" as "a changeful discourse" in which there is "a disconcerting mixture of rationalistic mechanics and romantic spiritualization" (76). The mixture is nonetheless coherent, a contention which can be supported by representing the imagery and the extended metaphors diagrammatically. This is possible because the dialogue, which takes the form of theme and variations, exhibits an oppositional structure that can be represented spatially. Guided by a pragmatic hermeneutic, we can ask: "If the essay on the marionette theatre is about the paradox of grace represented by purely natural laws, then does this diagrammatic representation accurately display a symmetry of the emblematic and narrative representations of the essay?"

186   Notes to pages 156–57

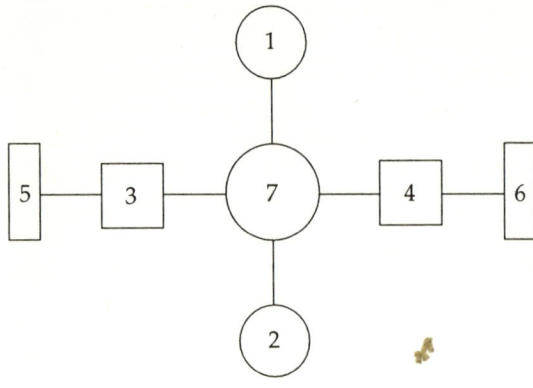

pantin	1. the puppet controlled by a single string the & 2. the peasants' rondo, à la Teniers
figures subject only to natural law	3. the *Gliedermann* & (numbers and their logarithms) 4. the "dancing" amputees
the anti-types of Grace matched to Innocence	5. the fencer vs. the bear & (ballet dancers portraying Daphne, Apollo, Paris) 6. the Spinario, before and after the mirror
the vanishing point which is infinity	7. sudden transformation: momentary resistance of the ground; hyperbolas and their asymtotes; the backdoor of Paradise; the point where the two ends of the circular world meet; the concave mirror; the parallel lines returning from infinity; eating again from the Tree of Knowledge and falling back into Innocence; the last chapter of mankind.

15 These moments are often signalled by *plötzlich*. In the fifth *Duino Elegy*, Rilke represents this sudden transformation in saluting the acrobats depicted in Picasso's great canvas, *Les Saltimbanques*, standing there forming the capital letter of *Dasein*. He imagines how they build a pyramid which suddenly springs apart:

Und plötzlich in diesem mühsamen Nirgends, plötzlich
die unsägliche Stelle, wo sich reine Zuwenig
unbegreiflich verwandelt – umspringt
in jenes leere Zuviel.
Wo die vielstellige Rechnung
zahlenlos aufgeht.

16 This principle is often enunciated by Sapir, as in the following: "Language is at one and the same time helping and retarding us in our exploration of experience, and the details of these processes of help and hindrance are deposited in the subtler meanings of different cultures" (1949:11).
17 There is a comic Kleistian moment when he observes that Mirabeau took his cues from his audience. Like all great orators, he did not know what he was going to say until he was saying it, letting himself be guided by what he saw in the expressions of the Assembly. Indeed, Kleist notes, it could be said that because somebody wiped an upper lip or adjusted his cuffs, the old order was overturned. Kleist's main emphasis throughout is on the dialectic of thought and language, not that of audience and speaker. It is inaccurate to describe this essay as "response to the modes of discourse and rhetorical interactions accompanying socio-political upheavals" (James Smith, "Dialogic Midwifery in Kleist's *Marquise von O* and the Hermeneutics of Telling the Untold in Kant and Plato," PMLA 100 [1985], 215n). There is no interaction, rhetorical or otherwise, in this comic description or at the beginning of the essay where a cure is offered for what we call "writer's block" – not being able to represent what it is that you know. Kleist advises that one should start talking to the first acquaintance you run into. He does not have to be sharp-witted. It will not be his job to question you substantially; rather, you will tell him. This defines very clearly the usual role of the narrator in the essay on the marionette theatre.
18 *The Philosophy of Symbolic Forms* (1929; New Haven: Yale University Press, 1957), III, p. 331.
19 *Heinrich von Kleist: Sämtliche Werke und Briefe*, ed. Helmut Sembdner (Munich, 1961), 6, p. 30.
20 Sembdner, 6, p. 30. The contempt expressed here is consonant with Herr C.'s insistent goal of getting rid of wire (*Draht*) or string (*Faden*). Manipulability – as in *pantin* as time-server – is the aspect of marionettes from which Kleist again and again takes flight. This letter antedates his essay on the marionette theatre in which he tries to liberate puppets from any and all control.
21 Sembdner, 6, p. 163.
22 I have commented on the images and themes shared by Cusanus and

Marvell in *The Resolved Soul: A Study of Marvell's Major Poems* (Princeton, 1970).

23 *The Vision of God*, tr. Emma Gurney Salter (New York: Ungar, 1978), p. 43. Cusanus's declaration that the Lord has inspired him "to do violence to myself" is puzzling, but both the rhetoric and the logic of the passage suggests that suicide is metaphoric of the conquest of a self-centered understanding. The discovery that "impossibility coincideth with necessity" seems simultaneous and correlative with the conviction that man's limited sight is only possible because there is Absolute Sight.

24 Cassirer's most extensive discussion of Cusanus is in *The Individual and the Cosmos in Renaissance Philosophy* (New York: Harper & Row, 1964).

25 "'Spirit' and 'Life' in Contemporary Philosophy," 1930; reprinted in *The Philosophy of Ernst Cassirer*, ed. Paul Arthur Schilpp (Evanston, 1949).

Author Index

Altieri, Charles, 79, 177
Anscombe, G.E.M., 174
Arnheim, Rudolph, 25

Bachelard, Gaston, 10, 160
Bakhtin, Mikhail, 10, 160
Barfield, Owen, 4, 17
Barth, Karl, 96–97, 178, 179
Barthes, Roland, 20, 22, 167–68
Baxandall, Michael, 38
Benamou, Michel, 174
Benjamin, Walter, 19, 51–52, 54
Berryman, John, 183
Berthoff, Ann E., 167, 188
Black, Max, 3, 50, 168
Bloomfield, Leonard, 105
Bohr, Niels, 69
Brandt, Richard B., 178
Browne, Sir Thomas, 15, 126–27, 132
Bruaene, Geert van, 74
Burke, Kenneth, 6, 22, 30–31, 72, 126
Burks, Arthur, 63

Campbell, Joseph, 135
Cassirer, Ernst, 8, 39, 50, 86, 92, 101, 102, 108, 111, 113, 115, 116, 126, 161, 165, 183, 188

Cavell, Stanley, 173
Chase, Stuart, 37
Citron, Pierre, 172
Chomsky, Noam, 114
Cohen, Morris, 65, 67
Coleridge, Samuel Taylor, 15, 25, 101, 135, 139, 176, 181
Couperin, François, 50, 172
Crews, Frederick, 3
Crick, Francis, 24
Culler, Jonathan, 6, 19, 35–36
Cusanus (Nicholas of Cusa), 134, 163–65, 188

de Man, Paul, 7, 17, 31–33, 90, 149–51, 178, 182
de Staël, Nicolas, 3, 50
Derrida, Jacques, 36–37, 39, 60–61, 135, 168, 171–72, 182
Dilthey, Wilhelm, 93, 96
Dinesen, Isak, 139
Droysen, Friedrich, 93

Eco, Umberto, 7
Ellis, John M., 3
Ellsworth, Phoebe C., 170
Empson, William, 37

Emerson, Ralph Waldo, 71
Esposito, Joseph, 7, 176

Ferber, Michael, 170
Fichte, J.F., 163
Fisch, Max, 7
Fish, Stanley, 6, 24, 175
Foucault, Michel, 44–45
Freire, Paulo, 85

Gadamer, Hans-Georg, 98
Gardner, Helen, 24
Geertz, Clifford, 112
Genette, Gérard, 102
Gilbert, Felix, 183
Gogol, Nicolai, 185
Gombrich, E.H., 40, 46, 172, 174
Graham, Martha, 139
Grimm, Jakob, 94

Haberman, Jürgen, 64, 176
Harpham, Geoffrey, 174–75
Hegel, G.W.F., 183–84
Heidegger, Martin, 99, 114, 133, 183
Heine, Heinrich, 147
Heisenberg, Werner, 37
Herder, J.G., 104, 109
Hirsch, E.D., 6, 24
Hoffman, E.T.A., 148
Holland, Norman, 177
Howells, William Dean, 57
Humboldt, Wilhelm von, 109
Husserl, Edmund, 26–28, 43, 168–69

Idhe, Don, 173

Jakobson, Roman, 26, 75
James, William, 113, 117, 167
Jameson, Fredric, 49, 170, 180

Janik, Allan, 173
Jastrow, Benjamin, 41, 44
Jolas, Eugene, 183

Kafka, Franz, 139
Kant, Immanuel, 87, 147, 162
Kermode, Frank, 20
Kevelson, Roberta, 176
Kierkegaard, Søren, 125, 133
Kimmerle, Heinz, 179
Klee, Paul, 41, 106
Kleist, Heinrich von, 10, 139–65, 183–88
Knights, L.C., 112
Kuhn, Thomas, 41
Kurock, Wolfgang, 143

Langer, Susanne K., 6, 9, 16, 26, 50, 82, 101, 112–24, 156, 170, 180–82
Lavoisier, Antoine, 92
LeCorbusier (C.E. Jeannert-Gris), 74
Lévi-Strauss, Claude, 181
Lewin, Bertram, 171
Lowes, John Livingston, 176

Magritte, René, 44–45, 174
Mann, Thomas, 146–47
Marcel, Gabriel, 126
Marty, Robert, 167–68
Marvell, Andrew, 163
Mauthner, Fritz, 49
Michaels, Walter Benn, 177
Miles, Josephine, 112
Morris, Charles, 127
Müller, Max, 170, 171
Munro, Robert, 178

Nelson, Beatrice, 182
Niebuhr, Richard R., 178

… Author Index   191

Ogden, C.K., 49, 72, 104, 180, 185
Onians, R.B., 171
Oppenheimer, J. Robert, 130
Ortega y Gasset, José, 71

Panofsky, Erwin, 178
Parry, Idris, 183
Peirce, Benjamin, 65
Peirce, Charles Sanders, 5, 7, 11, 19, 37–38, 44, 52, 57–71, 73, 76, 82, 87, 92–93, 107, 126, 128, 167, 176, 177
Percy, Walker, 7, 9, 57, 125–35, 182
Phillips, Antonia, 174
Piaget, Jean, 114
Picasso, Pablo, 186
Platt, John R., 167
Proust, Marcel, 31–33

Rawson, Claude, 178
Reiman, Donald H., 3
Richards, I.A., 6, 7, 11, 15, 17, 21, 22, 37, 49, 52, 69–70, 72–81, 104, 115, 129, 167, 174, 177
Riffaterre, Michael, 170
Rilke, Rainer Maria, 139, 186–87
Rorty, Richard, 67, 135

Samway, Patrick, 126
Sapir, Edward, 4, 8, 35, 97, 102–11, 119, 180, 187
Saussure, Ferdinand, 35
Schleiermacher, F.D.E., 8, 82–101, 134, 179
Sebeok, Thomas A., 7, 174
Shakespeare, William, 46, 67, 68, 70

Sheffer, Henry, 114
Shusterman, Ronald, 178
Silz, Walter, 144, 151, 183, 185
Smith, James, 187
Spivak, Gayatri Chakravorty, 171
Stam, James, 187
Steiner, George, 183
Sugerman, Shirley, 168

Tallis, Raymond, 3
Tate, Allen, 172
Todorov, Tzvetan, 22
Toulmin, Stephen, 173
Tuve, Rosemond, 182

Umiker-Sebeok, Jean, 7, 174

Vickers, Brian, 3
Vico, Giambattista, 92
Vygotsky, L.S., 10, 17, 50, 52–53, 88, 160

Waddington, C.H., 112
Waismann, Friedrich, 173
Welby, Victoria, Lady, 58–59, 63, 81
Welty, Eudora, 134
Wellek, René, 6, 28–30
Whitehead, Alfred North, 48, 50, 53, 112, 114, 116–17, 124, 126
Whitfield, Sarah, 174
Whorf, Benjamin Lee, 5, 35, 37, 102, 105, 180
Wind, Edgar, 168–69
Wittgenstein, Ludwig, 5, 41–44, 52, 89, 114, 172

OHIO UNIVERSITY LIBRARY
se return this book as soon as you have
        avoid a fine it must

A